PETRA
A Travell

Rosalyn Maqsood

With revisions by **Ann Jousiffe**

Garnet
PUBLISHING

With grateful thanks to Saleh Awad, Hussein el-Sudani and John Satterthwaite, who was the Bishop of Gibraltar in Europe, who gave me Jordan.

PETRA: A Traveller's Guide

Published by
Garnet Publishing Limited
8 Southern Court, South Street
Reading RG1 4QS, UK
Tel: +44(0)118 959 7847
Fax: +44(0)118 959 7356
E-mail: enquiries@garnet-ithaca.co.uk
Website: www.garnet-ithaca.co.uk

This edition published exclusively for the Jordan Distribution Agency, 2003

ISBN 1 85964 147 4

British Library Cataloguing-in-Publication Data. A catalogue record for this book is available from the British Library.

Credits
Editorial
Emma Hawker
Maps: Karen Rose

Design
David Rose

Production
Typesetting: Samantha Barden
Illustrations and maps: Janette Hill
Reprographics: Nick Holroyd

Photography
Ann Jousiffe: pages 3, 8, 67, 91, 93 (all), 95, 98, 101, 108, 109, 111, 112, 115, 117, 120 (middle), 121, 124, 135, 137, 138 (all), 140, 141, 150, 157
Jordan Tourism Board: pages 74, 76 (all), 77 (all), 78, 79, 81, 82, 87, 89, 90, 92, 99, 171, 180, 182

Printed and bound
in Lebanon by International Press

THE WATER CITY

Desert oleanders adorn a sandstone vista
to a clean swept plateau of white sand
and tiny unfrayed steps.
Looks easy to enter, but could ride
a cavalry of horsemen inside it, whose
giant but elegantly colour-washed interior
could perfectly seat a banquet, or recollect
a sofa, and rooms beyond this perfect vertical
wall, but also hides a receding echo of anxiety.
Trace past the momentary skirmishes
through these rooms, and you will see
a tidemark of another time, the key
to a water city
re-enacted in the rain
of its fiery sandstone and earth existence.

FRANCES KENDRICK

Contents

INTRODUCTION

Clinging to the reins of a serviceable nag one size too small, whose temperament suggests that it believes it was born for better things, I clatter nervously through the claustrophobic gloom at the bottom of an awesome zigzag cleft over a mile long, which splits a towering peak. An uncomfortable suspicion insinuates itself in my mind that humans are out of place here, that the mountains might shift again at any moment and crush any intruder. I am not, therefore, particularly consoled by the incomprehensible murmurings of the swarthy man, clad in a long shirt with an incongruous tweed jacket, who is sympathetically patting my knee.

Suddenly, I am blinded by a searing, almost neon, jag of pink light over 60m high. This is the first glimpse of one of the ornamental façades gouged out of the sandstone of Petra. It is a moment never to be forgotten. Now probably the world's most famous lost city, Petra lies in a deep valley east of the Wadi Arabah, enclosed on all sides by precipitous sandstone mountains. Once the floor of a prehistoric sea, the mountains were thrust up by tectonic movements, enclosing an inland lake; then primeval earthquakes created the Wadi Siyagh through which the waters passed and were lost in the arid stretches of the desert beyond.

The main site of the city lies in the Wadi Musa (Valley of Moses), a large open plain ringed by those silent peaks of pink sandstone which kept explorers guessing for centuries.

Petra is far more than a rock carving or two – it is an entire ghost town occupying a site of many hectares, not only the basin at the centre, but a whole network of gorges and ravines that wind off in every direction to various ancient suburbs, with tracks and staircases leading to altars perched on any number of 'high places'. The rock faces are riddled with cave-tombs sporting elegantly carved façades, graced with columns and urns. It is these thousands of carved tombs that have made Petra famous.

The other thing for which Petra is famous is its colour. An ecclesiastical writer, Dean John William Burgon, wrote a few lines of poetry which are quoted in every single article on Petra: 'the rose-red city half as old as time'. Do not quote these unfortunately unforgettable words and expect to be congratulated either on your originality or your scholarship.

In fact, iron oxide, carried by water, has stained the sandstone in shades of tawny reds and browns. Where the rock surfaces are old and weathered the hue is deep chocolate or dark maroon, in the excavated sections it is bright red, yellow, pink

The entrance to the Siq

or white, and in the best places looks like the ripples of watered silk. Burgon did not actually visit Petra until 16 years after writing the poem, and then had the embarrassment of realizing that his romantic description was wildly inaccurate.

The words of the intrepid seamen Captains Irby and Mangles are far more fitting to its atmosphere:

It is impossible to conceive any thing more aweful or sublime than such an approach: the width is not more than just sufficient for the passage of two horsemen abreast; the sides are in all parts perpendicular, varying from four hundred to seven hundred feet in height; and they often overhang to such a degree that, without their absolutely meeting, the sky is completely shut out for one hundred yards altogether, and there is little more light than in a cavern. It is somewhere amongst these natural horrors that upwards of thirty pilgrims from Barbary were murdered last year by the men of Wadi Mousa ... We followed this half subterranean passage for the space of nearly two miles, the sides increasing in height as the path continually descended ...

Irby and Mangles, *Travels in Egypt and Nubia, Syria and Asia Minor*

Having come through the Siq, here is Léon de Laborde's initial comment on the scene that met his eyes:

It was truly a strange spectacle – a city filled with tombs, some scarcely begun, some finished, looking as new and as fresh as if they had just come from the hands of the sculptor; while others seemed to be the abode of lizards, fallen into ruins and covered with brambles. One would be inclined to think that the former population had no employment which was not connected with death, and that they had all been surprised by death during the performance of some funeral amenities.

Laborde, *Voyage de l'Arabie Pétrée*

The ruins

At first, it is all too easy to believe that Petra consists of nothing but tombs – but one soon gets the message that these are simply the relics of the dead as opposed to those of the living, and of course, every dead celebrity who organized and carved a tomb for himself and his family was once alive and kicking, and enjoying the facilities of one of the most bustling and fashionable trade centres of the Middle East.

In its heyday, the city was the capital of the Nabataeans and gradually the veil has been lifted

The arch at the entrance to the Siq (Laborde)

from their remarkable civilization. A strong line of kings with sustained power in war and commerce gave Petra strength, riches, organization and wider dominion. Its fighting force numbered around 10,000.

There is a cluster of carved obelisks at the entrance to the tunnel in Wadi el Muslim, a branch of the Wadi Musa, which shows the Nabataean name for Petra – Raqmu, or Reqem. This was the name by which the city was known to the great Jewish historian Flavius Josephus (38–c.100 CE) and other ancient writers, and was also, incidentally, the name of the Petran king who refused permission for the Israelites to pass through his land (see Chapter 2). The name Petra, meaning 'The Rock', is Greek – it was given to the city by the Greek merchants who traded there in the first and second centuries BCE, at which time it was one of the premier commercial centres of the world and had a population of some 20–30,000 people.

The visitor to the ruins is obliged to exercise a little imagination, for Petra was not petrified, snuffed out in a moment of time like Pompeii, with its whole life sealed in a time capsule by the circumstances of its sudden demise. In Petra, all that remains of the heart of the city (the built ruins rather than the carved ones) is

the Cardo, a noble street paved with white limestone, with a lone crumbling temple to the sun-god Dushrat at the end of it. So the first impression of the actual city is rather disappointing – a vast, empty arena and a scattering of stones.

Some people are, frankly, disappointed by the place. Others feel strongly that they are being confronted by an enigma. Despite its emptiness, there is a powerful atmosphere in Petra, and any visitor with the slightest intuition for things which are supernatural begins to pick it up, either with delight or with distinct unease.

It does not take even the ordinary visitor long to realize that the Nabataeans were a deeply religious people. Some of the 'tombs' are not tombs at all but temples. All over the site can be found lumpen edifices, mysteriously called 'god boxes', obelisks, pyramidical-shaped stones, and other cultic sacred objects. Virtually every peak of every rocky massif is crowned by a site for either blood-sacrifice, the burning of incense, or contemplative prayer. Symbols of the deities mark every important feature and guard every possible sacred place. For those who have eyes to see, Petra is still a sacred place. Something of its mystical vibrations seems to linger, pervading the silent windswept peaks and the sudden springs, still untouched by the world.

Petra has been lucky. Having been for so long a 'lost city' it has not suffered the depradations of a continuous stream of foreign visitors. The last proper settlement here was in the twelfth century, at the time of the Crusaders. After they were driven out – by Richard the Lionheart's gallant enemy Saladin – there was no account (by any European traveller) of a ruin which could be identified for certain as Petra. Few non-Muslims were tempted to travel the territory of Arabia Petraea, and Petra was not rediscovered by Europeans until 1812 when the Swiss explorer Burckhardt, disguised as a Muslim scholar, set out to research the source of the River Niger in Africa by a somewhat circuitous route.

During the intervening 600 years the site of Petra was occupied only by a few Bedouin families, and that very depopulation has kept the ruins in the decent state of preservation they are in today. If any organized civilization had been maintained there, the ruins would certainly have been overlaid and spoiled.

However, since Burckhardt's time a masochistic yearning for adventures in impossible desert conditions seems to have become all the rage for people of a certain mentality, and a stream of eager and courageous explorers ventured forth in the face of the apparently alarming habits of the 'hostile natives' in and around Petra, who until recently certainly did display a hearty xenophobia. For example, when the Arab Legion set up a police post there to protect visitors from the tribesmen, the entire garrison was massacred. The main reason why the locals were so unwilling to advertise their lost city to strangers had nothing to do with romantic ancient lore, nor jealously guarded tribal boundaries, nor Islamic suspicion of the infidel, but was simply because of their trading interests. The merchants of Petra always had their eye on lucrative business, and knew how to turn a quick dollar. They were afraid that a host of sightseers would interfere with their live-lihood – which is precisely what has happened.

Nowadays visitors are encouraged. All are welcome, with no evidence of hostility, although there is still a kind of raffish buccaneering atmosphere amongst the young Bedouin – not to mention a certain triumphant swashbuckling amongst the tourists! Most visitors settle for either a day excursion, an overnight stop, or a three-day exploration. But a day tripper can do no more than see a sprinkling of the better monuments – to see the area properly would take weeks.

Petra's inhabitants today

The modern inhabitants of Petra are the Bedouin, traditionally nomadic Arabs who live by rearing sheep and camels. The word 'bedouin' is the Western version of the Arabic word *badawiyin* which means 'inhabitant of the desert'. The singular is *badawi* but the one word 'bedouin' is used for singular and plural, and is usually taken to apply to all nomadic Arabs, whatever their origins. The nomads usually refer to themselves as the 'arab', or 'the tribes'.

The tribes around Petra are mainly the Hejaya, Howetat, Ammarin (who are possibly descendants of the biblical Amorites) and the powerful Alawin. Historically the Alawin were the first to obtain the privilege of escorting pilgrims and travellers, from the Egyptian Government. The Howetat claim to be direct descendants of the Prophet Muhammad through his daughter Fatima and the Caliph Ali. They are also thought to be of old Nabataean stock.

The Petra ruins themselves were occupied until recently by the Liyatheneh, a turbulent bunch, possibly descendants of tribesmen who emigrated from Arabia after the Muslim conquests, who now live in and around Wadi Musa village; and the Bdul, who live within the Petra-Beidha basin. They have now been officially removed by the Government and resettled in newly built houses overlooking the city ruins – but it is one thing to build the accommodation and quite another to make the people live

there. Many tribespeople still prefer living in the caves or coolness of their tents in the summer as they have always done, and use the concrete houses as quarters for their livestock! The Bdul number about a thousand people, and the Liyatheneh many thousands.

With the advent of modern roads and transport, however, the nomadic way of life – following the trails across the deserts around Wadi Rum and down into Arabia, moving from grass to grass – is rapidly dying out. The Bedouin are adapting to more settled life and most young Bedouin now want to be educated and to make money in the cities. Most have taken paid employment of one sort or another (for example, running a taxi in town), and nearly every family will have a son working for the Government, and another in the forces or in business. The family menu is vastly enlarged by the availability of tinned foods from all over the world, which provide variety even though they are considered expensive. Tinned milk powder means better-fed children, and no starvation when flocks fail to produce sufficient.

The biggest problem is the widening gap between nomad and townsfolk, due to the discovery of Middle Eastern oil and all its associated industries. Little oil has yet been found in Jordan, but the boundaries of countries fixed by the parliaments of distant politicians mean little to nomads who cannot tell if a particular stretch of sand is in 'Jordan' or 'Saudia' or 'Iraq', and carry on driving to the various towns for work wherever it is to be found.

Other causes for the rich/poor gap are general illiteracy and the dislike of manual labour, which leave the Bedouin at a disadvantage when dealing in business, and restricts the type of work they can do in towns. However, driving offers many opportunities, and Bedouin men are often drawn into the police and armed forces. Service in the National Guard now provides the tribes with a large part of their income.

To the old folk, the ways of city dwellers and those who have become dependent on the tourists are regarded as inferior; they see the younger generation as being seduced into a foolish desire for material things, and the ambition to possess them renders them physically and morally corrupt. Occasionally there is some truth in this judgement. However, Bedouin are great pragmatists, and see no reason why they should not accept at least a few of the creature comforts without compromising their way of life. Unfortunately, many experts feel that the nomadic way will have gone completely in one more generation – although others disagree and argue that the culture is so strong and attractive, and the need for 'wildness' so ingrained in the tribespeople, that it will take more than a few roads, trucks and paraffin heaters to destroy it.

Lost cities

For most people, the idea of coming across a lost city in a remote place is full of romantic appeal. It seems impossible that something as large and vibrant as a city could really become lost, but they do (at least to the erudite scholars of the Western world, though not to the local populace) for centuries. They get smashed up by war and left as complete ruins. They may be eaten up by rampant nature, starved into submission by advancing desert or the disappearance of the water supply. They can be wiped out by disease or plague. Some cities are shaken to death by earthquake, swept away by landslide, buried by volcanic eruption, or engulfed by fire; others slide under the waves and are drowned. And some cities are cursed.

It is hard for us, perhaps, to imagine the psychological effect on a people of knowing that their enemies have called up divine power for the sole purpose of destroying them, of wiping them

off the face of the earth. The people of Petra had the misfortune to be among the most cursed victims of biblical priests and prophets. Not an easy thing to live with, and yet another reason why this particular city might have been abandoned.

Some cities, although not actually lost, are so plundered and neglected over long stretches of time that they sink to the level of mere heaps of rubble. Yet others survive as small settlements, or villages built on or near unexplained mounds, their former greatness quite forgotten until some strange people with a passion for grubbing about in the mud come along and reveal amazing streets, temples and treasures.

Any gardener who has tried to tame a certain space and create in it something of human taste and skill will tell you what a gigantic task it is to foist something so unnatural as a garden upon the forces of nature, which have a will of their own and a law from the beginning of time. There is an old story about the passer-by who stopped to congratulate a gardener on the beauty of his plot. 'What a wonderful job you and God have made of this,' he murmured. The gardener winked, and said, 'Yes, but you should have seen it when God had it to Himself!'

Like gardens, cities are not natural things, worked blocks of stone falling into position by themselves. They depend absolutely on the skills of those who dwell in them; on the success of such inventions as water channels and drainage systems; protective walls that will keep off enemies without falling down; viable roads over the deep ruts of winter mud, and orderly organizations of domiciles in which the citizens may live and be at peace with each other. When a city 'dies' and God gets the site back to Himself, the human traces soon begin to disappear.

Sometimes the only clues left are those in books. Six centuries passed since the end of the last Crusade cut the links between Europe and the Arab world, and in that time the entire history and 'feel' for what lay beyond Europe was itself lost. The well educated might be expected to know something of the Greek and Roman Empires but for the vast majority of Westerners geographical knowledge of the world stopped at the River Jordan. A few had 'bible-knowledge' of the Assyrians, Babylonians or Parthians, but it was not really until the nineteenth century that adventurous young men and women began to succumb to the urge to 'go East'. It is quite hard for us, living in a time of easy travel when hardly a patch of the earth's surface remains inaccessible, to grasp fully the sense of romance and mystery that obsessed the explorer of a hundred or so years ago.

THE FASCINATION OF THE PAST

Once people were bitten by the bug of rediscovery, the symptoms were dramatic. As Rose Macaulay put it:

the intoxication, at once so heady and devout, is not the romantic melancholy engendered by broken towers and mouldered stones; it is the soaring of the imagination into the high empyrean where huge episodes are tangled with myths and dreams; it is the stunning impact of world history on its amazed heirs … it is less ruin-worship than the worship of a tremendous past …

The Pleasure of Ruins

Petra's glorious past – when its temples and shrines drew streams of pilgrims from all over the Middle East, when its paved streets and public buildings gleamed so bright in the sunlight you could scarcely bear to look upon them, when its haughty tribesmen obliged the Romans to pay protection for their caravans, and when a saucy Petran prince led a legion by its nose and lost it in the unforgiving desert sands and got away with it – has been shrouded in mystery.

The discovery of Petra

BURCKHARDT

The 'discoverer' of Petra was Johann Ludwig Burckhardt (1784–1817), born in Lausanne, Switzerland, son of an army colonel. He had officially been hired by the African Association to get to Timbuktu and explore the source of the River Niger. The African Association had been founded in England for the humanitarian purpose of fighting slavery, and also to investigate the economic possibilities presented by this unknown continent. However, it so happened that the leading lights of the Association at that time were also the chiefs in the British Foreign Office. They had a further interest in information about the desert peninsula that lay between Europe and India. Burckhardt's movements therefore were dictated more by the Foreign Office than by the African Association.

Although the Age of Exploration was beginning to open up the world, jaunts to Africa and east of the Jordan were at that time regarded as undertakings requiring enormous fortitude and courage. Those places were considered to be as remote and dangerous as the surface of the moon, with local Bedouin (few of whom had ever seen Europeans) warring amongst themselves and highly suspicious of any stranger. As a result it was the normal practice of explorers to adopt disguises.

Burckhardt prepared himself for his delicate and dangerous task by going to Cambridge and learning Arabic, medicine and astronomy. With Teutonic application he practised sleeping on the ground and eating nothing but vegetables. He finally left England in 1809 and spent several years making a further study of the Arabic language and customs. In 1812 he left for Palestine and Egypt, having by this time completed his metamorphosis into Sheikh Ibrahim ibn Abdallah. Deliberately dressing as a poor traveller so as not to excite greed (which would have been dangerous), he set out.

Burckhardt paused briefly in Amman, then moved further south. Near Shaubak, he heard the villagers speak of a dead city in the Wadi Musa, and his curiosity was aroused; but as it was a deliberately hidden city, and the tribespeople were highly suspicious of strangers, he did not want to run the risk of his disguise being penetrated. There was a story that Moses' brother Aaron, venerated by the Muslims as the Prophet Harum, was buried near Petra. This information gave Burckhardt the opportunity he needed to explore the area. He

LADY HESTER STANHOPE

The most irritating thing for Burckhardt was to find that he was not a trailblazer. Other Europeans had been before him and spoiled the adventure. On the summit of Mount Tabor he had a particular disappointment when the Syrian peasant who came to greet him turned out to be another disguised wanderer – Michael Bruce, the lover of Lady Hester Stanhope, niece of Sir William Pitt the Elder. She had once

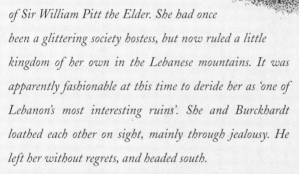

been a glittering society hostess, but now ruled a little kingdom of her own in the Lebanese mountains. It was apparently fashionable at this time to deride her as 'one of Lebanon's most interesting ruins'. She and Burckhardt loathed each other on sight, mainly through jealousy. He left her without regrets, and headed south.

In 1813 Lady Hester achieved her ambition, riding into Palmyra on a white horse, accompanied by Mr Bruce and Dr Meryon, her long-suffering physician. Once in Palmyra she investigated the ruins with great enthusiasm, tiring out the elderly sheikh who accompanied her on foot, and enjoying revels and feasts in the evenings. She died and was buried in the Lebanon, where the stories of her eccentric greatness live on. Her grave is now a tourist attraction.

knew that if he left the main route it would be interpreted as spying, and he would be in grave danger – but nobody would dare to argue with a pious Muslim intending to sacrifice a goat at the tomb of the ancient prophet.

The plan was successful, and he was soon approaching Petra, as most subsequent travellers have done, along the deep gorge of the Siq, watched by the suspicious Liyatheneh tribesmen. The guide had no intention of letting him loose to explore, or allowing him to find the vast stores of treasure supposedly hidden in the ruins. It was a hot and tiresome day, and by the time they had arrived at the foot of the climb up Mount Hor, Burckhardt had had enough. Most Muslims did not bother to make the arduous climb up, but made their sacrifice as soon as the white-washed *weli* came in sight, and Burckhardt decided to do the same (see Tour 11).

For all his excitement at the discovery of Petra, Burckhardt only stayed there one day. It had been a personal detour of his own, and was not the object of his mission, so he continued his journey without delay. In the end, however, the caravan to Timbuktu never did get organized. Burckhardt died in 1817, without ever carrying out the Sahara expedition. He was given a Muslim burial in Cairo in his name of Sheikh Ibrahim ibn Abdallah, in accordance with his status as *hajji* and scholar.

IRBY AND MANGLES

The next European visitors to Petra – in 1818 – were Charles Irby and James Mangles, both captains in the Royal Navy, accompanied by the artist Mr Bankes. They explored the ruins dressed in Bedouin clothing, but it was hardly an attempt at disguise. The business of dressing up had by now become one of the chief pleasures of travellers in these parts.

Their expedition ran into financial problems, which they blamed on the intrepid Lady Hester who they claimed had 'spoiled the market' by overpaying her retainers when she went to Palmyra. They seem to have enjoyed complete freedom of the ruins, but only stayed two days. Although they climbed Jabal Harun their biggest disappointment was that, although from its summit they had glimpsed the Urn decoration atop the monument later known as Ed Deir, they never discovered the way up to it despite valiant efforts (and presumably did not ask). The letters they sent home to their families were published in 1844 and became a bestseller.

LABORDE AND BELLEFONDS

Léon de Laborde, architect and explorer, reached Petra in 1826. He came from a very wealthy family (his grandfather had built the Paris quarter in which the Rue de la Borde lies today), and could afford to indulge his travel fantasies.

At first he tried to reach Petra from Syria, and then decided to start from Egypt after spending a year learning Arabic. He made plans for a caravan of sixteen camels, thinking this would impress the hostile tribesmen whose territory he would have to cross. Overcoming his fear of the Bedouin, he managed a triumphant eight days in the ruins, and was lucky enough to strike the correct route and go straight to Ed Deir on his first attempt. His travelling companions were Linant de Bellefonds (who later became chief engineer at the Suez Canal) and his family retainer Petit-Jean, a veteran of the Napoleonic Wars – an old man 'of iron constitution, on whom fatigue, wounds and illness made no impression', and 'whose only interests were in the temper of his sword and in the price of a good dinner' (Eydoux, *In Search of Lost Worlds*).

Laborde wrote a very detailed description of Petra with drawings, having never, according to his description, seen anything so remarkable or romantic. His was the first systematic study of the monuments, and three magnificent volumes were published in Paris in 1830. One of his pleasures was in reciting the appropriate biblical curses (*q.v.*) on Edom, apparently fast becoming another favourite pastime of these early visitors. He also gave sartorial recommendations to later travellers:

> Two shirts as well as the one being worn; every fortnight there is a chance to wash them; I had only one during the whole journey. Two pairs of pants; it is easier not to wear any. No socks, they cause astonishment.
>
> Eydoux, *In Search of Lost Worlds*

Later, Laborde had a brilliant career as aide-de-camp to the Marquis de Lafayette after the July Revolution of 1830, a member of Parliament under Louis Philippe, and a senator in the Second Empire.

Léon de Laborde

VISITORS OF NOTE

- The Reverend Edward Robinson, 'father of biblical archaeology', spent one day there in 1828 while touring the Bible Lands with his Bible open to identify the sites.

David Roberts

- The artist David Roberts went in 1829, and his beautiful and very accurate drawings are popular to this day.

Sir Henry Layard

- Sir Henry Layard (discoverer of Nineveh) visited in 1840, but got ripped off by the Bedouin, and took a poor view of the architecture which he found debased, of a bad period and corrupt style, wanting in both elegance and grandeur.

Edward Lear

- Edward Lear went there with a cook, one Georgio, whose famous culinary description of the rock as being like 'chocolate, ham, curry-powder and salmon' makes one feel even queasier than poor old Dean Burgon's Newdigate Prize poem.

HISTORY

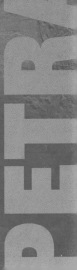

Petra in ancient history

Acity or region with such ancient associations and antecedents as Petra can have no really continuous and coherent history. The writer is forced to rely on the uncertain and fragmentary sources available. However, in the case of Petra, there are two invaluable sources which are also among the most widely read texts in the world: the Bible and the Qur'an. Threads of story and legend about the Petra region and its people are interwoven in both these sources, and include some of the best-known tales. What connection has Petra with the quarrel between Esau and Jacob, with the selling of Joseph into slavery, or with the fall of Jerusalem? How is it linked with Herod the Great, or Salome who danced and demanded John the Baptist's head as a reward? The following pages look at these stories (among others) to uncover part of the hidden history of one of the world's great commercial cities, and its links with some of the world's greatest literature.

PREHISTORY

The Petra region has been occupied since the earliest of times, and there was a settled community at Aklat and Baida (suburbs of the city in later times) as early as 7,000 BCE.

Our historical information about the people who inhabited the Petra region before the third millennium is very sparse, coming almost exclusively from the discoveries of excavators. In the seventeenth century BCE the Petra region was occupied by a Bronze Age people called the Horites (Deut. 2:12, 22). They were a primitive race who dwelt in caves and lived by hunting; they did not cultivate the ground or keep cattle and sheep; they did not know the arts of making pottery or weaving; their tools and weapons were of unworked flint which they later learned to work and polish. There is some evidence from archaeology that they cremated their dead – a practice abhorrent to Semitic feeling – and practised cannibalism. Early Egyptian records refer to a people known as the Charu – which maybe another name for the Horites. On the other hand, the reference to the Horites in Genesis 36:20, 29 implied that they were a Semitic people, so their identification with the cremated cave-dwellers is uncertain.

The Horites left numerous monuments of stone – menhirs (tall standing stones), dolmens (two standing stones with a horizontal stone lying upon them), and cromlechs (stones arranged in a circle). Dolmens are very common throughout Jordan. They were

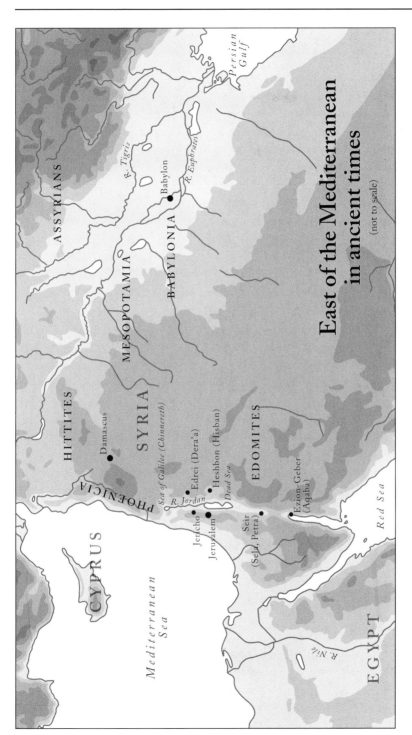

East of the Mediterranean in ancient times

(not to scale)

Persian Gulf

ASSYRIANS

R. Tigris

Babylon

R. Euphrates

MESOPOTAMIA

BABYLONIA

HITTITES

SYRIA

Damascus

Sea of Galilee (Chinnereth)

Edrei (Derʿaʾa)

Heshbon (Hisban)

PHOENICIA

R. Jordan

Dead Sea

Jericho

Jerusalem

Seir
(Sela, Petra)

EDOMITES

Ezion-Geber
(Aqaba)

CYPRUS

Mediterranean Sea

Red Sea

EGYPT

R. Nile

probably connected with the cult of the dead, and in some cases may have been used as altars.

From time to time the populations of the deserts to the east and south became too great to be sustained by their own produce, especially during dry periods. When this happened, they would cross the borders into the cultivated lands – Palestine was regarded particularly as a 'land flowing with milk and honey' – and seek to displace the existing inhabitants. One such invasion occurred in the fourth millennium BCE when the tide flowed over Mesopotamia and Syria. Another large migration in the next millennium filled Canaan with a Semitic population. The migrants were known in ancient records as Amurru, from which the Old Testament name Amorite was derived.

About a thousand years later came another wave, in which the Hebrews and their kinsmen – the Edomites, Ammonites and Moabites – reached Jordan. They eventually settled at Heshbon (Hisban) and Edrei (Dera'a), and their territory extended from the Dead Sea in the south to the Sea of Galilee in the north.

Historians and archaeologists have not yet agreed on the dates of the settlements of tribes in Jordan nor on the Israelite Exodus from Egypt. Estimates of the latter usually range from the fifteenth to thirteenth century BCE. Different historians have assigned it to the period of the Hyksos domination, to the Amarna Age (or Egyptian 18 Dynasty, c.1567–1320 BCE), to the period of the 19 Dynasty (Rameses II (c.1290–1224) and his successor Merneptah (c.1224–1216)), and to the time of the 20 Dynasty (c.1200–1085 BCE). It is impossible to be dogmatic on the subject, but if Rameses II was the Pharaoh who oppressed the slaves in Egypt, and his successor Merneptah the one who let them go, then the Exodus would have been in the mid-thirteenth century. However, the Israelites conquered a number of cities en route from Egypt to the Promised Land, and Kathleen Kenyon, the excavator of their most famous conquest, Jericho, dates its fall – which according to legend must have happened not long afterwards – towards the end of the fourteenth century.

Nothing certain is known of the history of Petra until the Iron Age (1200–330 BCE), by which time the region was known as Edom. The royal seals of four otherwise unknown kings have been discovered there: Qaush-malaku (747 BCE – in the reign of Tiglath-Pileser of Assyria); Malikram (705 BCE – reign of Sennacherib of Assyria); Qaush-gabri (681 BCE

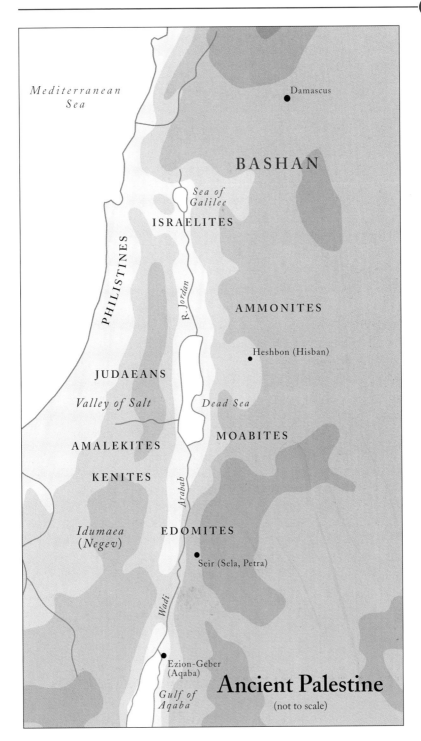

Mediterranean
Sea

Damascus

BASHAN

Sea of
Galilee

ISRAELITES

PHILISTINES

R. Jordan

AMMONITES

Heshbon (Hisban)

JUDAEANS

Valley of Salt

Dead Sea

AMALEKITES

MOABITES

KENITES

Arabah

Idumaea
(Negev)

EDOMITES

Seir (Sela, Petra)

Wadi

Ezion-Geber
(Aqaba)

Gulf of
Aqaba

Ancient Palestine
(not to scale)

THE EGYPTIAN TRIUMPH

The Egyptian name for the people of the Petra region was the Shasu. There is a famous relief depicting their defeat by Rameses III (1202–1170 BCE) on the wall of his temple at Medinet Habu. It shows a Shasu king with six other captive kinglets or sheikhs, kneeling in an uncomfortable attitude with his arms roped behind his back. The inscription reads: 'I plundered the people of Seir of the tribes of the Shasu. I plundered the tents of their people, their possessions, their cattle likewise, without number. They were pinioned and brought as captives, as tribute to Egypt. I gave them to the gods as slaves in their houses.'

Al-Khasneh Farun (Bellefonds)

– reign of Esarhaddon of Assyria); and Natnu (668 BCE – reign of Ashurbanipal of Assyria).

The importance of the region

The Petra region was of very great strategic importance. It was the land bridge between the continents of Asia and Africa, the major road from Egypt to the great empires of Babylon and Assyria to the north and east. Along it flowed all the traffic between these important commercial powers and not all that traffic was peaceful. There was inveterate rivalry between Egypt in the west and the empire of Babylon in the east, and for each of these rivals it was of utmost importance to control the King's Highway up from Aqaba through Petra to Damascus.

The routes passing Petra were conquered and controlled by the Hyksos (Shepherd) kings of Egypt (15–16 Dynasties) (c.1640–1532 BCE), and remained part of their empire until they were expelled from Egypt. Shortly afterwards the powerful female monarch Queen Hatshepsut and her successor, Thotmes III (c.1479–1425 BCE, 18 Dynasty) hurried to re-establish control. Egypt's main interest in the region was rather like Britain's interest in the Suez Canal – to keep the road open so that Phoenicia and Syria (Egyptian colonies at that time) could be defended against the rising power of the Hittite kingdom in the north.

BIBLICAL STORIES AND LEGENDS

The Petra basin was a nomadic tent 'city' from the very earliest biblical times, an important converging place for the nomadic tribes, being on the major trade routes and an important religious shrine. The tribespeople gathered with their tents in the large protected basin-like valley encircled by the mountains, with the massive rock now called Umm al-Biyara (Mother of Cisterns) as its natural fortress. But although Petra is so obviously important and placed in such a strategic position, it is not mentioned in the Bible. The reason is that the built city of Petra, with its tombs and houses carved in the rock, belongs to a period which comes after the biblical era, the period of the Nabataeans (see pp. 36–53). In biblical times the region was known as Seir or Sela, Petra being its Greek name.

The Bible is nonetheless a vital source of information about the region. The key to understanding its significance in biblical history lies in reading the Bible 'inside out'. The Bible concentrates on the descendants of Isaac's son Jacob, regarding all the other peoples of the land as being irrelevant riff-raff whose sole aim in life was to discomfit the 'chosen race'. But once you grasp the significance of the tribal relationships and become familiar with a basic map of the regions on the far side of the River Jordan, it becomes clear that the people of Petra played a singularly important role in the biblical narratives: read 'Petra' instead of 'Seir', 'Petrans' instead of 'Kenites', 'Horites', 'Ishmaelites', 'Edomites' and 'Esau'.

The first inhabitants of Petra who make their appearance in the pages of the Old Testament were Kenites (or Cainites), of the tribe of Cain the son of Adam – tillers of soil, as opposed to the sons of Abel (Habil), who were shepherds – the people now called Bedu. These Kenites were smiths and musicians (Josephus, *Jewish Antiquities*, i.2.2 and Gen. 4:21–22), and the Petra region abounds in old copper mines and metalworkings. The other early men of Seir were the menhir-building cave-dwelling Horites mentioned earlier, descendants of their founding father Seir the Horite. Their capital ('headquarters' would be a better word) was the Sela (Rock) (Gen. 14:6) with which Petra is usually now identified.

Descendants of Abraham

The history of Petra as told in the Bible concerns the descendants of the Prophet Abraham (Ibrahim) through his son Ishmail and his grandson Esau. Abraham was the Nomad of Mesopotamia, reckoned to be the founding father of all the tribespeople in that region – both Arabs and Jews. He was the man called by God, the man who became Al-Khalil (the Friend), who spent all his life following the commands of the Voice that guided him.

His religious enlightenment is revealed both in the Old Testament and in the Qur'an. According to the Qur'an, Abraham grew up amongst the Chaldaeans of Mesopotamia, who had great knowledge of the heavenly bodies, and who worshipped obelisks representing the moon, sun and Ishtar/Atargatis/Al-Uzza who was also the planet Venus (see pp. 54–61). But Abraham saw beyond the physical world to the spiritual world, and tried to teach his people the error of their ways. The faith of Abraham was the beginning of the long struggle of monotheistic worship against the Baal culture. These cults (discussed more fully on pp. 55–61) represented a much older form of religious life, one that worshipped a number of gods and goddesses representing the powers of life and nature.

Abraham had two famous sons: Ishmael (Ismail) and Isaac. Ishmael, his firstborn, was the son of Hagar, an Egyptian concubine, possibly of royal birth. Isaac, his second, was the son of his beloved wife Sarah – born in her old age after a lifetime of barrenness. The elder son, Ishmael, was the founding father of all the tribes known as Ishmaelites – an umbrella term covering the Edomites and Amalekites, tribes regarded by the Arabs as the senior descendants and heirs of Abraham.

Jacob and Esau

Isaac, the younger son married his cousin Rebekah and they had twin sons, Esau and Jacob. Isaac's favouritism towards Esau caused Jacob to plot against his twin brother who had married three powerful heiresses, one of whom was his uncle Ishmael's daughter Basemath (Gen. 36:1–5). Further, Rebekah could not bear the thought of the tribal inheritance getting back into the hands of Ishmael's family and plots were hatched. Jacob tricked his brother Esau out of his birthright (Gen. 25:28–34), and later tricked his blind father into giving him the tribal blessing which should have gone to the heir (Gen. 27). The rest of the Old Testament concentrates on the history of the Hebrew descendants of Jacob – whose name was changed to Israel after he wrestled with the angel (Gen. 32) – and is seen from their point of view. Because of this bias the descendants of Ishmael and Esau are relegated to a list of enemies of Israel, lumped together with all their tribal relatives – without any conscious realization of their equal, if not superior, importance in historical and religious terms.

Esau moves to Edom (Petra)

Angry after the second betrayal by his brother, Esau 'took his wives, his sons and daughters ... and went into a land far away from his brother Jacob ... and dwelt in the hill country of Seir; Esau is Edom' (Gen. 36:6–8). And Seir is Petra.

After such a history, it's not surprising that the Edomites were reckoned – along with their kinsmen the Amalekites, Ammonites and Moabites – to be the most intractable ancient enemies of the Hebrews. The list of Esau's descendants in the hill country of Seir is given in Genesis 36, plus the names of the eight kings who ruled in Edom long before the monarchy was established among the Hebrews (v. 31). It is most interesting that every one of those kings was an outsider. Exogamous marriage suggests strongly that descent must have been in the female line. Genesis 36:40–43 also gives a list of eleven of the tribal sheikhs, of whom the first five were women. This indicates the high status of women during a period and in a region where the Great Goddess was venerated (see pp. 57–59).

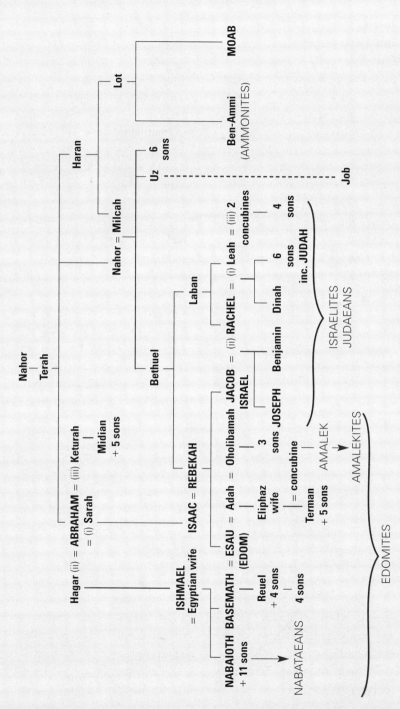

Family tree showing the relationships between the Israelite, Ishmaelite, Edomite, Amalekite, Ammonite and Moabite tribes.

Joseph's brothers sell him into slavery

One of the commodities that passed along the ancient trade route from Damascus down the King's Highway east of the Dead Sea to Petra and beyond, was slaves. The Israelites developed a reputation as slave owners and slave traders, and usually regarded any captives they took as having been given them by God. It must have amused the bitter patriarch Esau when his brother Jacob, in his turn, succumbed to the foolish desire to make one son his favourite, and the jealous brothers sold the young 'dreamer' Joseph to a caravan of Ishmaelites coming down to Petra from Gilead for 20 pieces of silver. Joseph was then sold to one of the military commanders of the Pharaoh of Egypt (Gen. 37:25–36). Joseph was apparently able to forgive his brothers for selling him, but he never forgave his Ishmaelite 'cousins'.

The Exodus

By the time of Moses and the Exodus some 400 years later (*c.*1350 BCE), the Edomites, Amalekites, Moabites and Ammonites had become full-blown tribal kingdoms, and continued to be bitter enemies of the Israelites.

The present-day Ishmaelites of Petra claim that it was in the mountains just outside the city that

Moses struck the rock when the Israelites were perishing from thirst in the desert (Num. 20:7–11). Moses then sent a message to King Rekem of Petra, requesting permission to pass through Edom and reminding him of previous Israelite military triumphs. In spite of this thinly veiled threat, the king would not allow them to enter his territory, and they were obliged to take a long route round. In fact the Israelites already knew that they could not take Petra. They had been told by God that they were about to

> pass through the territory of your brethren the sons of Esau who live in Seir; they will be afraid of you. Take good heed! Do not fight with them, for I will not give you any of their land. No, not so much as for the sole of the foot to tread on, because I have given Mount Seir to Esau as a possession.
>
> Deut. 2:4–5

They could only buy food and water from the Edomites. Before they left the region, Moses' brother Aaron died and was buried on Jabal Harun.

Despite God's ban, the Israelites – now led by the Israelite war hero Joshua – were itching for a fight. When they eventually got past the tribal territories of their kinfolk their savagery was horrendous. They slaughtered Sihon the Amorite king of Heshbon, and after him Og the king of Bashan:

And we utterly destroyed them … destroying every city, men, women and children, and all the cattle and spoils of the cities we took as our booty.

Deut. 3:6–7

Joshua, celebrated as a hero by the Old Testament, became a byword amongst the Ishmaelite peoples for merciless butchery in the name of his religion.

The Prophet Balaam, who was summoned by King Balak of Moab to curse the Israelites (Num. 24), is probably to be identified as Bela, son of Sheikh Beor; Balaam had apparently succeeded Rekem as king of the Edomites (Gen. 36:32). He may have been a sacral king, ruling as both king and high priest. His visions revealed only that their resistance to the Israelites would be in vain.

Moses curses Petra

The curses on Petra began during this period. Moses, in his final counsel before his death, reminded the Israelites of the great high place at Petra with its dangerous religious practices. He reminded them how the Edomites had,

stirred Him to jealousy with strange gods, with abominable practices they had provoked Him to anger. They sacrificed to demons which were no gods … I will heap evils upon them … they shall be wasted with hunger and devoured with heat and poisonous pestilence; and I will send the teeth of beasts against them, with venom of crawling things of the dust … they are a nation devoid of understanding; if they were wise, they would understand this! … For their rock is not as our Rock … See that I, even I, am He, and there is no God beside Me; I kill and I make alive; I wound and I heal; and there is none that can deliver out my My hand!

Deut. 32:15–39

Thus began the tradition of terrible curses that were to be heaped upon the region.

The Edomites were by now settled at Petra, so from now on we will refer to them as Petrans. With their rich mineral resources they thrived for the time being, and soon became masters of the arts of metalworking. The Wadi Arabah to the south of the Dead Sea is covered with ancient copper slag heaps which reveal the extent of their mining and smelting operations – Khirbet Nahas, for example, means 'Copper Ruin'. At the same time, the Philistines on the Mediterranean coast had the monopoly of iron. The Israelites, with no metallurgical expertise, were at a serious disadvantage. 'There was no smith to be found throughout all the land of Israel …

and there was no sword or spear in the hand of the people' (I Sam. 13:19–22).

The Hebrews defeat the Petrans

The first Israelite king was Saul (shortly before 1000 BCE). He proved himself a powerful warrior, fighting the Israelites' enemies remorselessly: 'when Saul had taken the kingship, he fought against all his enemies on every side, against Moab, the Ammonites, Edom [Petra] …' (I Sam. 14:47–48). Saul apparently made use of some of the Petrans he had conquered. His chief herdsman was Doeg the Edomite, who presumably looked after his flocks in the newly conquered Edomite territories and became a famous biblical villain. In the rivalry between Saul and David, Doeg took the part of Saul, and was involved in betraying David (I Sam. 21:7; 22:11–19).

After Saul's death, David (who was by then king of Judah) was accepted as king by the Israelites also. David (c.1000–960 BCE) then moved against the Petrans in order to gain control of the copper trade, and used Doeg's treachery as an excuse to attack. The campaign was an attempt at genocide which the Petrans never forgave: 'David slew eighteen thousand Edomites in the Valley of Salt, and he put garrisons in Edom, and all the Edomites became David's servants' (II Sam. 8:13–14; I Chr. 18:12). The Petrans who had survived, meanwhile, nursed their hatred and grievance against the Hebrews for four hundred years until the time of the downfall of Jerusalem (586 BCE).

Solomon (c.960–922 BCE), David's son, maintained his grip on the Petran territory. Not only did he benefit from the famous copper mines near Ezion-Geber (the Gulf of Aqaba) which, as we have seen, had been seized from the Petrans, he also realized that control of the shore of the Red Sea opened up enormous trade possibilities (II Chr. 8:17). He commissioned the building of a merchant fleet, and established trade with the coasts of Africa and the Queen of Sheba (in what is now the Yemen). This must have been a bitter time for those who had survived David's slaughter, who were obliged to watch Petra and its trade routes being taken over and run by the Hebrews.

The Petrans resist Judah

After Solomon's death, the united Hebrew monarchy of Israel and Judah could not be sustained, and the kingdoms were divided once more. The history of Petra then becomes bound up with that of the Kingdom of Judah. King Jehoshaphat of Judah (868 BCE) was hampered by tribal warfare: 'The Moabites and Ammonites …

came up against him for battle.' They told him, 'A great multitude is coming against you from Edom [Petra].' He appealed to God for help, and complained that 'the men of Ammon and Moab and Mount Seir, whom You would not let Israel invade when they came out of Egypt … behold they reward us by coming to drive us out.' After his earnest prayers, the Lord must have intervened to confuse his enemies, for:

> the Lord set an ambush against the men of Moab, Ammon and Mount Seir, destroying them utterly … for they rose up against each other, and helped to destroy one another … and when Judah came to the watchtower of the wilderness, behold, they were dead bodies lying on the ground.
>
> II Chr. 20

A generation later, in the reign of Amaziah of Judah (c.800–783 BCE), the people of Petra took a battering once again. Amaziah 'led out his people and went to the Valley of Salt, and smote 10,000 men of Seir [Petra]'. Then followed a horrific act of barbarity against prisoners of war: 'The men of Judah captured another 10,000 alive, and took them to the top of the rock and threw them down from the top, and they were all dashed to pieces' (II Chr. 25:5–13). Scholars argue about the numbers,

but nobody can argue that it was not an atrocity.

However, the king underwent an amazing conversion: 'After he came from the slaughter of the men of Seir, he brought their gods and set them up as his own gods, and worshipped them, making offerings to them' (v. 14).

The Petrans' revenge on Judah

In the late sixth century BCE, the smaller kingdoms of the Middle East were gripped by fear of the aggressive might of Babylon (modern Iraq), the superpower at the head of the Persian Gulf. In the face of this threat the Triad worshippers of Petra actually became allies of the Judaeans for a brief time, but this alliance was only superficial and when Jerusalem (then held by the Judaeans) fell to Babylon in 586 BCE after a two-year siege, the Petrans could not resist their glee as the city was burned and everything reduced to rubble. At last they were seeing their revenge for their ancient grievances. The Judaeans who managed to flee from the city were hunted down and shown no mercy. Their lamentations also contained a warning to the triumphant Petrans, who assisted the Babylonians in the decimation of the city and its inhabitants:

> Our pursuers were swifter than the vultures in the sky, they chased

us on the mountains, they lay in wait for us in the wilderness … [you may] rejoice and be glad, O daughter of Edom, dweller in the land of Uz; but to you also the cup shall pass!

Lam. 4:18–22

The Petrans jubilantly chanted 'Down with it! Even to the foundation' as the Babylonians systematically destroyed Jerusalem. Psalm 137 records the cry of one aggrieved Judaean against the Babylonians: 'Blessed be he who shall deal with them as they dealt with us! Blessed be he who shall take their little ones and dash their heads against the rocks!'

If the Petrans had truly helped or encouraged the Babylonians to seize fleeing infants and kill them in this horrific manner, one can understand the curses against them that were to follow. But any retribution for the Judaeans was yet to come – they were carried off captive, and the Petran Edomites immediately moved into the derelict territory and set up a new kingdom, known as Idumaea (now the Negev in Israel).

Any Petran sense of triumph, or hopes for freedom from the worry of their ancestral enemies were shortlived. In _c._500 BCE, in the living memory of some of the exiles, the Judaeans were allowed to return to their old homes

and the savage bitterness broke out again.

The curses on Petra

It was during this turbulent period that the biblical prophets began to launch their psychic campaign against Petra. The ancient hatred between the Hebrew (Israelite and Judaean) and Ishamaelite tribes was inextricably linked with the religious fanaticism of both sides, and the holy city whose gods and atmosphere had so impressed King Amaziah achieved the dubious honour of being the most cursed place in the Bible. Prophet after prophet ritually pronounced the most terrible dooms against it.

The attempts of the Triad worshippers to block the curses would come to nothing:

> And when they say to you, consult the mediums and wizards who chirp and mutter, should not a people consult their God? Should they consult the dead on behalf of the living? … They will be thrust into thick darkness.

Isa. 8:19–22

The Petrans were suitably nervous in the circumstances, and made conciliatory moves, but there was to be no forgiveness. 'They have sent lambs from Sela [Petra], by way of the desert, to the mount of Zion … but when Moab presents himself, when he comes to his sanctuary to pray, he will not prevail.' (Isa. 15–16)

Flee! Save yourselves! Be like a wild ass in the desert ... I will make you small among nations, despised among men. The horror you inspire has deceived you, and the pride of your heart, you who live in the clefts of the Rock (Sela), who hold the height of the hill. Though you make your nest as high as the eagle's, I will bring you down from there! [Petra] shall become a horror; everyone who passes by it will hiss ... no man shall dwell there, no man shall sojourn in her ... Hear the plan which the Lord has made against Edom ... at the sound of their fall the earth shall tremble, the sound of their cry shall be heard at the Red Sea ... the heart of the warriors of Edom [Petra] shall be in that day like the heart of a woman in her pangs!

Jer. 48–49

Ezekiel, the chief prophet of the exile, continued the onslaught:

Because you laughed over My sanctuary when it was profaned, and over the land of Israel when it was made desolate, and over the house of Judah when it went into exile – I am handing you over to the people of the East for a possession ... I will destroy you ... I will stretch out My hand against Edom and cut off from it man and beast; I will make it desolate; from Teman to Dedan they will fall by the sword ...'

Ezek. 25:3–7, 13–14

'Behold, I am against you, Mount Seir ... I will make you a desolation and a waste ... I will cut it off from all the nomads. And I will fill your mountains and valleys and all your ravines with the slain ... you shall be desolate, Mount Seir, and all Edom, all of it!

Ezek. 35

Their doom was settled:

Let the earth listen, and all that fills it ... the Lord has doomed them, has given them over for slaughter. Their slain shall be cast out, and the stench of their corpses shall rise; the mountains shall flow with their blood ... their land shall be soaked with their blood, and their soil made rich with their fat ... and the streams of Edom shall be turned into burning pitch; night and day it shall not be quenched; its smoke shall go up for ever.

Isa. 34

The most vehement curse was that of Obadaiah, reiterating some of the words of Jeremiah, which suggests that it was a 'floating oracle' – original curser unknown:

Thus says the Lord concerning Edom [Petra] … though you soar aloft like the eagle, though your nest is set among the stars, I will bring you down … Every man from Mount Esau [Umm al-Biyara] shall be cut off by slaughter. For the violence done to your brother shame shall cover you, and you shall be cut off for ever … you should not have rejoiced over the people of Judah in the day of their ruin; you should not have entered the gate of my people and gloated over his disaster … or stood at the parting of the ways to cut off his fugitives; you should not have delivered up the survivors in the day of distress. As you have done, so shall it be done to you, your deeds shall return upon your own head … There shall be no survivor of the house of Esau!

Obad. vv. 1–18

A shudder ran through the tribespeople of Petra. The clash was not an earthly one, but a confrontation of the gods themselves. If their gods failed them, they were surely doomed.

The Book of Job (Nabi Ayyub)
One of the most interesting theological works of the Old Testament is the Book of Job, the story of a noble and long-suffering sheikh of 'the land of Uz', who may have been a citizen of Petra at a time when it was a tent city.

There are two theories about this land of Uz, both of which favour identifying it with the Petra region. One suggests that it was the cult centre of the goddess Venus Al-Uzza, the chief deity of Petra, and the other is geneaological. According to the Genesis narrative, the firstborn son of Abraham's niece Milcah was called Uz (Gen. 11:27, 29). According to Josephus (*Jewish Antiquities*, 1.vi.4) Uz founded Trachonitis and Damascus, but it is generally accepted that the 'land of Uz' was further to the south, and that the Edomite territory extended into it (see Lamentations 4:18–22), where the 'daughter of Edom' who rejoiced in the downfall of Jerusalem was identified with the 'dweller in the land of Uz'.

The images employed in the Book of Job reveal a great deal about the inhabitants of his city. The kings and great men had splendid tombs, and great wealth in gold and silver (3:14–15); there were already rumours of ancient treasures concealed in the earth (3:21) – not so far-fetched in those days before banking (cf. Matthew 25:18, 25); they were keen gardeners, and worked the rock for water-channels (28:9–11). They protected their plots from wild creatures by traps and snares (18:9–10). Apart from rock carving, they also cut inscriptions with iron pens onto tablets which they then fixed with lead to the rock faces (19:24). Gold, silver and iron were mined, and brass was manufactured (28:1-2.) They valued the topaz of Ethiopia (28:19) and wore jewellery made of coral, pearl, rubies, crystal, onyx and sapphires (28:6, 16–18). They wore gold earrings (42:11) and admired themselves in looking-glasses of polished metal (37:18). Musical instruments were common – timbrel, harp and organ (21:11–12).

PETRAN TRIBES IN THE QUR'AN

The Qur'an is also a source of story and legend about the peoples who dwelt in and around the Petra region. Although they do not play anything like as significant a part in this text as they do in the Bible, they are connected with some of the best-known stories of the Islamic prophets.

According to the Qur'an (the revelations from God given to the Arabian Prophet Muhammad (c.570–632 CE), the people of the 'tent city' at Petra were the tribes known as the 'Ad and the Thamud. In Arab tradition, 'Ad was the son of 'Aus, the son of Aram, the son of Shem, the son of Noah. Nearly all the prophets accepted as genuine by Muslims are celebrities known from the pages of the Old

Testament – except two. The two known only from the Arabic tradition are Hud and Salih, the two sent specifically to the 'Ad and the Thamud tribes.

At the time of Hud (a figure from the time before Abraham), the 'Ad tribesmen had forgotten all about the One God of their ancestor Noah (known as the Prophet Nuh in the Qur'an), and had begun worshipping the Baal forces of earth and sky. Hud was sent to try to bring them back to the True Way. His mission was not successful, and the 'Ad tribesmen ridiculed his attempts to re-establish the religion and worship of Noah (Surah 7:66). The result of this was disaster. As also happened so often in the Old Testament tradition when the Hebrew tribes turned back to Baalism and adulterated their worship of the One God, the tribe was punished – by a terrible famine which lasted three years. It was finally wiped out – all but a small remnant – by a fiery wind-storm.

The few who survived became known as the Second 'Ad, or Thamud tribe. Tradition specifies that these survivors were actually the 'cousin' tribe to the 'Ad, for they were also descended from Noah. The first known archaeological inscription that identifies the Thamud tribe was carved by Sargon of Assyria in c.715 BCE.

They occupied the north-west region of Arabia, and Petra became their capital. It was a tent city rather than a city with erected buildings at this stage, although they soon began to chisel away at the sandstone rocks. Their territory included what was known as the *hijr* (rocky country) (Surah 15:80), and the fertile valley and plains of Qura, north of Medina. The Thamud grew very rich from their trade in frankincense from the Yemen, which was in great demand in the western Roman world and in Egypt. In fact all the goods bound for Egypt passed through the stronghold city of Petra. Verses from the Qur'an describe Petra and its wealth: 'You have made gardens and springs, cornfields and date-palms with spathes near breaking with the weight of fruit. And you carve houses out of the rocky mountains with great skill' (Surah 11:147, 149).

Inevitably, as so often happens when people become rich, the Thamud became godless and arrogant, and conveniently forgot that all blessings belong to no one as of right, but are bestowed *insha'Allah* – as God wills. The second of the prophets, Salih, was sent to remind them of their duty towards God, and try to bring them back to right thinking:

Remember how He made you inheritors after the 'Ad people,

and gave you dwelling-place in the land; you built for yourselves palaces and fortresses in the plains, and carved out homes in the mountains. Bring to your minds the benefits you have received from God, and stop your evil mischief on the earth!

Surah 7:74

Despite the fate of their cousins the 'Ad, the Thamud took no notice of the divine warnings, and their complacency led to the most famous story about Salih and the Petran tribes. It concerns the sign of the She-Camel, which is referred to many times in the Qur'an. When the Petran tribes were stricken by one of the inevitable droughts, Salih found to his disgust that the privileged classes of the city were saving their own skins by conserving all the water for themselves and preventing the poor from bringing their livestock to the few remaining springs. Muslims believe that a human being never really owns anything; he or she is allowed the temporary use of something by God. Therefore the claim by the rich of Petra that they owned the water supply was regarded by the Muslim prophet as an act of *shirk* – the usurping of the rights of God Alone.

Salih's sign involved letting loose a she-camel, and sending the thirsty beast on to Thamud land. Any true Muslim would have allowed the beast food and drink, but the wealthy Thamud took the point of view that since they, owned the wells and pasture and this was not one of their camels, they would not allow her to drink their water; so they slaughtered her (Surah 91:14; 54:9). God was so angry at this proof of their callousness and *shirk* that He destroyed them by means of a great earthquake.

The Nabataean period (sixth century BCE–106 CE)

The tribes of Nabataea, who took over from the Edomites (Idumaeans) as occupiers of Petra, claimed to be descendants of Ishmael's eldest daughter, Nabaioth, as opposed to the younger sister, Basemath, who married Esau. (Nabaioth is usually assumed to be Ishmael's son, but the name is a female one.) In fact, one could argue that the Nabataeans were simply a senior clan of Edomites. Their rise to supremacy probably coincided with the depopulation of Palestine by the Babylonian king Nebuchadnezzar in the sixth century BCE – although their civilization at Petra developed much later. They were first referred to as a people (the *Nabaaiti*) in 647 BCE in a list of the enemies of the last

great Assyrian king, Ashurbanipal, when their king was Natnu.

The next mention of them is in the fourth century BCE, when Alexander the Great's massive empire was divided up amongst his generals after his death (323 BCE). The Petra region became the border country between the Seleucid dynasty in Syria (created by Alexander's general Seleucus), and the Ptolemaic dynasty (created by another of his generals, Ptolemy) in Egypt. Continual rivalry between these two kingdoms ensured that the territories in between were rarely at peace.

The next reference to the Nabataeans (*Nabataioi*) was by the historian Diodorus of Sicily (first century BCE). He quoted an author of around 312 BCE who recorded an unpleasant bit of warfare between the Nabataean Petrans and the Seleucid emperor Antigonus, who was attempting to become sole ruler of Asia. He swept down the King's Highway and attacked Umm al-Biyara while the fighting men were absent; the Nabataean army then returned, ambushed and massacred them, and escaped further trouble by retreating into the desert. However, until 198 BCE the Egyptians, not the Seleucids, were dominant on the west side of the Jordan, until the Seleucids under Antiochus IV attempted to unite the whole region with Syria under a Hellenistic culture, by imposing a mixed Greek and Syrian religion, Greek language, literature, sports and dress. (This led to the Maccabaean revolt of 168 BCE.)

After 125 BCE the decline of both the Seleucid and Egyptian empires allowed the full development of the Nabataean state. They gradually extended their territory west into the Negev, east to the Euphrates and south along the Red Sea, a domain that stretched from Madain Salih (north of Medina in present day Saudi Arabia) all the way north to Damascus in the north.

TRADE

From very early times, Petra was closely associated with trade. However, it was in the turbulent century around the lifetime of Jesus that the historic situation arose which allowed the Nabataeans finally to develop an urban civilization on a magnificent scale.

When the Seleucid Empire finally collapsed in 64 BCE, the rival mights of Rome to the west and Parthia to the east (established in 247 BCE) confronted each other across a wild, bandit-infested no-man's-land. The inhabitants of Petra saw their opportunity and seized it. They organized a highly efficient force of 'desert police' to create a 'safe' route by which the caravans could travel from the East to the voracious markets of Rome and the West.

The luxury produce of India and China was much in demand on the shores of the eastern Mediterranean. Merchandise was brought by ship through the Straits of Hormuz in the Persian Gulf, to enter the Tigris-Euphrates delta and dock at Charax Spasinu. From there it would have been taken either up the Euphrates to Babylon, or across the top of the Nejd and Nefud deserts via Jauf (Al-Jawf) to Petra. Other routes to Petra went across the desert starting from what is now Kuwait, or Bahrain. Alternatively, the ships could go right round the south of Arabia and enter the Red Sea heading for the port of Ezion-Geber (now Aqaba). However, since most ships from the East could not sail against the very strong winds in the Red Sea, merchants regularly unloaded their goods on the Arabian peninsula, and carried them up the eastern shore by camel straight to Petra. To the west of Petra the routes fanned out, one road continuing west to Egypt, one branching north-west to Gaza, and the other heading north to Damascus.

The Nabataeans were effective highwaymen and made a good living by swooping down on the caravans and carrying off the luxuries of Arabia, India and East Africa to Petra. Outsiders were

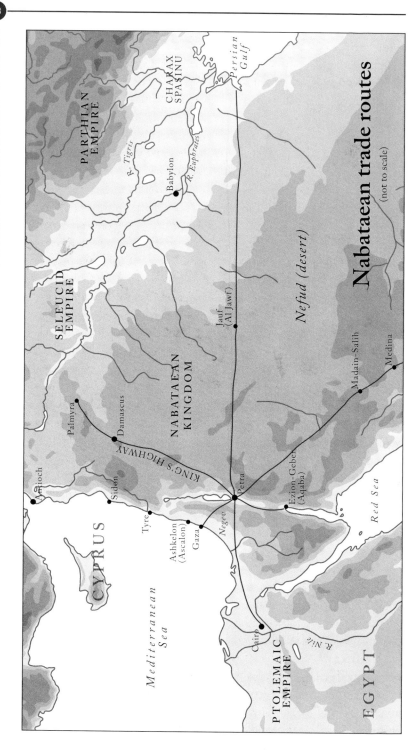

Nabataean trade routes
(not to scale)

PARTHIAN EMPIRE

CHARAX SPASINU

Persian Gulf

R. Tigris

R. Euphrates

Babylon

SELEUCID EMPIRE

Jauf (Al Jawf)

Nefud (desert)

Madain-Salih

Medina

NABATAEAN KINGDOM

Palmyra

Damascus

KING'S HIGHWAY

Antioch

Sidon

Tyre

Ashkelon (Ascalon)

Gaza

Negev

Petra

Ezion-Geber (Aqaba)

Red Sea

CYPRUS

Mediterranean Sea

Cairo

R. Nile

PTOLEMAIC EMPIRE

EGYPT

refused entry to the Petra basin and it became the storing place for plunder. As the trade route bypassed the actual city site this was quite easy to do.

Eventually, they found acting as 'customs officials' more profitable than brigandage, and offered their services on the road to the merchants as 'honest brokers', plus giving them protection from any other tribes with their own desert police – at a price. Subsidies were demanded as transit insurance, the money being paid to these other tribes (with whom they were generally in league) to stop them attacking and taking plunder. It must be said, however, that the interpretation of this system as a 'protection racket' is a Western one. In tribal eyes the Nabataeans were providing a fair service by 'smoothing the road'. Since all desert land was actually owned by the various tribes, it can be argued that they were only acting on a principle similar to our toll roads and bridges.

By these means Petra became the major caravan-city of the ancient world. The few classical references to the Nabataeans bolster this image. The Greek historian Strabo (c.54 BCE) had a friend who had been to Petra, who described their imports as copper, iron, purple-dyed cloth, styrax (a bush producing benzoin gum) and statues. A later historian, Pliny the Elder (23–79 CE), mentioned a valuable medicament called lycion, which was transported in unbreakable leather bottles.

Other luxury goods that came to Petra were henna from Ascalon (Ashkelon) near Gaza, glass and purple dye from Sidon and Tyre to the north, pearls from the Persian Gulf, fine silk (damask) from Damascus, iron and bronze from the West, ginger and pepper, precious woods and ostrich feathers, ivory, apes and slaves from Africa.

Gold, frankincense and myrrh

Everyone knows what gold is, but not everyone is familiar with those two extremely valuable commodities from the land of the Queen of Sheba (Yemen) – frankincense and myrrh. Some scholars believe that the wise men of the Christmas story must have been Nabataeans, since the Nabataeans had a monopoly in these perfumes at that time.

Frankincense and myrrh are sweet-smelling gum resins which are gathered from special trees growing mainly in Arabia. To obtain frankincense, cuts are made in the bark of trees of the genus *Boswellia*, and a white juice forms in teardrops of about 2.5 centimetres in length. When burned, these produce an exotic scent, and so frankincense was much in demand for worship of the various gods in their temples, including the great Temple of Jehovah in Jerusalem.

Myrrh is derived from a low-growing thorny shrub called *Commiphora myrrha* and exudes naturally, although cutting increases the flow. Walking in a garden of these trees is sheer joy, for the beautiful scent is given off even by the wood and bark. It was made into a special oil, used to scent clothes and bedrooms, and became the most fashionable fragrance in demand by wealthy women throughout the Roman Empire. It was also used in preparing the bodies of loved ones for burial, and apparently it had medicinal properties as a painkilling drug. Myrrh was sometimes allowed to be given to criminals about to be crucified, by tender-hearted Roman centurions. According to Mark 15:23, it was also offered to Jesus before his crucifixion, but he refused to drink it. Cleopatra, the Ptolemaic Queen of Egypt, was very fond of the scent and was once the landlord of Herod's famous myrrh garden at Jericho. Both the myrrh and the frankincense given to the infant Jesus would have been very expensive presents, just as valuable as the gold and possibly more so.

ROYALTY

Although most of what follows deals with the quarrels and intrigues of kings, it's worth bearing in mind that queens in the ancient world were often as powerful. It is this ignored aspect of the history that sometimes throws light on otherwise puzzling events. For this reason, this section begins by looking at the role of women in the royal houses during this period, so that parts of the history which follows will appear less surprising.

Female royal power in the ancient world

Most histories concentrate on 'male' history – the kings, politics and battles; but history from the female point of view is often highly intriguing. Family relationships become of vital importance, and a glance at the family tree or marital arrangements of a monarch can often supply the answers to perplexing motives for the course of history.

Families in ancient history were frequently based on the strength of the matrilineal bloodline. When studying the power of female royalty in the buffer states between Rome and Parthia 100 BCE–70 CE (i.e. the landblock from Turkey to Egypt), I hoped to find at least a few notable females who might be worth a closer look, such as Cleopatra and Queen Alexandra of the Jews. To my surprise I uncovered not just a few but hordes of magnificent and powerful queens. Female power was almost the norm all over the East.

The best way for a woman to suceed in obtaining power was to get started as a daughter of a favourite wife and mother's favourite, or senior royal princess who would at puberty become sister-wife to the intended heir. If he died prematurely, you simply married the next one. (Sister-wives had a far better grip on the monarch than outsiders as a general rule; kings' fancies came and went, a sister was a sister.) As soon as possible you would produce an heir, or choice of heirs, in view of infant mortality rates; and once you were safely on the throne (your brother's accession following the death of his father) you would then send your young king-warlord off into battle as soon as possible. When he got killed, as he inevitably would sooner or later, you would then rule as dowager for your son, who might be still only an infant if you were lucky, until he reached the age when he could take authority on himself – usually around 17 years old, at which time he would also, of course, be just right for starting military service too. During your time as dowager, you would closely supervise his training and that of your daughter who was destined to marry him; he would then marry your daughter and you would retain enormous influence

as queen-mother (The empress Thermusa of Parthia – originally a clever Italian slave-secretary – actually married her own son when he reached the age of 17.)

Alternatively, when your war-lord died, you could marry another husband of your own choice, and either go with him to his kingdom or, in a matriarchal system, draft him in as the new king of your kingdom. The Petran queens did this; so did Cleopatra – she got rid of two brother-husbands very rapidly so that she could enjoy the ambitious Roman warlords Pompey, Caesar and Antony. One of her predecessors married and was reign-ing queen five times, in different countries. The main trouble with bringing in outside blood was that it encouraged succession disputes.

Almost hand-in-hand with female power went the female aspect of trinity worship (see pp. 56–61). While monotheism cuts out the female, in a holy trinity or triad the mother is the lynchpin of the whole system. She combines virginal purity, the eager (and often scheming) lover, the fertile mother, the grieving mother or widow. She touches all sorts of Jungian archetypal chords. A devout Roman Catholic would understand the meaning of all this best – although the Catholic veneration of the Virgin Mary is ascetic and omits the archetypal passions of sexuality and fertility. Nevertheless, I should imagine the atmosphere of ancient Petra was not unlike Lourdes.

The early kings

The Nabataean kings were notable for three things: their rampant hatred of the rival tribes of Israel and Judah; their admiration for Greek culture; and their resistance to Roman red tape which threatened their independence and lucrative desert enterprises. Their early history is sketchy indeed. They were at war with the first Seleucid emperor, Antigonus, in 312 BCE; but by 217 there was a Nabataean named Zabdibelos who commanded a mercenary force in the Seleucid army of Antiochus III (the Great).

The first Nabataean king was Harith I (also called Haretat, or Aretas in Greek), the 'tyrant of the Arabs' mentioned in one of the Apocryphal books of the Bible (II Maccabees 5:8) for his refusal to protect the renegade Jewish high priest Jason who had been driven out of his own country. He was succeeded by three shadowy figures of whom virtually nothing is known – Zabdiel (or Zabelos), who murdered the Seleucid Alexander Balas in 146 BCE and sent his head to Ptolemy; Malik I (or Imalcue or Iamblichus), who raised the Seleucid Antiochus Theos as a foster-son; and the warlike Harith

II (Erotimus – c.100–96 BCE) whose attack on Gaza in 97 BCE was mentioned by the Jewish historian Josephus (*Jewish Antiquities*, 13:360).

The next king, Aboud I (Obodas, Obidath) defeated the Jewish warrior-king Alexander Jannaeus in c.93 BCE, and recovered Moab and Gilead which Alexander had previously captured. The whole of east Jordan had probably come under Nabataean rule by that time, since Nabataean pottery of this period has also been found in tombs in Amman. Rabbel I, who succeeded him, fought against Antiochus Dionysus in 87 BCE. Nothing else is known of him.

Herod the Great

The most famous Petran was undoubtedly that biblical villain Herod the Great. Herod was a Petran prince, his mother Cypros being a cousin of King Harith III of Petra (c.85–60 BCE) who had brought Herod up as a son. (She was the princess after whom he named the Cypros fortress in Jericho.) His father, Antipater, was an Idumaean millionaire. Herod's talents as a warrior and his friendship with the rising Roman star Mark Antony led to him becoming recognized as King of the Jews by the Romans in 30 BCE.

Herod is usually remembered only for his beastly role in the

Christmas story, when he tried to dupe the wise men and butchered all the male babies of Bethlehem. Apart from being a wily politician he was also a world-famous orator, debonair heart-throb of the Roman jet set, and brilliant athlete. In his old age he was made president of the Olympic Games – mainly because he paid for the athletes' village, the ruins of which are on view in Olympia to this day. In fact, this outrageous millionaire was the builder or benefactor of nearly all the Roman-type ruins to be seen in the major sites all over the Mediterranean world. Like many great rulers, he simply lived ten years too long.

Herod's uncle, Harith III of Petra, had conquered Damascus, the capital of Syria. He then became embroiled in the Jewish Civil War which broke out between two rival claimants for the Jewish throne, on behalf of Aristobulus, who was not backed by Rome. As a result Harith fell foul of the Roman governor of Syria, Marcus Aemilius Scaurus. In revenge, Scaurus set out for Petra with the supposed support of Herod's father, Antipater, who in fact was not too pleased about attacking Harith, as he was a relative. However, rather than risk the wrath of Rome, Antipater agreed to provision the Fourth Legion at his own expense and led them down to Petra – trusting that

they would find it impregnable. So it turned out. Scaurus was eventually forced to settle for a face-saving tribute from Harith of 300 talents, of which Antipater immediately volunteered to pay half (thus reassuring Harith, who had understandably not been too sure of his relative's loyalty in the circumstances). A Roman coin in the British Museum shows Harith on his knees with a camel in the background. Scaurus had evidently chosen to interpret this embarrassing stand-off as a Roman victory! The camel was presumably carrying the tribute-money. No doubt it wore its usual enigmatic smile. The Jewish prince Aristobulus, in whose cause Harith had challenged Rome, repaid him by ceding to him all the territory south of the Dead Sea (Josephus, *Wars*, 1.117–227). Harith was succeeded by Aboud II (*c.*62–56 BCE) about whom nothing is known.

Scaurus' successors in office were no more successful against the undaunted tribesmen of the region, until Gabinius (governor of Syria 57–55 BCE) scored a signal victory over them. Herod, who was then at the tender age of 16 a young cavalry officer in a unit captained by Mark Antony, got his first military experience in a battle against his own mother's people. The next Nabataean king, Malik II (Malchus), never forgave

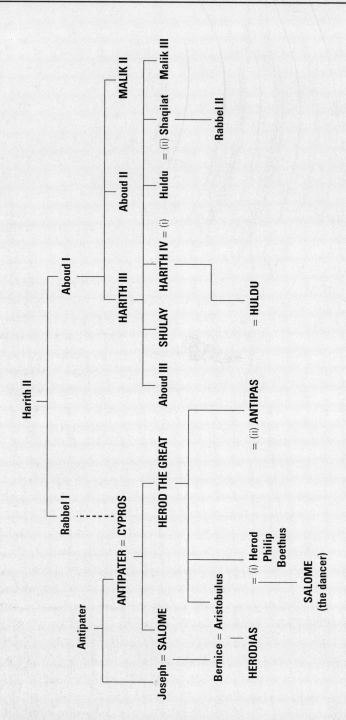

Family tree showing the relationship between the Petran royal house and Herod's family between about 100 BCE and 30 CE.

Herod, and they became bitter enemies.

Meanwhile, the handsome young Herod had caught the attention of Cleopatra of Egypt, and became possibly the only warrior-prince whose shrewdness overcame his ardour, so that he did not succumb to her charms. At one stage Cleopatra increased the animosity between Herod and Malik by giving Herod the lucrative monopoly in the bitumen trade on the Dead Sea instead of granting it to Malik.

Malik believed Rome could be overthrown, and backed her most powerful enemy, Parthia. When Parthia lost, he had to pay an enormous tribute to save his skin. Later, during the struggles between the various triumvirs of Rome, Malik sent cavalry to help Julius Caesar in Egypt, and proved so helpful he was mentioned in Caesar's famous dispatches (*Caesar De Bello: Alexandrino 1*).

Rome and Nabataea never rode easy together. Mark Antony gave a large part of Malik's territory to Cleopatra, and once again Malik had to dig deep to pay tribute. In revenge, he assisted in her downfall following her defeat in the Mediterranean by surrounding her ships as they were being hauled across the sands to the Red Sea (she no doubt cursed her short-sightedness in not having had a convenient canal dug to Suez). Malik fell on the helpless fleet, and fired the lot. Herod had warned his friend Antony of Cleopatra's dangerous ambitions, and as a result of its pro-Roman activity Herod's family received Roman citizenship and was granted immunity from taxation.

Salome

King Herod's reign was beset by tragedies and intrigues, and many historians acknowledge that the spiteful and jealous hand of his sister Salome lay behind everything – but they do not often suggest why she was so malevolent. My theory is that because of her Nabataean background, Salome was genuinely aggrieved that Herod did not marry her and make her his sister-queen as was common practice for the Nabataean and other Middle Eastern royal lines (see pp. 40–2) – notably in Egypt, Parthia and Commagene. Having spurned Salome, Herod fell disastrously in love with the Jewish heiress Mariamne. This led to horrendous plotting, and much of Herod's dynamic energy was frittered away coping with the intrigues stirred up by the bitter, rejected Salome. Until she died, she consistently removed all who came between herself and the throne – including the Jewish queen, her own two husbands, Herod's two best friends, and later Herod's two sons by Mariamne – to no avail.

Meanwhile, in Petra the sluggish but wily Aboud III (30–9 BCE) had succeeded Malik. Short of funds, he sent his slick brother Prince Shulay (Syllaeus) to do a deal with Herod. Shulay, who never ruled, was the most colourful character by far in Nabataean history. At one point he bamboozled Aelius Gallus – the greedy megalomaniac Roman prefect of Egypt – into undertaking an expedition into Arabia Felix (Yemen). It was a total disaster for the Romans, with thousands perishing in fearful torment from heat and thirst in the blistering sands. Shulay survived and profited from the débâcle.

Salome, a grandmother in her hungry forties by this time, pounced on her handsome young royal relative Shulay (aged not much more than 22), seeing in him the chance of becoming queen of Petra if she couldn't have Judaea. The scandal of their liaison became public; Salome appealed to the empress Livia for support and got it. Herod, who did not approve, agreed slyly to let Shulay have his sister on the condition that Shulay became a Jew. Negotiations ended abruptly; Salome was married off to a nonentity, and resumed blighting the lives of Herod's sons.

In 12 BCE Shulay reappeared on the scene, supporting guerrilla raids on Herod's borders on the King's Highway. The Roman governor Saturninus authorized Herod to take retaliatory action, and Shulay's brother Neguib (Nacebus) was killed together with a handful of warriors in a skirmish. Shulay instantly appealed to the emperor, putting out the chilling propaganda that Herod had invaded his territory without permission and slaughtered 2,500 people. Augustus chose to believe him, and Herod became *persona non grata* in Rome.

In 9 BCE the ineffectual Aboud III died, and Shulay's brother Harith, who was friendly with Herod, seized the throne in a *coup d'état* without applying for permission from Rome and got away with it. He succeeded largely because his case was argued by the greatest lawyer of that time, the famous historian Nicolaus of Damascus. Nicolaus had just embarked on a flattering biography of the emperor Augustus, and that had clout. Shulay didn't stand a chance. The débâcle in Arabia Felix was dredged up, and he was condemned. The fact that he had seduced the wives of half the gentlemen in the Senate did not do his cause much good either. Augustus was into modesty and decency just then. Shulay's Salome, who had hoped for success and a marriage to follow, stirred up further intrigues amongst Herod's offspring until he was eventually obliged to execute his favourite sons.

By a quirk of the Christian calendar, Herod's death is dated to 4 BCE, although it is believed that the infant Jesus was nearly two years old by this time. Salome briefly achieved her ambition and became the ruler of his kingdom, concealing the news of his death until the young princes she favoured were ready to take control. She then retired, took up gardening, and lived to be over ninety – tending the vast orange groves she had planted at Jaffa, raising her granddaughter Herodias, and supporting her favourite nephew, Antipas. She died in c.10 CE, and left her fortune to the empress Livia.

The Petran monarchy and Herod Antipas

Harith IV Philodemus, 'Lover of Rome', ended up with a reprimand for his precipitate coup, but was allowed to keep the throne. He reigned for nearly thirty years (9 BCE–40 CE) in the mercantile heyday of Petra, his reign spanning the New Testament period. He proclaimed his ineffectual dead brother Aboud to be a god, and buried him in a new city, Oboda or Avdat, which was raised in his honour. He married two of his sisters, first Huldu, then Shaqilat. One Nabataean inscription at Petra lists several members of his family:

'For the life of Harith, king of the Nabataeans, lover of his people, and Shaqilat his sister, queen of the Nabataeans, and Malik and Aboud and Rabbel and Pesael and Shaudat and Higru his children, and Harith son of Higru.'

Prince Herod Antipas, who became Governor of Galilee at the age of 17, strengthened his ties with Petra by marrying a daughter of Harith IV, probably named Huldu after her mother. She remained his only wife for 20 years, despite the fact that she bore him no children – which indicates a powerful love match. It ended tragically however, for at the age of 50 he could no longer deny his feelings for his niece Herodias, who had married his half-brother Herod Philip Boethus and lived in Rome with their daughter young Salome. Antipas agreed to divorce Huldu if Herodias would leave Rome and marry him. She did, and the distraught Huldu fled home to her father, Harith, who never forgave Antipas.

It was Antipas' weakness for Herodias that led to the death of the biblical prophet John the Baptist. Herodias' 24-year-old and still unmarried daughter Salome was the princess who did the famous dance at his birthday party (Mark 6:14–29). She is not named in the gospels, but is known from Josephus. The results of it were twofold: John (who had been a respected prisoner in the Machaerus fortress for some time) was beheaded; and Antipas' other half-brother, Philip the Tetrarch – not to be confused with Philip Boethus, Salome's father! – governor of the region round the King's Highway to Petra – fell in love with Salome and married her (he was 55 at the time). The excitement killed him – or at least, he died shortly afterwards in 34 CE. Salome the Dancer survived further marriages and ended up as queen of Lesser Armenia in 54 CE. According to legend, she died in c.61 CE whilst skating on the ice of a frozen lake. The ice gave way, and the returning movement of the floes sliced off her head. The Stichometry of Nicephorus considered this a just punishment for her sins.

Harith IV still thirsted for revenge for his daughter Huldu's suffering. In 36 CE, while Antipas was absent, he stormed up the Highway and invaded his territory. Since Antipas had always been a loyal supporter of the emperor Tiberius, the Romans were ordered to sack Petra on his behalf. The Roman governor, Vitellius, who disliked Antipas and happened to be a friend of Herodias' abandoned husband, Philip Boethus, stalled as long as possible.

When at last battle seemed inevitable, and Harith had bid a poignant farewell to those who were going to march out and be martyred with him in the stand against the invincible Romans, news broke that Tiberius had died and Caligula was now emperor. Vitellius used this as an excuse for not going any further until he received fresh orders. Herodias' ambitious brother Agrippa, also a friend of her abandoned husband, was allocated the King's Highway region in the shake-up, plus the coveted rank of king.

Furious that Antipas had been slighted so publicly by these arrangements, Herodias persuaded him to go to Rome to demand equal kingship with Agrippa. While they were there, Harith finally had his revenge by getting Antipas arrested for treason. He had apparently gathered an arsenal of weapons large enough to arm 70,000 men. This could only mean he was planning to rebel, or go over to the Parthians. Antipas was banished to Gaul and his kingdom fell into Agrippa's greedy hands. Harith died, thus avenged, in 40 CE.

Harith also had trouble with the Christians, incidentally. It was one of his governors who tried to arrest St Paul in Damascus (II Cor. 11:32). The Nabataean guards keeping watch at the gate were hoping to seize him, but he was secretly let down the wall in a

---

basket and escaped. The suggestion has been made that Paul took refuge in Petra, and spent his 'hidden years' there before he appeared again in Jerusalem (Gal. 1:16–18), but this seems unlikely.

Malik III (40–70 CE) succeeded Harith, and was probably his brother. Like Harith, he also married a sister-wife named Shaqilat, probably Harith's widow. If so, it would indicate the power of a Nabataean queen, for this lady occupied the throne during three reigns – Harith's, Malik's and later as regent for her son Rabbel. Malik hated the Jews so much that he went in person to aid the Romans in 67 CE, and was present during the siege and capture of Jerusalem (70 CE) along with Agrippa's daughter Berenice (Veronica) and her lover – the future emperor Titus.

The end of the Petran monarchy

It was the trade in incense from southern Arabia and Somaliland that proved to be the eventual undoing of the Petran monarchy. Emperor Trajan (c.53–117 CE) could not resist the lure of the Nabataean wealth, and ordered his governor of Syria, Cornelius Palma, to annexe the kingdom and incorporate it into the Province Arabia. The last king, Rabbel II (70–106 CE), seems to have been a minor when he came to the throne, for his coins show him first with his mother, Shaqilat, and later on with his wife, Gamilat. The Romans may have done a deal with him, for Nabataea kept its independence during his lifetime and was handed over peacefully. There was no evidence of a fight to the last. Petra was incorporated into the Roman Empire on 22 March, 106 CE.

THE LATER HISTORY OF PETRA

Roman Petra

On the death of Rabbel II, Trajan annexed the Nabataean kingdom to the Province Arabia and appointed Cornelius Palma as governor. The city of Petra struggled to preserve its splendour, but its trade weakened every day, resulting in the gradual exodus of the wealthy merchants. The administrative capital of the province was moved to Bosra (in present day Syria) and the Fourth Legion was garrisoned a few miles north of Petra. They took over from the Nabataeans the role of policing the trade routes.

Petra's economic decline was caused partly when Trajan started a great paved road from Bosra through Philadelphia (now Amman), Karak, Shaubak and Udhruh to Aqaba (some still visible), connecting Syria with the Red Sea and bypassing Petra. In addition, discoveries in navigation made the journey up and across the Red Sea easier and merchant ships could now safely

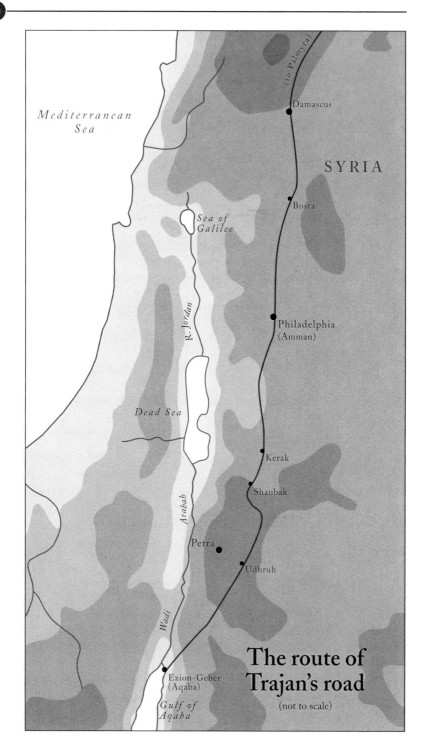

Mediterranean Sea

SYRIA

(to Palmyra)

Damascus

Bosra

Sea of Galilee

R. Jordan

Philadelphia (Amman)

Dead Sea

Kerak

Shaubak

Arabah

Petra

Udhruh

Wadi

Ezion-Geber (Aqaba)

Gulf of Aqaba

The route of Trajan's road

(not to scale)

reach port on the Egyptian side. Another trade route from the east went up the Persian Gulf and thence by caravan up the Euphrates and across the desert to Antioch. Trajan's activities encouraged the use of this route, which increased the wealth and prosperity of the Syrian city of Palmyra as Petra declined. The more astute Nabataean merchants had long since quietly diverted their traffic to Palmyra anyway, to avoid putting their money in Roman pockets. Once the Romans shifted their attention to Palmyra also it was confirmed as the commercial centre and Petra sank into obscurity.

In 131 CE the emperor Hadrian (76–138 CE) visited Petra and granted it the name Adriana Petra, but during the late Roman period it really only served as a religious centre for Trans-Jordan and southern Syria and its trading importance ceased altogether. When commerce departed

with it departed the opulent inhabitants who had animated by their presence the magnificent edifices which their sumptuous taste had raised – those edifices now everywhere in ruin. The rural tribes returned without any reluctance to a purely nomadic existence, mingling without any sense of transition with the Arabs who had never abandoned that kind of life. The change in the

social constitution of the country, however, brought with it some variation in their habits; they plundered where before they trafficked; they traversed the desert as bands of wanderers, not as those lengthened lines of peaceable caravans which had for so many ages given life to the wilderness

Laborde, *Voyage de l'Arabie Pétrée*

Emperor Diocletion (*c.* 230–316 CE) reorganized the province, and Petra became part of the Province of Palestine (Palestian Tertia).

Christian and Muslim Petra

Christianity came to Petra in the fourth century CE, when it was the seat of a bishopric wealthy enough to support a community of anchorites (hermits) in the cliffs surrounding the city. The Byzantine era was one of steady population growth and urbanization thoughout the area Jordan now occupies, but Petra's decline apparently continued. Excavations show that the Street of Columns (the Cardo) became just a dirt track, and small shops and hovels were built over it. The Urn Tomb became a church sometime before 447 CE; and the last reference to a bishop of Petra was to Athenagoras, a nephew of Emperor Maurice in the sixth century.

After the Arab Conquest (seventh century CE), Petra was

only partially occupied, and fell further into obscurity. It may have been shaken by the same earthquake that destroyed Jerusalem and Jerash in 747 CE. Further damage may have been done by Caliph Yazid II (720–24 CE), who ordered the destruction of all human images in Muslim lands. The nomadic tribes had always resented Roman and Byzantine dominance, and welcomed the Muslim forces as liberators.

There is no information on the history of Petra in the first centuries of the Arab period. In later Arab sources the town appears under the name of Al-Asuit. When Muslim power shifed to Baghdad with the Abbasid caliphate in 750, the entire land of what is now Jordan declined into a neglected, sparsely populated district.

Little is known of Petra after this, except that in the twelfth century under Baldwin I, king of Jerusalem, the Crusaders occupied it and built a fort there. Baldwin went there in 1101 in response to the plea of the Greek anchorites on Jabal Harun for protection, since Aaron's shrine was claimed as a holy place by the Muslims as well as the Christians. The area east of the Dead Sea was known as Oultre Jourdain, and Baldwin built a string of fortresses between Jerusalem and Aqaba (Alia) including Shaubak (Mont Real or Mons Regalis) and

La Vaux Moise (Valley of Moses) at Petra. A fortress on the summit of Al-Habis was a solitary lookout. Both were abandoned at the end of the twelfth century. When the Crusaders were finally defeated Petra was ruled by Saladin's brother Al Adil, and then by An Nasir in 1229. In 1253 it passed to Izzidin Abek, the Mameluke ruler of Egypt. The last Muslim leader to visit Petra was the savage Sultan Baybars in 1276, who luckily for the Petrans was only passing through.

The mountains surrounding Petra became its shroud. The city became 'lost' and entered the realms of legend. When rediscovered in the nineteenth century by Burckhardt the wheel had turned full circle, and Petra was no more than a ruinous waste held by Arab robbers.

The religion of Petra

As we saw earlier in this chapter, the religious worship of Petra called forth violent antagonism from the Israelites. This was not because it was a load of meaningless rubbish. Their cult was feared because it provided a viable and attractive alternative to monotheism. The gods were not austere and remote: any sensitive persons could have knowledge and experience of them for themselves and were not

Al-Khasneh Farun
(Laborde)

expected simply to accept priestly dogma in an attitude of blind faith. The attitude of those who worshipped the Triads was elitist and confident: 'to faith add knowledge'.

Any information we might have about the gods or spirit-powers of Petra comes to us from three main sources: from surviving written documents including the Old Testament; from the reports of travellers and ethnologists who study the beliefs, mythologies and practices of primitive peoples who still exist, and who believe that some kind of comparison can be justified; and from the esoteric teachings of present day mystics and seekers after truth who claim to have some direct knowledge of natural religion and the initiation into what are widely known as the 'Earth-mysteries'.

No one with any knowledge of Egyptian religion can fail to be struck by the vast range of deities, idols of metal, stone or wood, receiving homage and ceremonial offerings or performing ritual gestures for the benefit of their worshippers; but in Petra one searches in vain for any such representation. It is true that in Roman times there was apparently a huge statue of the sun-god Dushrat in the city temple, but this is of late date and Roman influence.

LIGHT AND WATER: SYMBOL AND REALITY

Like all people in antiquity, the Nabataeans explained everything by the intervention of their gods, and for them there was nothing that was not capable of containing supernatural power. In particular the Nabataeans venerated the primeval forces of light (the sun, moon and the planet Venus) and water.

Light is the nearest thing to God in this dense world of material things and phenomena. It is the subtlest, most intangible of things which humans can register by means of the five senses, the most ethereal element science can handle. According to the Old Testament, the first thing created by God was light, and it is a perfect symbol: out of the blackness of despair light brings us hope and consolation; out of our ignorance and bewilderment, light brings us awareness and direction. And since our light comes from the sun, it is God as the sun which symbolizes the archetypal burst of power, and becomes in many ancient mythologies the Father and Creator of all things, the Maker, the One, the Self-Born.

Similarly, the veneration of water, especially springs and rivers, is one of the most ancient and universal forms of worship, and also one of the most persistent because it originates in such a basic human need. Neither the spiritual nor material resources that humans can offer are sufficient to control it. The smiting hammer of the sun and the gentle mystic blessedness of the evening star seem very close in Petra; and the sanctity of water, the dependence on its vital force, is absolute.

NABATAEAN MYTHOLOGY

The supernatural entities which affected the everyday life of every Nabataean were divided into three categories. First, there were the ancestors, the lingering identifiable residue of those who once existed as normal human beings; the Nabataeans had absolute belief in the existence of the human soul and its ability to survive separately from the human body. Second, there were the gods themselves, divinities who were eternal and transcendent, and who had never existed as humans. Third, there were certain forces, elemental powers or *jinn* that were less than gods but possessors of strange and sometimes malevolent powers. The *jinn* were not spirits of dead ancestors but something quite different – they were entities which had real existence but were inferior to the gods. The Assyrians and Babylonians called them *utukku*. They could have a force either for good or for evil, and played a significant role in the daily life of humans.

Little is known of the minor Petran deities. The names of Qaush, Habalu and She'a-alqum have been recorded, the first being represented by a crescent moon, or by a sun beetle like the Egyptian god Kheperi, and the last being a guardian of caravans. There was a goddess Manat, or Manathu, who appears to have been regarded as a daughter of Dushrat and was the 'Genius' or hearth-goddess of the city.

The Triad

Since the Nabataeans had contact with so many different cultures, it is not surprising that their theology shares many aspects and beliefs with those of their desert neighbours – the Egyptians, the Aramaeans, the Syrians, Assyrians and Babylonians, the Canaanites, the Hebrews. It was a form of what the Old Testament calls 'Baalism' – the worship of the supernatural powers that lay behind the natural forces which enable life to exist on our planet. The word 'Baal' simply means 'Lord' or 'Master', or 'Great One'.

The Sun-god

The chief god in most triads was the Sun, and this seems to have been so in Petra (although some will argue that the major deity in this vast shrine was the Great Goddess). His four complementary powers were Atargatis, the goddess of grain, foliage, fruit and fish; Allat, the goddess of the moon; Al-Uzza (Al-Udha), the Evening Star, or goddess of the planet Venus, who represented human devotion – both romantic and religious; and Manat, (referred to above) the goddess of fate or fortune. Al-Uzza was also patroness of water (especially springs or 'living' water) and fertility in general.

Because assimilation was widespread, there is confusion as to the exact relationships within this hierarchy. Atargatis is usually reckoned to be the Great God's consort, and the other three goddesses his daughters. In Petra, however, Allat is sometimes depicted as the Virgin Mother of Dushrat, and Al-Uzza seems to have been assimilated with both Atargatis and Allat; she may, indeed, have been worshipped as his equal sister. If so, this would have reflected the relationships in Nabataean royal culture, where it was vital that these heiresses did not marry beneath them and, as we saw earlier in this chapter it was usual for kings to marry their sisters. In the Nabataean cult the Sun was known as Dushrat (Dusares, Dushara), the Watcher, the Eye that Saw, a deity of strength and creative force also associated with springs and water.

The Sun had many aspects but three were paramount. In the first aspect Dushrat represented the primeval source of power. He had existed before the creation, a formless spirit which bore within itself the sum of all existence. However, for our universe to exist at all, light must triumph over darkness and order over chaos. In this second aspect, the Light Triumphant, the solar deity is frequently symbolized by a stone object in the form of an obelisk, which represented a materialized beam of light reaching down and striking the earth.

In the third aspect, of being the cause of change, Dushrat is also 'He who becomes', represented as the rising sun which emerges from its own substance and is reborn of itself; the god of all the transformations of life which is forever renewing itself. The symbol was often the black dung beetle rolling the solar disc between his front legs.

The distinctive qualities of solar worship were active rather than passive; Dushrat required commitment and loyalty to a mystical ideal, vigour and courage. God the Sun triumphed over night and put winter to flight. He was god of justice – his bursting light chased away the shadows where crime was rampant. He was also the god of divination – through soothsayers he revealed the secrets of the future.

Dushrat was also commonly associated with the seasonal aspect of nature because plant life depended on the warmth and light of the sun, and was either urged into growth or – especially in the desert – destroyed by it. The solar deity was therefore closely linked with the spirit of vegetation which dies with the harvest and is reborn when the grain sprouts. In this aspect, the vegetation god is usually thought to be an incarnation of the sun-god himself, or his son.

Sun cycles were daily, seasonal and annual, so the fact that he encountered and conquered darkness (symbolizing death) led to his being accepted in some cosmologies as the god of the dead, and the conqueror of Death. He was the light which vanished in the shadows every evening to reappear more brilliantly with each dawn. Thus he represented the struggle of good against evil – the war between the desert and the fertile earth, the drying wind and the green vegetation, the darkness and the light.

The Great Goddess
Turning now to the female divinities, the second person in the Triad was the divine power that symbolized response and receptiveness. The response could take the form of quiet, passive devotion (representing and accepting the self-denying submission of the worshipper), or it could manifest as the source of the fierce all-sacrificing zeal of the missionary disciple.

The Great Goddess of the East had many forms and guises. Just as with talented women everywhere the roles of sweet virgin, pure maiden, beloved wife, sexual fulfiller, vigorous supporter, honoured mother, protective nurse, grieving widow-mother, venerable grandmother were all really aspects of the same entity. Four 'mysteries' were bound up with the concept of female divinity: virginal purity and chastity; the hunger and passion of voluptuous female sexuality; the self-sacrificing beneficence of motherhood and fruitful love; and the grief of a mother or widow.

It seems that the Great Goddess was originally called Allat (simply meaning 'the goddess'). She had as many names as she had local manifestations, in Petra she took the name Al-Uzza (the Mighty One). Sepulchral evidence at Palmyra equated her with the virgin-warrior Pallas Athena, the Maid, showing her helmeted with one hand holding a spear while the other rests on a shield. The symbol of the Goddess was usually the Moon, or the planet Venus – the Evening Star – and her sacred animals were the cow and the lioness, and sometimes the snake.

In the aspect of fruition, she symbolized the receptive living earth flowering and fruiting in due season. This role was closely bound up with the dying and rising god myth, the Goddess being either the stricken lover/widow or mother of the deceased.

Al-Uzza was the divine personification of Venus, the goddess of morn and evening. As the war-goddess she was Lady of Battles, valiant among goddesses. What we call sacred prostitution was part of her cult. She was goddess of both love and destruction. A very ambivalent character, she could be fickle, insatiable and cruel, gobbling up her numerous lovers and emasculating if not destroying them. She was therefore greatly feared as well as venerated. She was the 'Star of Lamentation', making brothers quarrel among themselves and friends forget their friendship.

She regulated the course of the heavenly bodies and controlled the alternating seasons. She killed or tamed wild beasts. It was she who caused the products of the soil to flourish, gave men riches, protected them in battle, and at sea guided them on their adventures.

Sometimes she was depicted as a beautiful nude, sometimes her statues wore a Cretan-type dress with flounced skirt and bare bosom. Sometimes she was assimilated with Diana (Artemis), the twin sister of Apollo (the sun), a virgin-warrior who advanced, escorted by a lion, striking the ground with her spear. Sometimes she was the symbol of procreation, with huge broad hips, pressing her raised arms to breasts heavy with milk. The Nabataeans and their Bedouin descendants depicted her only as a stone or obelisk, perhaps with a rudimentary face.

What did the Nabataeans believe about life after death? The dominant belief current in the Middle East at that period was the depressing one that under the earth lay the infernal dwelling place, the land of no return. To enter it, you had to penetrate seven gates, abandoning at each a part of your apparel, the symbol of your humanity. When the last gate had closed behind you, you were naked and imprisoned forever in the land of shadows. In this region of eternal darkness the souls of the dead, 'clad, like birds, in a garment of wings', were all jumbled together, irrespective of rank or merit.

> In the house of dust
> live lord and priest,
> wizard and prophet …
> dusk is their nourishment
> and their food is mud.

This sad picture was described by Enkidu to his friend Gilgamesh in the famous cuneiform epic discovered in Babylon.

It was not a pleasant prospect, and this miserable abode was not likely to attract anyone. If that was the human lot, no wonder dead loved ones were mourned, and death was feared. Countering this grim belief, the Triadic mystery cults burst upon dejected humanity like water pouring onto the desert, like light in darkness. Worship of the Triad made sense of life, gave purpose and direction. No matter what your personal misfortunes, if you struggled to do good and lived a life submitted to the gods, after you left the earthly body behind you would pass through judgement to eternal bliss. If you deserved punishment, on the other hand, then that in justice would be your lot. The cult of Al-Uzza/Atargatis was one of the chief examples of these religious systems.

The Divine Son

The third person in each divine Triad was the saviour-hero, the virgin-born son of God, meta-physically impossible to distinguish from the Father since he was an incarnation of Himself. Mystical and intuitive knowledge of this offered salvation and eternal life to those who were worthy and capable of receiving it. At the time of King Harith IV, the doctrine of salvation can be summarized roughly as follows. Humanity was in the grip of sin and the Evil One,

a thraldom which could not be broken by any moral effort on the part of any human, since the moral nature of humanity was too weak. Consequently humanity was doomed to everlasting punishment. But God in His mercy provided a way of release by sending a Divine Son into the world to show the way and suffer a cruel death which atoned for the collective sin of humanity. The myth contained the following standard elements – the depressing sense of hope-lessness about the moral condition of humanity; the descent of a virgin-born divine saviour-hero into a human body; the violent sac-rificial death of that saviour; and the resurrection, immortality and divinity of that saviour, followed by the vicarious atonement effected by the divine death for all those who had faith in its efficacy, and the promise of their personal resurrection and immortality.

The reader may be forgiven for jumping to the conclusion that this description refers to Christianity, but it was the mythology that lay behind the Dushrat/Al-Uzza cult, the Baal cults and fertility religions of the Old Testament, the mystery cults of Isis, Osiris, Dionysus, Attis, Tammuz, Demeter and Persephone, and – above all – Mithras, the most popular elitist cult favoured by the Roman military. It was precisely this seductive mythology of Triad worship that the prophets of Israel inveighed against throughout the Old Testament, and which is condemned by the Tawhid or Unity of God in the Qur'an:

They do blaspheme who say God is one of three, in a Trinity; for there is no god except One God.

Surah 5:76

They make the *jinn* equal with God, though God did create the *jinn*; and they falsely attribute to Him sons and daughters … To Him is the primal origin of the heavens and the earth; how can He have a son when He has no consort?

Surah 6:100–101

All these systems involved mystical identification with personal saviour-gods, and ritually undergoing the personal sacrifice, death and resurrection experience of this saviour – whose prime function was to stir the heart and then show the way. It meant undergoing a stringent programme of fasting and long nights of prayer intended to produce actual experience of psychic phenomena, and in particular the 'out-of-body' experience. In some cults, the neophyte was sealed up in a cave or 'womb', to remain in a foetal position until this experience was achieved.

There was one basic difference between a member of such cults and an outsider. The members knew that life after death and the personal survival of the soul outside the physical body was not just an illusion brought about by our wishful thinking and reluctance to shuffle off our mortal coil. They knew it was reality because they had experienced it. This awareness was not based on a person's circumstances of birth, background, wealth, or intelligence. One person could search a lifetime for the answers and not find them; on the other hand, another might stumble on the truth as if by accident. It was the duty of pious humans simply to be ready by attention to the conduct of their lives, and when enlightened, to submit. The secret knowledge involved various psychical powers along the way and it was considered dangerous to put this knowledge into the hands of the unworthy or those not ready to receive it. Therefore neophytes were sworn to silence.

Everyday life in ancient Petra

Everyday life in Petra in Nabataean times combined all the riches of Greek and Roman culture, the mystery of the oriental religious systems, the wheeling and dealing of international playboys, and the makeshift pragmatism of desert people who have to live beneath a blistering sun.

What remains of Petra is fascinating in its own right, but it can give the visitor little idea of what life was like in ancient times. What follows is the author's own reconstruction based on records of contemporary documents of the Middle East in Roman times.

HOUSES AND DOMESTIC LIFE

Houses were packed close together and the streets were narrow and dark, as they are everywhere in the Middle East. Things were arranged so that the greatest amount of shade could be obtained. The houses of the poor were simple square buildings of mud-brick and straw, the size of the room depending on the length of wooden beam available for the roof.

Since trees were a valuable commodity in this desert-encompassed region, anything made of wood was looked after, and such things as roof beams, doors and window-frames would be passed from person to person, and have a lifetime much longer than any particular house. Beams were usually fairly short, so the average room could not be wider than 2.5m or so. If a solid roof was laid over the beams, the family could use it as further living space, and it was often preferable to the stuffy darkness below. For most of the year families would have used the roof as the bedroom.

The simplest of houses with roofs consisting of no more than an overlay of dried mud enjoyed the springtime phenomenon of having green roofs after the rains, when grains of seed in them sprouted. This little crop was soon polished off by goats clambering up, and if they were too lively, threatening to bring the whole lot down.

By contrast, the wealthy people of Petra had grand and spacious villas, built in stone brought on wagons from the quarries. Their rooms were doubled or trebled in size by having central pillars and supporting walls that could support a second or third length of wooden beam, and upper storeys. These grand establishments were home to large extended families that included not only numerous relatives but also household slaves. Most houses presented a blank wall to the street, and did not encourage unwanted attention from the passer-by. It was only when one had passed the door and gone into the courtyard that one could appreciate the loveliness or friendliness of a house.

Slaves

A well-organized household would have enough people to cope with its smooth running – cleaners, gardeners, cooks, handymen, agricultural workers, maintenance men, drivers, and a motley assortment of children who could sweep up, skim the flies off pools, pick fruit, carry a message, and so on.

Urban slaves did not fare badly. Most did not do any more work than the average housewife does today. In ordinary times a slave who was a craftsman, entertainer or cook would fetch a high price at auction. After wars, however, there was often a glut on the market and prices slumped. Household slaves purchased in the market were a bit of a gamble, since one had no way of telling (apart from the vendor's assurances) what sort of return one might get for one's outlay, but since they cost good money, there was no point in wasting an investment by ill-treating them or neglecting them when ill.

Slaves who had been born in households, whose families might have been with that household for generations, were quite a different matter. They were usually treated as part of the family, and might have quite a pleasant life, depending on their owners. Some, who were loving nurses and noble tutors and were more or less treated as honorary aunts and uncles, became beloved friends.

Most slaves were allowed to marry, carry on their own businesses and even to accumulate a fund called the *peculium* with which they might eventually buy their freedom if they wished. Many slaves who were granted freedom chose to continue living in the establish-

ments of their birth. It was not considered dishonourable to be a slave – it was just the way things were. People could even put themselves into slavery for agreed periods to pay off debts. At the end of the session they were free to go.

Water

The dwellers at Petra were particularly aware of water, since the surrounding region was so arid and lifeless, the nearby Dead Sea so poisonous, and the actual Petra basin so totally dependent on its springs and the careful husbandry of its infrequent rains. Relatively speaking Petra was very generously supplied. The abundant springs of Ain Musa never ran dry, and the Nabataean engineers channelled all the water that fell on their mountains through the Siq and around Jabal al-Khubtha to the Nymphaeum. Huge tanks and cisterns were constructed to conserve the spring flood-waters.

Jars for water were made of rough earthenware and left unglazed; they were therefore slightly porous in order that gentle evaporation from the clay left the water inside cooler than the air outside. Fetching water was generally the woman's work, although men sometimes did it. It was not considered burdensome, but rather an opportunity to get out of the household, meet friends and have a gossip.

Dining

In dining rooms, the guests and family did not sit upright on chairs to eat but reclined on couches, which sloped slightly downwards, away from the table. The usual arrangement was very formal, with couches on three sides of the table on which the food was placed. The three couches gave the room the name *triclinium*. Each couch usually held three people who reclined at an angle across it.

Dining rooms were small, and servants could only serve from the open end. They were expected to keep an eye on the guests, and it was tactful to make sure that any cushions were covered with clean sheets. In that enclosed space, one of the first duties of the slave at mealtimes was to wash and dry the feet of the guests.

The places on the couches were decreed by custom. The first place on the lefthand couch went to the master of the house, next to him would be his wife and son or freedman. Near to the master on the middle couch was the chief guest. Other guests occupied the remaining places. They ate with their right hands. Eating with the left hand was socially unacceptable, because the left hand was always used for 'dishonourable' purposes, especially the washing of private parts after visiting the toilet. If a thief was punished by having

their right hand cut off it meant that the person would never again be acceptable company at the dining table.

It was not considered polite to empty the plate, since after the meal any food left was passed back to the servants, or other household members not present at the meal. It was quite normal in these massive dinners for much of the dish to be left untouched, so the servants did not do at all badly in a reasonable household.

A BIBLICAL TEXT COMES TO LIFE

It was precisely while reclining round a table being looked after by servants that Jesus ate his last supper:

[Jesus] rose from supper, laid aside his garments, and girded himself with a towel. Then he poured water into a basin, and began to wash the disciples' feet, and to wipe them with the towel with which he was girded. He came to Peter, and Peter said to him: Lord, do you wash my feet? Jesus answered him, What I am doing you do not know now, but afterwards you will understand. Peter said to him, You will never wash my feet! Jesus answered him, If I do not wash you, you have no part in me. Peter said to him, Then not only my feet, but my hands and head also! …

When he had washed their feet and taken his garments and resumed his place, he said … I have given you an example. Truly I say to you, a servant is not greater than his master; nor is he who is sent greater than he who sent him … and he testified, One of you will betray me. One of his disciples, whom Jesus loved, was lying close to his breast. So Peter beckoned to him and said Tell us who it is of whom he speaks. So lying thus, close to the breast of Jesus, he said to him, Lord, who is it? Jesus answered, It is he to whom I shall give this morsel when I have dipped it.

John 13:4–26

FOOD AND DRINK

Food was generally fairly simple, consisting of flat bread, beans, salads, onions, olives, yoghurt, dates and figs, eggs, fruit such as grapes and pears, poultry, rabbits and fish. In such a market town as Petra all kinds of foodstuffs were available and the feasts of the wealthy were just as exotic as those in Rome.

Like the Egyptians, Nabataeans used to soak wheat in pans to create a strong alcoholic drink or beer. This was extremely popular, and there are records of Nabataean 'drinking-messes' in which each round was drunk from a different

MENUS OF THE PERIOD

Delicacies included:

- Dormice in honey, sprinkled with poppy seeds, sliced damsons, olives and pomegranate seeds.

- Hare served with sow's udders.

- Female wild boar with a small basket dangling from each tusk, one with fresh dates and the other with dried. Clamped to this boar's udders were small suckling pigs made of marzipan, arranged as if they were feeding.

- Boiled calf, or tender baby goat.

- Fat chicken and goose eggs.

- Quails rolled in flour and stuffed with nuts and raisins, served with quinces stuck with prickles to look like sea urchins.

golden vessel. These references may have been to ritual occasions.

Beer-making was simple and remains unchanged to this day. Strongly leavened bread is crumbled and mixed with water, then warmed for several hours over a slow fire. When removed from the heat, water is poured over it, and it is left for two nights to ferment. The name often given to it is *Om Belbel*, or 'Mother of Nightingales', because it makes the drunkard sing. Sometimes it is drunk with the crumbs of bread still in it, in which state it is reckoned to be as good as a meal. Similarly, date wine is still made by throwing the fruit into large earthen boilers with water, and boiling for two days. The clear juice is poured into jars which are buried underground. After only 10–12 days the wine is fit to drink.

GARDENS

Well-to-do houses always had a garden enclosed within a wall. These walls were occasionally painted with *trompe-l'oeil* scenes of waterside, woodland and greenery, a trick to make the gardens seem larger and cooler. Gardening was highly fashionable in Rome during this period and we can be sure that many exotic plants passed through Petra on their way to the world's capital, and that some remained in this flourishing transit town.

Plants grew at amazing speed in the spring, when the air was fresh and pleasant but required skill and constant attention to keep them going during the scorches of summer. Tough plants like the pink, red and white oleanders generally did well, and so did tangles of the heady-scented white jasmine. The formal garden usually had a peristyle with elegant colonnades where one could shelter in heat of the day.

Courtyards would have a water supply and tubs containing grape vines, figs or the large spreading leaves of cucumber plants trailing a bit of welcome shade over a trellis roof, where every householder might sit 'under his own vine or fig tree' (Micah 4:4). A smart household would send a servant to dust and spray these every evening. They might have a date palm, and would certainly have pots of herbs for the kitchen and for making infusions for drinking. St Matthew's gospel mentions mint, dill and cummin (Matthew 23:23) which were available in virtually every household.

THE STREET

When one looks at the deserted scene in Petra today, it is hard to imagine that this was not only the focal point for endless streams of pilgrims, but also one of the world's greatest market towns, bustling with Nabataean and foreign merchants, the stink and snort of camels, the motley thousands of milling hangers-on. Respectable mechants would walk briskly up the Cardo in the fresh cool of the very early morning to organize their caravans and do their business deals. Shopkeepers would open their doors, expectant of another good day if a caravan had recently come in, and put out whatever they used to lure the customer inside – 'no charge for looking!' Touts and confidence tricksters would shake themselves into wakefulness after a hard night of shady dealings and come haunting the public places looking for a quick profit. There was money to be made both by the citizens of Petra and by those passing through. The massive influx of outsiders led to the proliferation of taverns, bars and shops, far more than would be needed by the inhabitants of the town. Food shops, shops selling metal utensils, earthenware, leather goods and cloth were everywhere, providing the necessary for a vast clientele. They usually had masonry counters with earthenware pots (*dolia*) set into them for grain, dried fruit, liquids and spices. There was a constant supply of cooked delicacies – savoury breads, sticky sweets, cakes coated in honey, meatballs, grilled snacks – ready at any time of the day.

One interesting place of work was the fuller's shop, for the finishing of manufactured cloth. This was usually easily identified by the large pot outside the front door into which passers-by were invited to urinate. Fullers, like tanners, needed large quantities of this basic commodity, and similar pots were placed on street corners. The emperor Vespasian (69–79 CE) actually put a tax on this, with the result that everyone laughed at his meanness, and public urinals got the nickname of 'Vespasiani'.

The main commercial area, as in any town, was the forum – the centre of government, business and law. Where commerce was life, the three were barely distinguishable. The forum acted as gentlemen's club, law court and stock exchange. The other chief gathering places were the baths and the theatre.

ENTERTAINMENT: THE THEATRE

An amphitheatre was a valuable civic asset, bringing in spectators and income from all the nearby towns. The beautiful sandstone structure in Petra is one of the most outstanding buildings that remain, even though any marble that may have lined the seats has long since been taken away. It is a large theatre and seated 7,000; what sort of performances might it have staged?

Cardo Maximus

Some theatrical events of that period were serious cultural occasions, lectures, readings of verse, displays of visiting rhetoricians. It was nothing at all for an audience of that time to gather and listen to some good locutor holding forth for five hours at a stretch. Having said this, the larger theatres like the one at Petra were not often used for tasteful declamations. Like today's commercial ventures they needed to make money and were places of popular entertainment. Patronage based on popular taste did not usually make for a very high level of theatre. The three main types of shows a Petran audience would have enjoyed were farce, mime and pantomime.

Farce was very similar to medieval street-theatre – bawdy, topical, wholly lacking in sophistication, with a lot of audience participation. Mime usually involved strolling performers who could juggle, sing or dance. Pantomime was the most sophisticated with the entire action in the hands of a single player, the *pantomimus* (literally 'one who imitates all things'), supported by chorus and musicians. A top-ranking *pantomimus* was the idol of the public. However, in the eyes of the law acting was a dishonourable profession, and although top actors were rich and famous they were disqualified from holding public office.

Displays of gladiators or exotic beasts were very popular as stage shows. By the very nature of things, these shows stirred up excitement and passions, and could often be dangerous. The audience did not pay its money in order to sit there knitting. What they wanted was blood, and lots of it – pitting ferocious wild beasts against human victims, or against each other. The more unusual the contest the better they liked it. Gladiators often fought with mismatched weapons, or a dwarf might be brought out to fight against a woman. Human performers were either condemned criminals exposed to some form of sophisticated butchery, or trained gladiators who might be slaves, prisoners of war or lesser criminals. Professional gladiators were the most dramatic; they were usually organized into schools (*familiae*) under private or public ownership, and were highly skilled.

It was a matter of concern that the youth of the day preferred the arena to their studies. Tacitus remarked: 'Really, I think that the passion for gladiators and horses is conceived in the mother's womb! Few indeed are to be found who talk of any other subjects in their houses, and whenever we enter a classroom, what else is the conversation of the youths?' (Tacitus *c.*55–120 CE)

69

HISTORY

AGRICULTURE

Most of the agriculture around Petra was wheat and other grain, vines and olives, and the raising of goats and sheep. The agricultural tasks were those found everywhere in the region at that period. Many of them remain unchanged to the present day. Ploughing was particularly hard work as the soil was full of rocks. It was usually done by the farmer with two animals yoked to a wooden plough with a metal blade. If the farmer was considerate he would always use animals evenly yoked to avoid causing sores to his beasts. God's law, in Deuteronomy 22:10, stipulated that 'you shall not plough with an ox and an ass together'. Unfortuantely this law was frequently broken, and still is to this day.

THE CULT OF THE DEAD

Many ancient peoples practised a cult of the dead. This can most readily be seen whenever graves are excavated, and evidence is found of deposits of food and other necessities, for the use of the dead loved one in the afterlife. Certain objects of value were often buried with the dead, as if the dead still had the power to own them. Care lavished on the dead was not always a labour of love, a duty performed by the relatives left behind to grieve their loss. Sometimes it was done to encourage the favourable

disposition of that dead person towards the living, to soften possible hostility or to put the departed in a position where they could do no harm. Sometimes it was to make sure they really had departed.

While an enemy lived, at least one knew where he was and what he was doing. Once that enemy died, he could come at you when you least expected him, and you were at a great disadvantage. People who had died through human violence would certainly harbour resentment against their slayers and could extend this ill-feeling against their families, tribes and distant descendants. In those cases, burial customs were measures of protection against the deceased, and the tombs were intended to imprison them. The souls of the dead who had not been appeased or whose funeral rites had been neglected avenged themselves by tormenting the living, although once their presence was suspected they could be appeased by making a libation of water or offering a funeral repast. Petra was full of banqueting halls (*triclinia*), where such funeral meals were celebrated in honour of the dead.

However, the practice of mummification, practised by the Nabataeans as well as the Egyptians, indicated a love and respect for the dear departed; the object of keeping a corpse intact (if not recognizable)

MEDICAL TIPS

These titbits gleaned from the *Natural History* of Pliny the Younger (*c.* 61–113 CE) were all the rage throughout the Mediterranean world in the Nabataean period. Try them if you dare!

- *Aching bones and joints* A poultice of grass or herbs against which a dog has lifted its leg, plucked without touching iron.
- *Aphrodisiac* Stir the genitals of an ass in hot oil seven times, and rub it on. Or drink the ashes of the said member. A more palatable aphrodisiac – take artichoke in wine.
- *Bee-sting* Slap on your own ear wax.
- *Bites of mad dog* Take pills made from skull of a hanged man.
- *Cataract* Rub urine on, especially that collected first thing in the morning.
- *Chin* To soften the hair on a stubbly chin, rub on a paste made of crushed ants' eggs.
- *Diarrhoea* Dried camel's tail powdered and drunk.
- *Ears* If runny or wormy, drink a jar of urine in which leeks have been boiled.
- *Epilepsy* Camel's brain dried and drunk with vinegar.
- *Hair* To make it curl, use camel dung reduced to ashes and mixed with oil.
- *Headache* Dry the genitals of a fox and wear them round the head.
- *Poison* A good antidote is to eat a toad baked red hot between two plates; but not too much – some patients have died of the remedy.
- *Sciatica* Cut an earthworm in half, stitch up again with an iron wire, rinse with water and bury it; drink the water.
- *Snakebite* Apply the hair plucked from a hanged man, soaked in wine.
- *Tooth decay* Take the worm found in bearded wheat, cover it in wax and put it into the hole in the faulty tooth.
- *Toothpaste* Use the ankle-bones of asses or goats powdered into ashes.

was to give the deceased's *ba* or soul a contact point with this world so that communication between the living and the dead could still take place, usually via a medium or priest. A soul which remained near to a well-preserved corpse was a kind of guardian spirit able to communicate with the living, avenge wrongs done to its body, and retain enough tribal feeling to assist in guarding the storage-places of tribal plunder. Like the Egyptians, the Petrans believed that so long as the mummy remained intact, the soul or 'life-force' of the deceased could be drawn back into the cave tomb and be visited by the bereaved relatives, who would thereby gain consolation. If a loved one's soul came back, summoned or unsummoned, it would derive considerable satisfaction from the knowledge that the diligent descendants were still keeping them in mind. The spectral presence could be picked up by anyone with psychic ability and its advice asked on important matters.

In Petra there was a sharp difference between the burials of the rich and those of the poor, and obviously it is mainly the tombs of the rich that the visitors see and marvel over. However, behind both forms of burial lay a deep respect for the dead and a confidence that their souls lived on, and would bless the living with their continued loving and guiding presence.

Burial of the rich

Wealthy people in Petra mummified their dead, laying their pickled and dried-out remains to rest in stone coffins in the cave-tombs. The mummification process followed the same principles as in neighbouring Egypt.

At first the body was laid out in the house for a few hours, for relatives to come and bid farewell to the corpse. Bodies were not left unattended by the embalmers for long, because the heat of the climate started the process of rotting very quickly.

When there was a death it was traditionally polite for mourners to come from far and wide, and for all the local people to gather to add their sympathy, swelling the ranks of relatives, household and neighbours. Weeping and tearing their hair and garments, they would mill about outside the house of the deceased in a frenzy of grief, throwing dust upon themselves and wailing loudly. A wealthy Petran might also feel obliged to hire extra ceremonial mourners – not that they were needed, but in order not to be thought stingy or lacking in respect. St Mark (5:38) gives a picture of such a crowd present at the house of a synagogue official in Capernaum within moments of the death of his 12-year-old daughter, who had passed away while Jesus was being sent for.

Once death was certain, all the inhabitants of a house where there was a dead body unknotted all their clothes and hair, and opened windows and doors – all part of the ritual to speed the soul on its journey to the Great Beyond. The householder would summon a funeral company, much as we do today, to take over the care of the dead. When the immediate family and friends had finished paying respects, the corpse was taken in procession to the embalmers, and the relatives touched or kissed the deceased for the last time, bid farewell, and went off to their mourning and cleansing ceremonies. Mourners would continue to arrive for several weeks after the actual burial. No one need fear solitary grief and distress. After forty days there would be a farewell feast held in one of the *triclinia*. Such feasts are still the tradition in many societies in the Middle East.

Embalming and entombment

Meanwhile, behind a tactful curtain at the embalmer's establishment, the body would have been laid out on a large table. First the brain was removed, then all the internal organs except the heart. These items of human offal were carefully treated and placed in special jars. The corpse was cleaned out and temporarily stuffed with packing material to keep the natural outline

of the loved one. Toenails and fingernails were tied on with fine cord. (Tutankhamun's were wrapped in gold leaf.)

It was always hoped that the embalmers would work with respect, although sometimes there were scandals. It was not unknown in the ancient East for the bodies of young girls to be abused before the embalming began if they were not 'chaperoned' by priests who could be trusted. Any embalmer caught in the horrifying act of desecrating a corpse was instantly put to death.

The corpses were then pickled in natron, which took around thirty days. Some embalmers worked a system with one large vat of natron solution for each day of the month, each vat holding about five corpses. The day's work would entail the preparation of the five corpses that were to go into the natron that particular day, followed by the removal of the five due to come out in the shift after lunch.

The cranial cavity was stuffed with resin-soaked linen, and the body emptied of its temporary packing and stuffed with linen bags of sawdust and myrrh soaked in resin. The abdomen was sewn up and the surface of the body rubbed with a mixture of cedar oil, wax, natron and gum, and dusted with spices. The orifices – nose, ears and anus – were plugged, and special attention paid to the area under the eyelids. Skilled embalmers tried to keep the eye region from shrinking away, and this was done either by inserting pads of linen, or frequently by the use of a conveniently sized onion. The whole body was then coated with molten resin to close the pores and protect the surface, and finally bandaged and wrapped in a fine shroud. Spells and amulets were frequently included in the wrappings to take the deceased safely through the underworld.

The mummies were laid to rest in stone sarcophagi, not decorated like the ornate wooden Egyptian ones, or with a portrait of the deceased painted on the front, but in plain, solid stone coffins with little horns at the edges. (A collection of these sarcophagi is on display along the side of the road at the top of the Acropolis in Amman.) Once the body was finally laid to rest on the shelf in its carved sandstone cave, everything that had touched it, including all the embalming materials, was gathered up and buried too.

Burial of the poor

So far we have considered only the mummification of the wealthy. What about the ordinary people? Some were interred in caves, but the procedure was different. They were reverently washed and anointed with spices and perfumed oils and wrapped in grave-cloths, then simply sealed inside and left to rot. If the cave entrance was small enough the seal would sometimes be a large grindstone that had worn out. These could be rolled in and out fairly easily so that other bodies could be put in. (This seems to have been the case for the grave of Jesus.)

Since bodies were buried so soon after death, a guard was usually kept near the tomb for three days, in case there had been a mistake and the corpse was still 'quick', in which case it was a simple matter to roll away the stone and rescue the unfortunate person. Some months later, relatives would go back into the tomb, gather up the remains and boil them to clean the bones of any remaining residue of decaying flesh. The women would scrub out the tomb and shelf, leaving it ready for the next incumbent. The boiled bones of the deceased were reverently laid in chests known as ossuaries and stored in communal vaults. No one who wanders in and out of Petra's monumental tombs today need feel embarrassed that they are about to stumble upon the treasured remains of the long-deceased. The tombs are bereft and empty, gaping mouths undermining the cliffs and riddling the hillsides.

WALKING
TOURS

3

Travelling from Amman

If you are arriving at Amman there are several places of interest to see on the drive down to Petra. Depending on the amount of time you have available you can see all or some of the following.

The Dead Sea

At the lowest point on earth the Dead Sea remains a geological

Dead Sea

freak. With 33 per cent salinity no plant or animal life can survive in its mineral-rich waters – hence the name. The sea is of course famous for its unusual qualities for swimmers: the high salt content makes conventional swimming impossible; at best buoyant swimmers bob gently on the surface like corks. At Suweinah on the northern shore of the Dead Sea is a health resort where you can try the various Dead Sea mud treatments (supposedly very good for skin complaints). A word of warning: don't get the salty water into your eyes – it can sting like mad. Wear goggles if your eyes are sensitive and definitely take

plenty of fresh water (a couple of litres per person) to wash the salt off your skin after swimming. Better still, stick to the resorts where showers are available.

Madaba

Just 30km south of Amman is the town of Madaba, famous for its extraordinary Byzantine mosaic depicting a map of the known world in the floor of St George's Church. The mosaic is fascinating and shows many places including Alexandria, the Dead Sea and the Nile, but it is the map of Jerusalem which is unique. The church opens daily from 8.30 am to 6 pm except Friday and Sunday when it opens later at 10.30 am. Other mosaics from the town can be seen in the archaeological park, open from 8.30 am to 5.30 pm.

St George's Church

Don't miss the museum which incorporates several private Madaba houses where mosaics have been discovered, often when the owners were doing some routine building work in the garage!

Mount Nebo

The views from the top of Mount Nebo are stunning. If the air is clear you can even make out Jerusalem on the far side of the Dead Sea. The mountain is primarily famous for the site of the tomb of Moses. The summit is the site of an ancient church undergoing some archaeological restoration. It is open from 7 am to 7 pm in summer and to 5 pm in winter.

Mount Nebo

Ma'in Spa

Further to the south, near the shores of the Dead Sea, is the hot spring and thalassotherapy resort at Ma'in. The springs have been recognized for their therapeutic

properties since Roman times. The hot water tumbles down a waterfall on the side of the wadi and is open to all – most refreshing after a long drive. The spa resort and hotel on the other hand are expensive and need to be pre-booked. Tel: (08) 545500 for information.

Hot springs, Ma'in

Kerak

The ancient town of Kerak has been associated with the trade caravan route for millennia. Much of what you can see today dates from the time of the Crusaders who fortified Kerak which is in a strategic position between Showbak and Jerusalem. The drive up to Kerak from the King's Highway is eyepopping. The huge gorge of the Wadi

Fortress at Kerak

al-Mujib practically disappears as you climb more than a kilometre from the wadi floor. Once up in Kerak itself the *qasr* (castle) is the place to go for views across the town and surrounding countryside. Open daily from sunrise to sunset. There is also a museum within the *qasr* which is open from 8 am to 5 pm except Tuesday.

Dana

This is a new experiment to attract 'green tourism' to the area. Dana is a village set within a nature park and visitors can stay at the Dana Guest House (Tel: (03) 368497) and explore the park within limited boundaries (there are designated walking trails). There is also a camping ground in the park. Apart from its wildlife conservation programme Dana also has a number of craft workshops run by local people. The park is run by the Royal Society for the Conservation of Nature. Tel: (03) 837931.

Dana village

Showbak

This Crusader fortress overlooks great swathes of desolate land-

scape. It is a vast structure undergoing restoration. It was built in 1115 CE and changed hands several times during its history. Elaborate Arabic inscriptions over some of the doorways date from Saladin's occupation, but much of the later building dates from the time of the Mamelukes who largely rebuilt the *qasr* in the fourteenth century.

Travelling from Aqaba

Wadi Rum

The one great place of interest on the way north from Aqaba is Wadi Rum. It really is worth spending a day (and a night too) if you can spare the time to explore this wonderful desert region. The dramatic scenery is so photogenic that it has appeared in several films, most famously in *Lawrence of Arabia*.

There is no hotel at Rum, only the Government Rest House where if you wish you can camp. Alternatively you can hire a mattress and blankets and sleep on the Rest House roof. Beware though, the temperatures can plunge at night to freezing and below. Meals are available at the Rest House or you can bring your own food with you. There is a JD 1 per person entrance fee to Rum (JD 4 per vehicle if you bring your own). This goes towards the maintenance of the Rest House, where you are entitled to a free cup of tea. Rum is also home to the famous Desert Patrol who traditionally 'walk the beat' on camels. These days, sadly, 4WDs are starting to take over.

How much time you have will dictate what you do at Wadi Rum. There are walks within the vicinity of the Rest House, to the Nabataean temple for example or to see Lawrence's Well, both just a couple of kilometres.

Various excursions on camel, foot or by 4WD are available and the prices are posted up inside the Rest House. These range from half an hour to a full day. Those who really want a desert experience should consider travelling off the road all the way from Aqaba to Wadi Rum. This can be arranged by local travel agents in Aqaba who

will provide the vehicle, driver and guide. All you have to do is sit there and enjoy the scenery. This route is definitely not recommended for those with their own 4WD unless they take an experienced guide with them. The route is between 50 and 70km depending on the route used. A recommended agency specializing in this sort of expedition is Qutaish and Sons (Tel: (03) 2012295, Fax: (03) 2014679).

It is possible for the independent traveller to leave Amman around dawn, make it to Petra by car in about three hours, take in a couple of excursions and be back in Amman the same evening; but this requires a reliable motor, and stamina in inverse proportion to sensitivity and interest. Most visitors prefer to stay overnight there, and see more.

Wadi Rum

An overnight itinerary

A great deal depends on how energetic you are, and how good you are at scrambling up mountain tracks.

The best overnight itinerary is probably to leave Amman after an early breakfast, lunch in Petra and 'do' Ed Dier (see Tour 10) in the afternoon. Sunrise the following day from the summit of the High Place (Tour 2) is breathtaking if you can get there; alternatively, go through the Siq to arrive at Al-Khasneh (see Tour 1) for the best light at 10 am. Tour 6 (the Urn, Palace and Corinthian tombs) is the best excursion to follow when time is limited. Return via the Theatre and Al-Khasneh (Tour 1) at around 4 pm, back up the Siq before nightfall and return to Amman for dinner.

If you want to include at least one climb to a high place, the High Place of Sacrifice (Tour 2) is the most convenient, Ed Deir (Tour 10) the most stupendous, and neither involves mountaineering – steps are cut into all the steepest places. If you like views, the Wadi Siyagh (Tour 4) is the prettiest walk. The Silk Tomb (Tour 6), the interior of the *triclinium* of the Roman Soldier Tomb (Tour 2) and the Carmine Tomb (Tour 7) make the best colour photos. The Renaissance Tomb (Tour 2) gives the best ornamental façade that fits neatly into an amateur's viewfinder (most are too large without a wide-angle lens). The Royal Tombs are the grandest buildings, Al-Khasneh and the Theatre (Tour 1) are the pinkest. The City Ruins (Tour 3) and the Royal Tombs (Tour 6) should also not be missed – but if your visit is only a short one you will have to choose.

The best use of a 24-hour stay

If you arrive at Petra in time for the evening meal, and you are lucky enough to have a full moon, why not attempt to see at least one Petra ruin by moonlight? Best is the Theatre.

MORNING. Walk down the Siq and arrive at Al-Khasneh (Tour 1) between 10 and 11 am when the stone is at its pinkest in full sun.

Next, if you can manage a climb, go up several hundred rock-cut stairs over the Attouf Ridge and see the High Place (Tour 2), descending via the Wadi al-Farasa. The average tourist could cope with this ascent without too much difficulty (estimate two hours) although it is strenuous, steep in places, and would obviously not be advisable for anyone lacking in stamina, with bad legs or a medical

Al-Khasneh Farun at night

condition. The only tricky bit is a stretch of some one hundred metres at the very top, where you need your hands free.

If your legs are not up to this, amble along the Wadi Musa past the Theatre (Tour 1) to the city centre sites (Tour 3). Both these trails end at Nazzal's Camp near the Hotel Forum restaurant.

AFTERNOON. After lunch, you could either do the Royal Tombs (Tour 6) (walking only), or strike out for Ed Deir (Tour 10) – which involves a stiff climb (808 steps) and is always best done in the afternoon when the sun has moved round. The trek to Ed Deir and back presents no dangers, but takes at least three hours.

For the following tours a guide is necessary, plus hired horses for the trips to the suburbs. These can be arranged from the Visitors' Centre.

The most challenging local climb is the full-day excursion to Umm al-Biyara (Tour 5). The ascent is tricky, and takes an agile person about three hours. The ascent of Al-Habis and back (Tour 4) takes around two hours and is much less strenuous. The trek out to Jabal Harun (Tour 11), with or without the climb, or Wadi Sabrah (Tour 9) is a full-day trip. Visiting the suburbs of Baidha and Al-Barid (Tour 8) needs half a day if you go by car.

Don't forget that everything takes longer in the hot season (May–September), since one tires much more easily, and more frequent rests are necessary if one is to avoid heat exhaustion.

Note. If you are travelling independently by car and are happy to take longer over your journey, then the trip down the King's Highway via Madaba and Kerate will take you eight hours including sightseeing.

Detail of
Ed Deir

The Siq Gorge

How long this takes will depend on how long it takes to get organized – waiting for your Arab guides or your tour group, for example. Allow 40 minutes if you're taking things gently or an hour if you want to dawdle, but it can be done in 20 minutes. It's nearly 3km from the Forum Rest House to the city centre. You can ride as far as the Siq entrance, or walk. Private vehicles do not go through it. The gorge approaches Petra from the east. It is a chasm over 1.5km in length, inhabited by thousands of sparrows that set up a great noise as evening descends. There are other ways into Petra on the far side, but this is by far the most dramatic, and you would miss one of the great experiences if you do not explore it.

For hundreds of years tales had been told of the strange cleft in the wilderness that led to a fabulous City of Rock – but the few adventurers who set out to solve the mystery never returned, and horrible rumours ran that they had had their throats cut, sacrificed on the high places by the bloodthirsty devotees of the sun-god, Dushrat. A constant watch was said to be kept on the gorge day and night by hawk-faced warriors, and all the lesser ravines were guarded by military outposts. Never had any fortress possessed so impregnable an entrance as this Siq gorge – a natural trap for invaders or spies. In fact, the air of romantic mystery was a matter of shrewd, practical business. The less outsiders knew about the inhabitants' mountain stronghold, the safer they were from attack and investigation.

Petra really begins before you enter the gorge at Ain Musa (Spring of Moses), said to be the spring that burst forth from the rock that Moses struck with his staff (Ex. 17:1–7). Consequently the course of the river that flowed forth is called the Wadi Musa (Valley of Moses). The spring has been enclosed now in a small building with three white domes (it looks like a

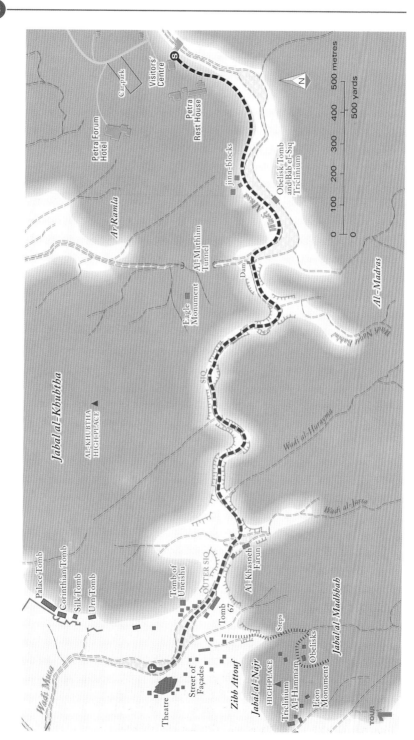

mosque) and bubbles out from under a stone wall along a pebbly channel. The clear water is safe to drink. Many tourists fill their bottles here in honour of its ancient association with Moses. In Nabataean times the place was regarded as being especially holy, since this was the water on which the whole existence of the city depended. The flow from this sacred spring was collected in two interconnected pools (Al-Birka), seen just beyond the car park of the Petra Forum Hotel, and channelled by pipe and conduit right round Jabal al-Khubtha to feed the nymphaeum, a huge ornamental fountain at the head of Petra's main street. Other channels, one rock-cut and one of ceramic pipes, went through the Siq.

Beside the spring is the Bedouin village of Wadi Musa (Al-Ji), once a very important outlying suburb of Petra, but unexcavated as yet, since the Arabs have built over it. The spring is still a place of sacrifice, for the mountain-top *weli*, or tomb-shrine in honour of the prophet Harun (Moses' brother Aaron) is just visible from here. Most Muslim pilgrims would make their sacrifices here, rather than climb all the way up – hence the native suspicion about Burckhardt's 'religious enthusiasm' (see p. 12). Communication with the locals is not 100 per cent. On asking to see the inside of the 'mosque', I was shown into the loos!

The scenery around Wadi Musa consists of smooth humps of white limestone hills, their smoothness accentuated by the jagged dark red peaks of the Petra range beyond. As yet, there is no hint of the lost city. The first Nabataean monuments to be seen are three enigmatic, solid carved cubes of rock some 6m high, and a 9m free-standing tower-tomb, with carved pilasters. The tombs are visually more photogenic, but the solid cubes are in other respects more interesting. They are described in Arabic as *sahrij* (water-tanks) – apparently rather a whimsy since they are perched up a hillside as dry as a bone. Twenty-three similar blocks have been identified elsewhere in Petra, and they seem to be massive 'god-boxes' or 'jinn-blocks' (see p. 55) – places in which Nabataean spirit-guardians dwell. They all occur near places of running water, hence the Arab name. (The Western mind needs to press a certain mental switch in order to understand Arabic – it is all too easy to dismiss things as gullible nonsense, without realizing that in fact you have a linguistic barrier to cross. In English 'water-tank' implies a reservoir to keep liquid in. The Arab searching for the concept of container has come up with 'tank', but it is a container of the god-power not the water, but these are specifically water-tanks because the inhabiting spirit forces happen to be standing guard over a source or flow of water.)

You wait below these monuments on a grey-white road strewn with small boulders that is really the river-bed, until a sudden echoing clatter indicates that your horses are about to arrive out of the Siq – which at this stage you cannot even see. Suddenly you are surrounded by tribesmen who seem to have appeared out of the solid wall of rock like Ali Baba and the forty thieves. It is a stirring sight when they come rampaging up at full gallop in a cloud of dust, with encouraging whoops and yells. The horses, these days, are only allowed to take the riders along the river bed as far as the Siq entrance.

The ride is memorable. You can fall off the horse if you try, but they are used to tourists and the owners generally lead them for you unless you are an experienced rider. This is half to protect you and half to protect the horse, which is after all their livelihood.

Once mounted, visitors usually miss the first minor but interesting sights and ride their tentative first 200m to the Obelisk Tomb perched above the dark entrance to a big cave, so named because its façade features four Egyptian-type obelisks some 4.5m high. The obelisks are in fact pillars known as *mazzeboth* in the Bible and, like the 'water-tanks', represent the presence of Nabataean gods, either as

Obelisk Tomb

symbols or as focus points 'anchors' in which their protective power could reside. This obelisk façade with its bristling display of psychic armour is the only one of its kind in Petra and of great importance because it guards the entrance to the Siq. Had it been in Egypt one might have expected to find a sacred *uraeus* (serpent) lurking somewhere ready to spit its psychic fire. Indeed, the guides point out an odd-looking rocky lump vaguely coiled about a huge block nearby, and say that it is a serpent. It may well be.

Obelisks carved on walls (as opposed to the free-standing variety) are referred to in Nabataean tomb incriptions as the *nephesh* of the buried person. *Nephesh* means 'soul' or 'spirit'. Just as Egyptian tombs had false doors carved into the tomb wall though which spirits could enter the world of the living, so it seems likely that the *nephesh* was a link-point of the departed Nabataean spirits.

The cave gouged out beneath is known as the Bab el-Siq Triclinium (*Bab* means 'gate'). A *triclinium* in this context, of which you are about to see many more examples, was a specially dedicated hall in which banquets were held in honour of the dead. The signpost to Al-Madras indicates a hike to a suburb of Petra, much of it through carved passageways, that ends just before Al-Khasneh. Very few visitors try it.

A modern dam now blocks the entrance to the gorge and diverts the waters of Wadi Musa down a smooth-sided tunnel that goes off to your right. You would be forgiven for wondering at this apparently superfluous feature if you go into Petra when it is dry. The reason for it is that after rainfall, when the wadi is in spate, the waters hurtle down the gorge and would trap and drown anything in their path were it not for the dam. The tunnel was built by the Nabataeans centuries ago to conserve every drop of that precious water. It is well worth a look, just to get a first close-up of the skill of the stone-carvers. You can comfortably walk in it without bending. It is guarded by many carved obelisks and a solitary jinn-block. From this point you must dismount and negotiate the Siq on foot, unless you are elderly or infirm, in which case a horse-drawn calêche will take you down into the city.

Once past the dam, the dark cleft of the Siq looms before you, and you plunge into its unaccustomed gloom. The long, narrow canyon, sometimes only wide enough to take two horses abreast, twists between sheer multicoloured rock walls that rise higher and higher as you go deeper into the heart of the mountains, reaching about 100m at their highest. It is eerie and cool, and in some places the sky is completely obscured by the looming overhangs. Here the gloom deepens, and the crunch of footsteps echoes between the sheer walls. Pebbles kicked up clink like glass in the enclosed space. However, although it is very narrow, it is not true – as some have claimed – that you can touch either side in one arm-stretch.

Most eerie and atmospheric of all is to walk through the Siq at dawn, when you can hear creaking noises, and an odd humming sound. It may be the *jinn*, disturbed by the intruders, or it could be the action of the rising sun stirring its warmth into the sleeping mountain.

The Siq

The Siq

The Siq is rough travelling these days but it was once beautifully paved with limestone blocks at the expense of those two millionaires, Herod the Great and Harith IV of Petra (see Chapter 2). There was a monumental arch straddling the entrance until its collapse in 1896. You can still make out the remains of the pediments on either side. Nowadays only traces of the pavement are left – visible in some places where the flash-flood torrents have gouged through the stones to reveal the gleam of white below. The Ministry of Tourism has reconstructed part of it – and threatens to repave the entire length (which will surely spoil the wild beauty). The Ministry has also contributed an irritatingly intrusive length of black telephone wire – that wretched and ubiquitous bane of all photographers of wilderness views!

On either side you can see the rock-cut Nabataean water-channels, and here and there are niches with a god-symbol, either a cube or an obelisk carved into the wall. Occasionally, where the gorge is more open, there is a sudden splash of brilliant sunshine, and the green of oleander bushes. Go in the spring, and you will see the strongly scented white *retm* (broom) in full flower, and the pink oleanders alive with colourful butterflies.

The prickly plant underfoot is the aloe, so beloved by makers of skin-care products.

Just when you are beginning to wonder whether the gorge will ever come to an end, you turn the final bend and are suddenly dazzled by Al-Khasneh Farun, especially if you arrive at around 10 am. No matter how many times you return, the brilliance of its sunlit façade is always startling. This is the best-preserved monument in Petra, carved in a rock face secluded from wind and rain, retaining its lines as fresh and sharp as if they were sculpted yesterday. (The façade, *c.*28m wide and 40m high, was restored by the archaeologist G.H. Wright in 1960.)

Legends abound. Khasneh Farun means 'Treasury of Pharaoh'. A large urn decorating the top is riddled with bullet-holes, and tourists are told that these are from potshots taken by gullible Bedouin in attempts to release the treasure hoarded within. Don't bother sneaking back after dark with rope and tackle – that urn was thoroughly checked out centuries ago and is a solid lump of rock. Any present day firing of rifles is for bravura display only.

Most scholars believe Al-Khasneh Farun to have been the tomb of King Harith IV. If St Paul ever did come to Petra as one legend maintains, he may very well

Approaching Al-Khasneh Farun through the Siq

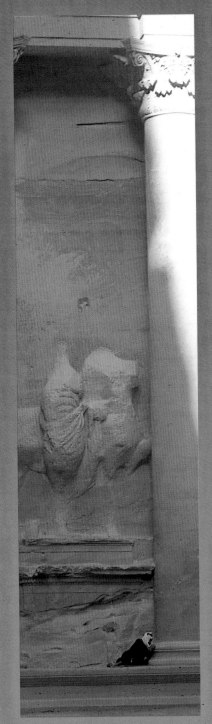

Opposite and this page
Details of Al-Khasneh Farun

have seen it being carved. Others maintain that in such a key position Al-Khasneh must have been a temple of the Great Goddess Isis, in Nabataean nomenclature the goddess Al-Uzza. The central figure on the decorative façade certainly appears to be female, but has been battered beyond recognition by either Christian or Muslim iconoclasts. Al-Khasneh may have degenerated into a treasury or toll gate, a convenient place in which to stash the Petran cut of whatever merchandise was allowed to pass up the Siq.

The fact that the façade is 40m high (over six times the height of a house) does not really impress you until you begin to draw near, and finally stand gazing up one of those mighty columns. (Try to ignore the hash of brickwork that was used on one pillar in an early attempt at reconstruction.)

In comparison the interior is disappointing – as are most Petra interiors: one plain chamber flanked by two smaller ones that do not seem big enough for the grand exterior, and an even smaller room at the very back. The walls are smooth and square, and display vivid stripes of colour (however, you will see much better examples elsewhere). The best thing about the interior is the view out of it, across the sprinkle of oleander bushes to the black split of the gorge in the rocks opposite. One can get an interesting photo using the massive doorway as a frame – wait until a camel or contractor's Range Rover positions itself nicely, to give the impression of size. If you are agile you can scramble up the rocks opposite Al-Khasneh to get a bird's-eye view.

Bedouin collect in this valley to barter with the tourists, rather like the touters of religious bric-à-brac outside some great cathedral. You may buy trinkets, jewellery, pottery and be photographed on a camel richly caparisoned in vivid dyed-wool tassels. If you want souvenirs, go ahead and buy here or along the Cardo Maximus, although a lot of the 'antiques' are the products of modern Damascus artisans. Best buys are

Al-Khasneh Farun

Arab silver necklaces, usually of very fine and intricate strands of the metal convoluted into beads, boxes and chains, intermingled rather oddly with plastic or glass bead-work. Worst buys are the daggers which, sensibly I suppose, are not sharpened and not genuine.

Beyond Al-Khasneh the gorge narrows again, and as you pass along it there are tiers of monuments on either side including Petra's largest *triclinium* (4m²). It is worth having a close look at a couple of them before your appreciation for the smaller tombs is dulled by the grandiose monuments to come. The Street of Façades on your left is a collection of over forty tombs arranged into four 'streets' or levels. (There is another collection of tombs in two streets just beyond the Theatre.) On your right is the least known of the Royal Tombs (see Tour 6), known as the Tomb of Uneishu. It can be reached by scambling over the rocks. The inscription indicates that Uneishu was the brother of Shaqilat (probably Shaqilat II). The tomb was apparently used by other members of the royal family for three decades. Beyond the courtyard was the tomb chamber with 11 *loculi* and an adjacent *triclinium*.

Some of the majestic burial caves are as large as temples, sculpted in the style of imperial palaces; smaller tomb-caves or towers were modelled on the style of the square cottages of the working folk. Incidentally, not all these 'tombs' were tombs – some were houses, and many regular tiers of them can be seen in the cliff faces around Petra.

The exterior height of many tombs rises to over 20m – the biggest are well over 30m – with skilfully shaped porches, windows and outside altars for offerings to the spirits. In all these tombs the inside walls are now unadorned, but they were originally plastered. There is some evidence that many of the tower-tombs were sprayed with a kind of stucco. You will hear buffs talk about the 'typical crow-step' design, sported by over half of Petra's tombs. They are referring to the crenellated tops or battlements. The mummified corpses were placed in hollows along the sides and in graves in the rock floor, set closer as the generations passed. When they were full, new family tombs were excavated, the changing styles reflecting the passage of time. The oldest show Egyptian influence, then Assyrian followed by Persian, Greek, Scythian and Roman – all in no particular order.

All along the side of the gorge you can see surviving evidence of the water channel made up of short lengths of Nabataean pottery pipe set in lime plaster. The Nabataeans were masters of hydraulic engineering; today in the Negev desert the land is being irrigated using exactly the same methods the Nabataeans perfected. At the height of Petra's prosperity, it is estimated that the earthenware piping laid into the city could cope with the water demands of a population of some 20–30,000 people.

In crevices of the rock little geckoes watch you pass, their dusty grey colour flecked with rose-red, exactly matching the sandstone to which they cling with padded feet. If you are lucky, you might see the Sinai lizard which is a bright turquoise blue.

About half a mile beyond Al-Khasneh, you arrive at the Theatre, also a good pink, which seated between 7,000 and 8,500 people in 40 rows cut from the living rock. Behind the top row a high wall assisted the acoustics and carried a drainage gully. Like Al-Khasneh, this was probably built by Harith IV; it was modified by Malik II and refubished in the Roman era, but virtually destroyed by a single earthquake in 363 CE. It was excavated and the stage partially restored, by the American Mission from Princeton Theological Seminary in the 1960s. Their finds included a headless statue of Herakles, now the showpiece of the small museum.

When the Theatre was built the constructors sliced through many *loculi* (hollows carved in the rock for storing dead bodies). Their gaping mouths form the theatre backdrop – a unique setting for Aeschylus'

The Theatre

tragedies, or the cynical comedies of Aristophanes. The later Nabataeans were culture vultures. Take a moment to imagine the stage bestrewn with corpses in a saga that out-Hamlets *Hamlet*; normally staid elders leaping around dressed in green for Aristophanes' *Frogs* or wearing diaphanous wisps of gauze for *Clouds* or yellow and black striped vests for *Wasps*. The 'wasps' were equipped at the rear end with 'stings', phallic protuberances which could be swung round to the front if the slapstick required it! An old joke was inviting someone up from the audience and extending the artificial phallus as a convenient handhold for helping them up.

It is traditional to show off here by declaiming your own piece, a performance known as 'testing the acoustics'; either have a speech learnt in advance for such an occasion, or have one ready on paper. One performance here on a grand scale was the recital on a £20,000 Steinway by the concert pianist John Briggs in May 1989. He commented that 'the acoustics easily matched Carnegie Hall and the Sydney Opera House.'

An archaeologist has suggested that this Theatre, like others in the Nabataean kingdom, was not for buffoonery but served for the performance of funeral rites, and was probably built by Harith IV for the performance of these rites after his own death. It does seem rather remarkable that a theatre in the Graeco-Roman sense should have been constructed for entertainment in the midst of a necropolis which was still being used for burials. However, the Petran attitude to life after death may well have been such that they believed the surviving souls of their dead enjoyed watching the odd show with the living.

You have now penetrated to the heart of the mountains, and the hills fall back to reveal an open space over a mile long and half a mile wide where the city once stood. Visitors have to choose whether to proceed to the City Ruins (Tour 3), go round to the right to the so-called Royal Tombs (Tour 6) or climb up to the High Place on the Attouf Ridge (Tour 2) and rejoin the city route at the head of the Cardo (Paved Street) (Tour 3).

Beyond the Theatre and stretching down the Cardo are numerous tented cafés, souvenir-sellers, an information office and some lavatories.

Detail of the colourful cliffs

A TYPICAL GLADIATORS' CONTEST

The event commenced with a public banquet the evening before the show, in which all the contestants participated. Fans came to eye their favourites and gamblers to estimate odds. The following morning came the *pompa*, a flashy parade or procession in stage costume (rather like modern American wrestlers), the more colourful and outrageous the better, heralded by trumpets and horns. This procession included the sponsor of the games in a special chariot and all the fighters, who usually entered the amphitheatre by the north gate and left by the south.

The show opened with pretty tame preliminaries – mock fights with wooden weapons, and so on. This gave the fighters a chance to warm up and the audience ample time to settle.

The first pair on usually fought to the death, to get things going; but good losers were often allowed to live. It depended on what kind of mood the crowd was in. If they gave 'thumbs down' the defeated fighter would be finished off, either by the man who had beaten him or by an official dressed as Charon, the mythical ferryman of the dead to the underworld, who came on and smashed his skull with a large mallet. The corpses were then dragged through the death gate with hooks.

Midday was a slack period, with more mock fighting, displays, executions of criminals, and lunch. The afternoons were usually made over to the *venationes*, wild animals goaded into fighting against each other, or against trained *bestarii* (animal fighters).

The whole business was raucous, with continuous blowing of horns, trumpets, pipes, drums, water organs and voices.

The High Place of Sacrifice (Jabal al-Najr)

TOUR 2

The climb to the High Place and down the valley the other side will take you about two hours. Wear trousers not skirts if female: it's very windy at the top. This climb is not to be attempted if you are not physically fit, and is always best done in the morning with the sun behind you. You need a guide unless you're confident at reading the maps, although if you're staying longer than a day or two you'll soon get your bearings. The drop over the edge at the top is fatal but the views are splendid.

The route up to the High Place

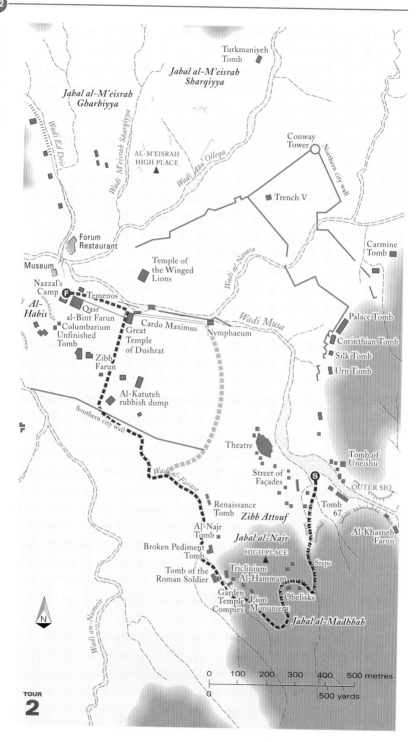

Turkmaniyeh Tomb

Jabal al-M'eisrah Sharqiyya

Jabal al-M'eisrah Gharbiyya

Wadi Ed Deir

Wadi M'eisrah Sharqiyya

AL-M'EISRAH HIGH PLACE

Wadi Abu Olleqa

Conway Tower

Northern city wall

Trench V

Forum Restaurant

Museum

Carmine Tomb

Wadi al-Nasara

Temple of the Winged Lions

Nazzal's Camp

Al-Habis

Temenos

Qasr al-Bint Farun

Columbarium

Unfinished Tomb

Zibb Farun

Cardo Maximus

Nymphaeum

Wadi Musa

Great Temple of Dushrat

Palace Tomb

Corinthian Tomb

Silk Tomb

Urn Tomb

Al-Katuteh rubbish dump

Southern city wall

Theatre

Wadi al-Farasa

Street of Façades

Tomb of Uneishu

OUTER SIQ

Tomb 67

Renaissance Tomb

Zibb Attouf

Al-Najr Tomb

Broken Pediment Tomb

Jabal al-Najr

HIGH PLACE

Steps

Al-Khasneh Farun

Tomb of the Roman Soldier

Triclinium

Al-Hammam

Garden Temple Complex

Lion Monument

Obelisks

Jabal al-Madhbah

Wadi an-Numeir

N

0   100   200   300   400   500 metres

0   500 yards

STONES AS SYMBOLS

The worship of Petra's gods did not consist of bowing down to representations of humans or animals. The worshippers were far more aware of the forces of nature themselves, and the presence of their gods was symbolized by obelisks or blocks of stone known as *mazzeboth*.

The sacred stones were more than symbols; they were also the places in which the powers of these chief gods and their attendant lesser entities collected, guarding specific locations, or bringing down the protective power of the deity on a particular natural feature and those who went there to bow in worship. They also represented the throne or seat of the deity – the place where the 'presence' of the god alighted, and could therefore serve as altars.

The stone blocks of Dushrat had the dimensions of 4 x 2 x 1, no matter how big or how small the blocks were. Dushrat's other stones were tapering obelisks, as were those of the female deities. (Even as far away as Cyprus, at the chief shrine of Venus/Al-Uzza, the goddess is shown on coins as a conical obelisk.)

This is undoubtedly one of the chief powerhouses in the psychic network that charged the city, and is a favourite spot for people with a psychic talent. These standing stones vibrate (for those with the right touch) and react strongly for dowsers. Many who approach the obelisks claim to be aware of strange forces and a tingling sensation like a mild electric shock when touching them, especially the relatively undamaged one. The author knows personally an elderly lady who was knocked flat when she placed her hands upon it. Whether these effects are caused by imagination or by a lingering ancient malice, it undoubtedly underlines the fact that it can be dangerous for the unwary to dabble with forces they do not understand. This was why priests were so important and powerful.

One of the results of having such an experience is that the surprised recipients' appreciation of what is usually regarded as ignorant and superstitious paganism is dramatically altered, and they begin to get an inkling as to why it was our intelligent ancestors were prepared to bend the knee and make blood sacrifices to bits of stone and wood.

If you are coming from the Siq, the trek up the 'pilgrim way' begins at an easily visible rock-cut stairway on your left guarded by several jinn-blocks. (The Theatre is about 200m beyond it.) The going is reasonable, with some steps recut in modern times although many are original. There are plenty of places to pause and catch your breath and watch the tombs at ground level along the Wadi Musa gradually shrink to toysize. At times the way leads alongside a sheer drop, but it is quite safe so long as you don't teeter near the edge.

Jabal al-Najr is a double summit on the Attouf Ridge, the first lower than the second, because the entire peak has been sliced away and levelled in order to leave two 6m *mazzeboth* or obelisks, some 30m apart. (The rubble may have been used to build the fortification across the gully to the north, which may have been a lookout or a stately entrance to the High Place.) This extraordinary labour created a large terrace with the two gigantic slivers of rock from the heart of the mountain piercing the open sky – sacred pillars of Dushrat (Dusares) and either his consort Atargatis or his daughter Al-Uzza (or the pair combined). A different theory is that the two obelisks represent the 'horns' of either the Great Goddess or the Edomite deity Qaush.

Since the obelisk shape is rather an obvious symbol representing the worship of fertility, the life force, the place is popularly known as Zibb Attouf. (Use the Bedouin name with caution – *zibb* means 'phallus'.)

Many visitors take a brief look, but unaware of its significance and overcome by the climb they make straight for a solitary tree at the far side of the terrace, just before the start of the final ascent, where there is just enough shade in which to huddle, and a Bdul tribesman selling drinks. His wife may spread out a blanket on the rocks and offer you various artefacts, daggers and jewellery. This is a good place to obtain a genuine Bedouin souvenir.

The last part of the climb up to the place of sacrifice is tricky, and one needs hands free to scramble over the smooth rock surface, since there are no steps here. Once again, the summit – some 1000m above sea level – has been sliced off by human endeavour to form a hewn platform (3m x 20m).

Just before you get to the altar, you pass a large pit excavated in the rock, a ritual cleansing bath, the green and putrid contents of which would have a hard time cleansing anything these days. It may have been used for the purification of priests or initiates – or it may have been where they washed the sacrificial implements. It certainly bears no resemblance to a store of drinking water.

Jabal al-Madhbah, the actual place of sacrifice, is set in a shallow courtyard (14.5m x 6.5m). This is quite a small space, suggesting that it was never intended to admit crowds for public worship. Built in *c*.7 BCE, it bears the dedicatory inscription of one Natayr'el who erected it 'for the life of Harith, King of the Nabataeans, who loves his people, and for the life of Huldu his wife'. Coins bearing portraits of this devout royal couple can be seen in the museum on the Acropolis in Amman. Harith's wife Huldu was also his sister, and these were the parents of the discarded wife of the biblical Herod Antipas (see Chapter 2).

The altar itself, where the priests cut the throats of their victims, is a plain and serviceable block about the size of an average church altar, approached by three hewn steps. You can see clearly the square indentation in the centre which held the black stone, possibly a meteorite, that symbolized Dushrat and channelled his power, and which would have been anointed with fresh blood every time it was shed.

Beside the altar to the left are the drains for the blood from the sacrifices. Each beast would have shed over a gallon. There are no signs of any fires which would have been needed if burnt offerings were being made, either here or on any of the other High Places in Petra.

DUSHRAT: THE SUN-GOD

Dushrat's original name in Petra was Dhu-esh-Shera, or 'He of Seir', Seir being the name of the mountains of the Petra neighbourhood. His shrine-symbol was a black stone, which was probably smeared with sacrificial blood. Such sacred stones were located at all of Petra's High Places, as well as in niches at the start of sacred staircases and by natural features such as pools, and in people's homes. It may, incidentally, be one such stone which is incorporated into the wall of the Ka'aba sanctuary in Mecca – the famous Black Stone. Such a stone still exists near the Tomb of Harun (Aaron) up the Jabal (Tour 11) where it is claimed the body of this patriarch has been interred.

RITUAL SACRIFICE

The second century philosopher Porphyry reported that a boy's throat was cut once a year at the Nabataean town of Dunat, less than 30km away from Petra, and it seems reasonable to suppose that the chill in the air as you stand on the summit of Jabal al-Najr, contemplating the drains that received the blood of sacrificial victims, is caused by more than just the stiff breeze.

It is not known whether the sacrifices here were animal or might have included humans, but it is certain from a Nabataean inscription at Madain Salih that human sacrifices were sometimes made. 'Abd Wadd, priest of Wadd, and his son Salim, and Zayn Wadd, have consecrated the young man Salim to be immolated to Dhu Gabat. Their double happiness!' (There were drawbacks to being a priest's son!)

Why sacrifice? The consecration of any life force was a very powerful psychic stimulant, and none more so than the offering of a human life – but it was worthless if the victim had to be dragged there kicking and screaming. It was not intended to be cruel or a punishment. The human sacrifice had to be willing, and to regard the honour of being thought worthy of being given to God as the greatest of all honours. The individuals concerned might not particularly want to die, but they had to submit of their own free will. Confident that death would be swift and painless and sublimely sure of being welcomed in a life after death, the victim would then accept death with serene dignity.

Western people, most of whom eat meat, but will never have seen animals slaughtered, can be very squeamish and sentimental about the whole business of sacrifice, a quite misguided reaction. The true spirit of sacrificial slaughter keeps the animal in a loving and caring atmosphere, well-tended and not knowing its fate until the moment it dies. Death is accompanied by prayer, and the animal's jugular vein severed quickly with a very sharp knife – possibly less painful than being shot in the brain by a large bolt after being stunned helpless by an electric shock.

In front of the altar is a small platform only 12cm high, a Mensa Sacra equivalent to the Israelite shewbread table, for bloodless offerings. Instead of this bare stone, useful only for standing on when taking yet another snap, try to imagine it laden with good things – perishable food offered in thanksgiving for harvests, the treasures of the wealthy, or perhaps the mites of poor widows (Luke 21: 1–4).

One can experience claustrophobia in Petra itself amongst all the tombs beneath those towering cliffs, but up here – in the intentional bareness of a shrine with limitless horizons – one feels a blissful sense of space, at one with the eagles under an open sky and the all-seeing eye of God. Down there you are just one of the masses, a nameless face in the crowd. Here there is just you and He who watches you, who neither slumbers nor sleeps (Psalm 121, and Qur'an 2:255). On a peak in the distance you can see the white-domed *weli* (shrine) of Moses' brother Aaron (see Tour 11).

The descent from the High Place has been much facilitated now by rock-hewn steps recently cut by the Department of Antiquities; they are perilously steep but there is a handrail. You go down the far side of the mountain, via the Butterfly Valley, or Wadi al-Farasa (it takes after its name – there are butterflies). There is a choice: you could climb down the water gully, which is a short route down off the peak, but very tricky; those with more sanity take the obvious, easier but more circuitous route, littered with inscriptions (could they but read them) wishing 'Peace, to so-and-so, son of so-and-so', occasional carved god-blocks, and some of the very best rock striations in Petra.

Just off the route is a small god-block set in a niche, guarded by two pillars surmounted by crescent moons, horns uppermost – symbols of Al-Uzza/Venus, the Morning Star, and not Dushrat the Sun as is generally supposed. Another monument is the medallion and block relief, the medallion being the weathered bust of the goddess.

The High Place of Sacrifice

The altar at the High Place of Sacrifice

Where the 'pilgrim way' meets up with the water gully one is confronted by a sculptured lion, the sacred beast of Al-Uzza, in its present weathered state looking more like an elephant or baboon. The 4.5m long beast with its faceless head turned to glower a warning at visitors was once a fountain with water pouring from its mouth. Remains of the piping can be seen above it. Originally the lion had a head cast in metal, which is why it seems so inexplicably weathered and blank now. The head has long since gone. It's a pity it doesn't work any more – a drink here would be much appreciated by today's pilgrims. No doubt the ancient pilgrims, toiling up this way from the city in reverse order to our tour, would have used the fountain for ritual cleansing before approaching the High Place.

Continuing down, next comes Al-Hammam (the Bath), a very large sacred reservoir 6m x 18m x 3.5m deep, where the water streaming from the lion's mouth collected. Here the initiates would have been cleansed by total immersion in the pure running water. (See St John's Gospel, chapter 4 – the difference between 'living' water and 'standing' or 'dead' water is very obvious in the Middle East.) Once again, there are many Nabataean pilgrim inscriptions carved in the rocks, some looking as if the pious 'vandal' was there but yesterday. The cistern now has a large leafy tree growing in it.

Beyond the Bath, a flight of very weathered steps leads down to the so-called Garden Tomb, really not a tomb at all but a small temple set in a carved terrace. Like the sacred cistern, it is somewhat improved (to the romantic eye) by having green plants burgeoning from the collected dust of ages. The steps are quite tricky but even the local donkeys manage them somehow.

Down another hundred metres to the next level, and you are at the Statue Tomb, otherwise known as the Tomb of the Roman Soldier, which has three

niches with statues on its façade including one of **The Garden** a headless legionnaire, and an interior very much **Tomb** blackened by Bedouin campfires. The open space in front of the tomb was once a rock-cut colonnaded courtyard, occupying every centimetre of the space between the two massifs.

At the far side is a very fine *triclinium* or sacred hall. Don't miss the interior – it is no less than 3.25m², and contains the only carved interior decoration in Petra – fluted Ionic columns that seem, like Michelangelo's famous figures, to be trapped within the rock. Unlike his tortured shapes, however, these stately frauds – for there is no need of any pillar to bolster the sheer solid-rock walls – give the air not of torment, but of a moment of magic – as if they had slipped gently back into the mountain, and then been arrested in a moment of time. If you look at a certain angle, you get a *trompe l'oeil* effect, as if you are looking down a corridor lined with these columns. The hall is well worth photographing inside for the

View from the Renaissance Tomb

colours alone, remarkable striations in fantastic pinks, reds, buffs, purple and blue, bands of colour that spread across walls and columns alike. The columns at the entrance reveal the violence of the weathering effect of wind and water – one has been nearly completely worn away in the middle. It will look most odd when Nature finally completes the process – unless restoring busybodies spoil it.

Carrying on down the track towards the City Ruins, you pass the Broken Pediment Tomb, presumably damaged by earthquake, and could take a short diversion of a few hundred metres round the Jabal al-Najr to see the Al-Najr Tomb. This is hardly ever visited or mentioned, probably because most walkers are too tired to bother by this time, and it has nothing particularly different to offer but its isolation and an impressive interior. Returning, you come back to the so-called Renaissance Tomb with its neat, sophisticated façade – one of the more ornate tombs in Petra.

Warning. By this time you will have ridden, walked and climbed three strenuous miles, and will be very hot and possibly faint. It is safer not to lose sight of all members of your party as they straggle out once they leave the Attouf Ridge and amble at varying speeds over the easy terrain down the Wadi al-Farasa. You would not get lost, as the trail is pretty obvious, but if you fainted you might not be missed for some time and rescue could be a very dodgy matter.

Once clear of the massifs, you have a choice of route – veer right for the city Main Street and then follow it down to Nazzal's Camp (about 2km – the itinerary is described in Tour 3); or keep left, for the road straight to the Camp (about 1.5km). If you have limited time in Petra, you should try to find the energy to do the City Ruins (Tour 3).

However, if you continue to follow the Wadi al-Farasa down towards the clearly visible Great Temple you come to the remains of Al-Katuteh rubbish dump, once the housing complex of a wealthy merchant, now only rubble. It was abandoned suddenly after the Roman annexation in 106 CE for no known reason – but the official Roman Petra rubbish dumps (still unexcavated) were created virtually next-door, and may have sent the worthy gentleman off in a huff.

Zibb Farun – a free-standing pillar next to a fallen one – is virtually all that remains of a nearby temple. It is not known why this particular phallic symbol is attributed to Pharaoh. (As hinted at earlier, if you use the word *zibb* in front of your Bedouin guides, it will trigger off a fit of giggling, if not other reactions.) Your hike ends as you come out behind the Great Temple and arrive at the refreshments on offer at Nazzal's Camp at the end of the Main Street.

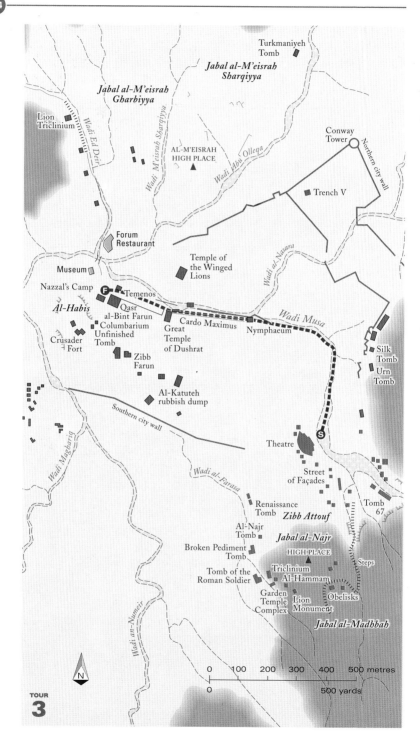

The City Ruins

This is a walking tour that requires no climbing. If you walk down the Siq from the Forum Rest House, continue down the Wadi Musa to the Theatre which is the starting point of the tour. You do not need a guide. If you have the time and energy, you could turn north first and visit the Royal Tombs which would add at least another hour to your hike (see Tour 6).

About 200m beyond the Theatre, the wadi takes a sharp turn to the west, to the open bowl of a large valley, the site of the City Ruins. You may wonder where all the dwellings have gone, but anyone who has visited rural villages in the Middle East will probably guess why there's so little to be seen. The usual building material for the houses of ordinary people was (and still is) mud, which was readily accessible in quantity and could be easily moulded into bricks

The view across the Cardo

and then sun-dried or baked in kilns. Needless to say, over time this is less than durable. Stone was rarely used because it was expensive and had to be brought from a distance.

However, the few limestone features remaining in Petra are very impressive. The first important site is the Nymphaeum, which was once a focal shrine in Petra sacred to the life force symbolized by water. It sported a very grandiose ornamental drinking fountain fed by the waters of the Wadi Musa, upon which the life of the city depended. The site is now occupied by a large, solitary tree (known as Al-Butmeh, 'the oak') and a Bdul drinks seller offering hot Coca-Cola and fizzy orange that has more than likely lost its fizz – a bit of a comedown but nevertheless immensely welcome.

The Nymphaeum is at the head of the Cardo Maximus (or Colonnaded or Paved Street), that runs alongside the river-bed. The street (10m wide and over 225m in length) was created from large, dazzling white limestone blocks, so bright in the midday sun that they really hurt the eye. It was excavated in 1955 by Diana Kirkbride (who became Mrs Hans Haelbek), one of several female archaeologists who have fallen under the spell of Petra. Miss Kirkbride spent many months here on her own, and her efforts are legendary in these parts. On the south side are the remains of Byzantine shops, built when the Cardo had been buried by dirt and rubble. The date that the Cardo was built is still not known for certain, but some authorities put it as late as the reign of Trajan (98–117 CE). There was a triumphal arch dedicated to Trajan in 114 at the entrance to the street. More recently support has been growing for those who favour an earlier date, in the reign of Harith IV (9 BCE–40 CE). In the rooms excavated alongside the Cardo (now below ground level) a great deal of pottery has come to light, dating back to about 300 BCE.

The Cardo Maximus

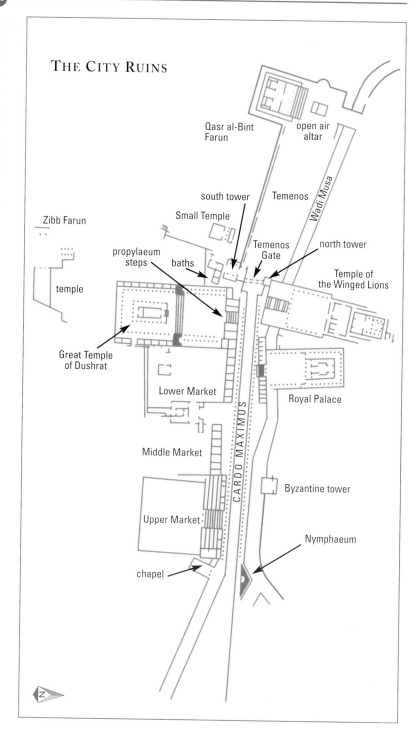

THE CITY RUINS

Qasr al-Bint Farun

open air altar

Wadi Musa

south tower

Temenos

Small Temple

Zibb Farun

Temenos Gate

north tower

propylaeum steps

baths

Temple of the Winged Lions

temple

Great Temple of Dushrat

Lower Market

Royal Palace

CARDO MAXIMUS

Middle Market

Byzantine tower

Upper Market

Nymphaeum

chapel

N

NABATAEAN POTTERY

Nabataean pottery was of a wafer-thin fineness, a terracotta decorated with feathery leaves – its delicacy and fineness only equalled by the very best porcelain; yet it was all thrown on the wheel and smoothed down afterwards – whereas porcelain is normally cast in a mould. Not only that, but the commonest Petra shape was a shallow open bowl – which happens to be the most difficult shape to throw on a wheel, even when the final product is as thick as a flowerpot. Nevertheless, the way it was treated suggests that it was not regarded by the Petrans with any special amazement.

A large complex of pottery kilns was found northeast of the Forum Rest House, a centre of intensive production for several hundred years. There was a gradual decline in quality as commercial demand brought about mass production techniques.

There were at least two bridges over the wadi, and it is possible that the river may have been completely vaulted over the entire length of the street. A wall was constructed along the edge of the torrent to reduce erosion from flash-floods. The slopes on both sides of the Cardo are positively littered with dressed sandstone blocks – all that remains above ground of the houses and temples. In the distance on your left you can see a massive temple, the only surviving free-standing (as opposed to rock-cut) monument in Petra, known as the Qasr al-Bint Farun (Castle of Pharaoh's Daughter). On the northern side of the street (on your right as you face the temple) are the sites of a Byzantine tower, a royal palace and the Temple of the Winged Lions – but very little remains of these now and they have not been fully excavated. Opposite the Nymphaeum, on the southern hillside, is a wide flight of steps leading up to unexcavated areas thought to be three markets, now rather prosaically known as the Upper,

Qasr al-Bint
Farun viewed
from Wadi Musa
(Laborde)

Qasr al-Bint
Farun

Qasr al-Bint
Farun from the
rear (Bellefonds)

Middle and Lower Markets. The trek up the Cardo is very exposed with no shade at all. Since visitors do not usually arrive here until around midday, they do not linger. It is impossible, in the hot season, to walk barefoot upon the pavers, but you could fry an egg on them.

Just beyond the 'market' areas on the southern slopes a dramatic ruined grand staircase leads up to the holiest shrine within the city of Petra itself, the Great Temple of Dushrat, the Watcher, the Almighty Father. Little can be said about the Great Temple as it has not been excavated. It must have been a grand and impressive structure judging from the size of the fallen columns. (It has also been suggested that this was not a temple at all, but the city's forum or agora.) Beyond the temple are three domed and interconnected chambers, known as 'the baths' because pendentives (circular domed roofs on a square room) became a popular shape for Middle Eastern bathhouses. These are the earliest-known pendentives in the world; maybe they were invented here. If you climb the steps to the Great Temple and follow the sign to the baths you can peer

Mosaic floor in the Byzantine Church

down into these chambers through an opening in the roof. It seems most likely that there were three major temples here: the Great Temple of Dushrat, the Temple of Al-Uzza his consort, and the Qasr al-Bint, which may have been the 'birth house' of the third person in the Triad – Dushrat the virgin-born son, the incarnation of himself.

The recently discovered so-called Temple of the Winged Lions, the temple of Atargatis Al-Uzza, is on the opposite hillside, across the Cardo. It gets its name from the carved lions on the column capitals – lions being one of the sacred beasts of Al-Uzza. Arches and porticoes from her temple extended right down to the wadi and across the bottom to the temple of Dushrat on the other side. It is interesting to note that the Great Mother's temple was actually placed at a higher vantage-point than that of the Great Father. The temple contained Egyptian statuettes, Nabataean god-blocks, and painted figures of humans, animals and geometrical motifs. Nearby were the workshops of painters, metalworkers and marbleworkers. All the inscriptions found mentioned Harith IV.

The entrance to the sacred precinct of the Qasr al-Bint complex was a stately triple-arched Temenos Gate (Monumental Gate) straddling the Cardo, once thought to be a triumphal arch erected by Trajan, but now dated much earlier. The arch remains but the gate has long since disappeared. If you look carefully at the pavers under the archway you will see sockets in the ground, which indicate that the original wooden doors faced east, into the rising sun. Part of this arch was rebuilt in 1960, under the direction of the archaeologist G.H. Wright, who also saw to the re-erection of some of the columns flanking the street. The Department of Antiquities, helped by British and American scholars, is still excavating the area – there is enough to keep them busy for decades. Many sculptures have been found in the Gate area – shields, heads, eagles, busts of Nabataean deities, some of which can be seen in the museum.

THE TEMENOS GATE

One wonders if the doors might have been overlaid with gold leaf, like the doors of the famous Temple of the Father at Jerusalem. If you have ever been spellbound by sunlight flashing from a window, you will appreciate immediately the symbolic relevance of the blinding light that would have shone from this barrier to the sanctuary, making it impossible for approaching worshippers to raise their eyes and stare immodestly. The door of a temple always represented that which stood between the spiritual and the material world, and functioned both as a barrier and as a means of access. Christians will be quite familiar with the words of Jesus when he compared himself to 'the door' (John 10:7–9).

The Temenos itself is a large courtyard in front of the Qasr, with two tiers of seats on the southern side for the spectators at the ceremonies. Excavations have revealed that the upper tier was added at a later period, and since one of the blocks at this level was once a statue-base dedicated to Harith IV it means that the temple ruins predate this, and therefore probably belong to the reign of Aboud III (30–9 BCE). Aboud was known to have been extremely devout, and in fact was deified by his brother Harith, who built a new city (Oboda or Avdat – now in Israeli territory) in his honour and named it after him.

On the same axis as the temple, at the foot of its steps, is a large rectangle of masonry (13.5m x 12m), believed to be the altar platform. Modern Christians, used to the idea of altars enclosed at the focal point inside expensive buildings, often forget that the original purpose of the stone block was for the releasing of the life force of a sacrificial victim which always was a messy business. For this reason no ancient altars were erected within the precious fabric of holy buildings.

The large limestone building is known for some reason as the 'Castle of Pharaoh's Daughter' or Qasr al-Bint Farun. It may have been the inner sanctum of the Temple of Dushrat if the building identified as the Great Temple was really only the Forum – or it may have been his 'birth house'. The local story about the name is that an Egyptian princess once lived here who gave herself in marriage to the man who succeeded in bringing a water-supply into the complex. However, it is also possible that the story may have originated in the performance of a 'ritual marriage' between a high priestess and a priest of Dushrat (representative of the spirit of fertility, the supplier of water) in order to produce a god-child who might be sacrificed in due course.

The Royal Tombs viewed from the Temenos Gate

The 'castle' is approached up a wide, monumental staircase, where a dedicatory inscription of Shuudat, daughter of Malik, was found. At present the building is under reconstruction. It has been in a very precarious state for some time, since at least two of the horizontal strata in the walls were not made of stone but of wood. This was presumably an anti-earthquake device, but once the wood started rotting away the walls became very unstable and might easily have toppled down. The upper layers used to lean outwards alarmingly.

The interior is in a ruinous condition, but it can be seen that the whole building was originally decorated with carved stucco or plaster (remains of it are visible on the back wall), and the layers of large stone blocks were painted in bands of bright colours. During the excavations part of the hand of a statue was found, four times life-size, suggesting a god-image some 6m high, which would nicely fit the Holy Place. One wonders what became of the rest of the statue of Dushrat. It is ironic that only the outstretched hand remains – for that was the very symbol of the bounty and grace of the Light of the Universe. (The reliefs at Tel el-Amarna in Egypt, for instance, often show the rays emanating from the Aten (the sun-disk) with little hands at the end, bestowing blessing.) The temple went out of use in the Roman period, and in later times was used as a stable. A ramp was built up to the main door to allow carts to be driven in.

This excursion usually finishes at the little shop quaintly signposted as the Bedouin supermarket. It doesn't sell all that much, mainly canned drinks and basic food supplies, and you may find the proprietor is more interested in buying – I could have sold my watch a thousand times, and was constantly asked for lipstick. An ideal place for a spiv to set up a couple of suitcases. The area is known as Nazzal's Camp, and lies at the foot of the massif Al-Habis, which off-puttingly means 'The Prison'. Just beyond the shop is the museum set in a large cave which also houses the workshops of the Department of Antiquities. The cave was originally a shrine marking the start of another important processional way leading to another mountain-top sanctuary. Opening hours seem to be very random, and it often stands defiantly shut behind ghastly red metal doors, but if you can get in there is a collection of statues, pottery, jewellery and various artefacts. It's worth a quick look. The two major features seem to be the Arts and the Drains – the headless statue of Herakles from the Theatre, and an assortment of Nabataean earthenware pipes. This area is riddled with cave-sepulchres, some done out with beds on which you may take a nap if you wish. Visitors usually recover here, see the exhibits in the museum, then walk back up the Cardo to be reunited with their horses for the return journey up the Siq.

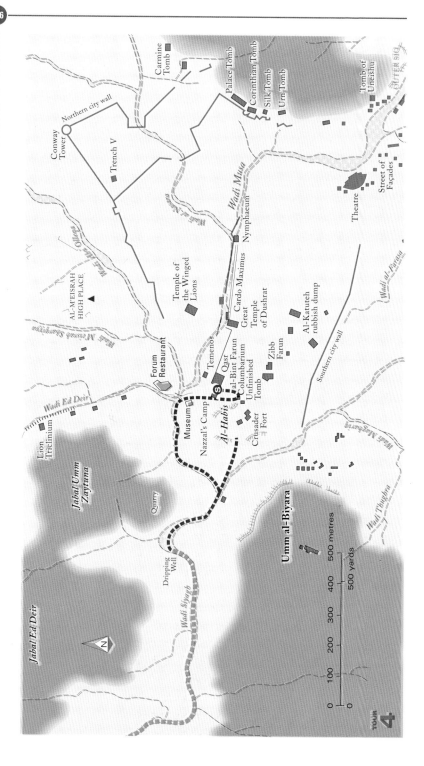

Carmine
Tomb

Palace Tomb

Corinthian Tomb

Silk Tomb

Urn Tomb

Tomb of
Uneishu

OUTER SIQ

Northern city wall

Conway
Tower

Trench V

Wadi al-Nasara

Wadi Musa

Nymphaeum

Theatre

Street of
Façades

Wadi al-Farasa

Al-Wa'arah Shanfara

Olfaa

AL-MEISRAH
HIGH PLACE

Temple of
the Winged
Lions

Cardo Maximus

Great
Temple of Dushrat

Al-Katuteh
rubbish dump

Southern city wall

Forum
Restaurant

Temenos

Qasr
al-Bint Farun

Columbarium

Zibb
Farun

Wadi Ed Deir

Museum

Nazzal's Camp

Al-Habis

Unfinished
Tomb

Crusader
Fort

Wadi Mataha

Lion
Triclinium

Jabal Umm
Zaytuna

Quarry

Umm al-Biyara

Wadi Thughra

Dripping
Well

Wadi Siyagh

Jabal Ed Deir

N

TOUR
4

0   100   200   300   400   500 metres

0   500 yards

Al-Habis and the Wadi Siyagh

TOUR 4

Starting from Nazzal's Camp, you can explore the immediate façade of Al-Habis, or walk all the way round the base (1km, no guide needed). You can combine this with a walk down the Wadi Siyagh, which is a pleasant excursion and not at all strenuous. Don't be fooled by the small size of Al-Habis in comparison with the towering massif behind it (likened locally to 'a cat beside a camel'). It is a safe climb, but still only for those who are fit. For those who would like to do at least one climb, and can't face the more strenuous ones, the ascent of Al-Habis is the one to do. For safety, it should be done with a guide, and you can usually pick one up at the camp. Give yourself two hours.

To inspect the façade of Al-Habis, first climb the slope behind the Camp, and you will arrive at an unexplained edifice known as the Columbarium or Dovecote. In archaeological terms, *columbaria* are not nesting-boxes for pigeons but tiers of niches for small funerary urns. However, the niches here are only 25cm x 25cm and very shallow; any urns would have fallen out! Maybe little god-blocks went there, or votive tablets. It does look rather like a post office sorting grid.

Working your way back, you see the Unfinished Tomb, which gives away the engineering methods of those ancient stonecutters. They first chiselled a vertical face into a cliff. At its top they cut a ledge wide enough for the craftsmen to fashion the highest point of the façade. When work had progressed down to where a door or window was desired, stonecutters tunnelled all the way to the proposed depth of the interior rear wall. Then they either tunnelled up to the ceiling, or cut out blocks downward to the floor. Carving of the façade proceeded simultaneously at the same level.

Just south of the Camp is a monument called Al-Thughra, a free-standing block surmounted by what is supposed to be a coiled serpent, although this is so weathered it takes a good eye to see it. This presumably had cultic significance, and may have symbolized the raising of psychic power or the protection of the shrine from the profane. The function of the sacred serpent of Egyptian mythology, the *uraeus*, was to defend; it sensed evil intent in anyone approaching and spat 'psychic fire'. In Earth-mystery thought anything with coils – like the sacred ring-dance or many of the puzzling 'mazes' associated with ancient sites – was intended to raise power.

Beyond the museum lies Wadi Siyagh. Five kilometres there and back – allow two hours – is probably enough for the average tourist, although the wadi itself continues on much further. It was a highly select suburb in Nabataean times, featuring some fine examples of rock-cut houses. The valley heads down past a sheer cliff face known as the Quarry cut and smoothed to a very considerable height.

The walk down is visually very rewarding as oleanders grow thickly here, and a beautiful spot to make for is the natural pool and waterfall known as the Dripping Well. The trickle and splash of water, the surrounding silence, and the breeze stirring the bushes all give a sensation of the place being alive and haunted by spirits. You are wafted along on the same cool breeze that rustles the oleanders (in flower in March–May) and which no doubt attracted the well-to-do citizens here in the first place. The colours of the rock are magnificent in late afternoon. In the winter, it is a different kettle of fish. The waters that come crashing down the wadi can be extremely violent and dangerous.

ASCENT OF AL-HABIS

Coming back from the pool, a small tomb on the south side marks the place where you could begin the ascent of Al-Habis. (There are also rock-cut steps leading to the top starting from the base of the hill on the rise behind Qasr al-Bint.) The main feature to explore is known as the Convent, a rectangular sunken courtyard excavated through the rock to a depth of 6m. It is now reached by a flight of steps which begin at the tomb. Do not attempt the main entry staircase – through a 'garden' with an enormous god-block – it is so badly eroded that it is too dangerous to use. All round this courtyard are carved little 'cells' – which presumably gave rise to the name Al-Habis meaning the Prison, and it would certainly make an excellent gaol – but the chambers were probably the dwellings of the priests who served the High Place perched on the western flank of the mountain, over to Wadi Thughra.

There is little to be seen at the top of Al-Habis but the remains of a small crusader fort, and some evidence of occupation from Iron Age times, various settlements excavated by Miss Kirkbride. It seems that people did not really want to be continually dragging up those steps, so such hilltops were never permanent living quarters but served as places of refuge when the city was under attack. The view over the city ruins is wonderful. The High Place is similar to the one on the Attouf Ridge, but much smaller – only 5m x 3.5m and you have it all to yourself. Walk round the south side of the the sunken court and it is on the rock ledge immediately behind the prominent tomb with the crow-steps.

There is a theory, incidentally, that many of these subsidiary high places were for ritual exposure of the aristocratic dead, in the Persian or Sassanian manner, the bodies being laid out in state to await 'sky-burial' – the rather gruesome disposal by vultures instead of worms; but there is no evidence to support this.

PETRA: A TRAVELLER'S GUIDE

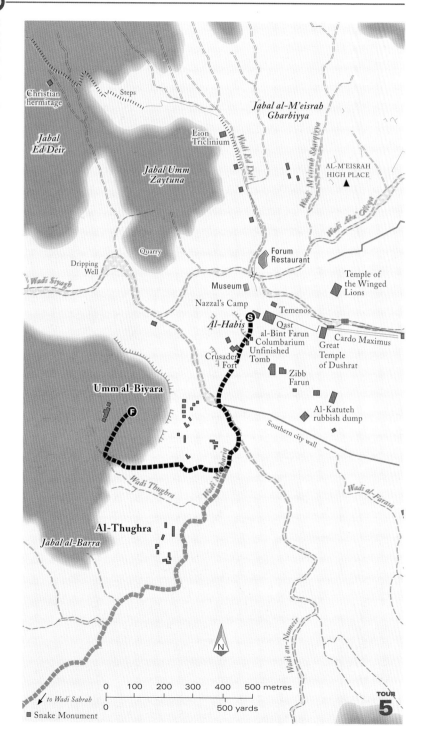

Umm al-Biyara

TOUR

5

his is a full-day trip and is the most hazardous and arduous climb, only for the very agile. The ascent should not be attempted before midday in the summer; in the afternoon the climb is in shadow and you would probably camp overnight at the summit. You must have a guide with you, because the going is not only dangerous but sometimes difficult to follow, and you won't want to fall or get lost. The ascent alone takes an average person about two hours. Leave by 2.30 pm to come down in daylight. Take water and provisions.

If you wish to enjoy the flesh-creeping experience of standing where thousands of hapless condemned prisoners of war were made to peer over a sheer drop of 300 metres before being launched to their doom, Umm al-Biyara (Mother of Cisterns) is the place. Towering behind Al-Habis, the enormous, sinister massif dominates every aspect of Petra. The walls are so sheer as to make it look inaccessible, but it can be climbed from the south-west. It is called 'Mother of Cisterns' because of the many water cisterns hewn out on the summit – a sensible precaution for anyone wishing to cut himself off from the world and stay up there for any length of time. This massif was the natural fortress used by the Edomites, their retreat when under attack, and the place where they regularly stored their valuables.

To reach the top, you labour up a narrow carved path/staircase that was originally closed by a gate. The first part is up a couloir or ramp of unstable scree, followed by a steep walk up a smooth and very impressive ramp cut in the rock. Beyond the couloir the steps are badly eroded and dangerous, and there are precipitous drops on your left. Here you have to scramble on all fours. Be very careful.

At the summit is a scrub-covered plateau with an Edomite settlement (*c.*700 BCE), featuring the eight

Massacre and Revenge

According to Diodorus, when the Seleucid king Antigonus swept down the King's Highway with his army, eager for conquests, his spies reported that the fighting men of Petra, 'Arabs called Nabataei' who 'neither sow corn nor plant any fruit-bearing trees, nor use wine, nor build houses', had gone off en masse to a tribal jamboree, leaving behind only unguarded old men, women and children. He seized the opportunity and sent his soldiers sweeping up to the rock, killing without mercy. They captured the entire Nabataean stock of frankincense and myrrh, plus an enormous booty of silver (five hundred talents – a talent is about a wheelbarrow full). The alarm was soon raised, and the furious Nabataeans hurtled after them and mowed them down in their camp, taking vengeance by massacring all but fifty people.

Honour satisfied, the Nabataeans apparently did not wish to stay on bad terms with Antigonus, but accepted his overtures of friendship. However, he was only fooling, and sent reinforcements to have another go at them. This time the lookouts were more alert, and after making their valuables secure with a corps of elite warlords on the rock, the entire population withdrew into the desert where the Syrians, who did not know the whereabouts of their carefully concealed cisterns, could not follow. The Syrians sensibly gave up and went home.

huge bell-shaped cisterns which gave the mountain its name. The reservoir mouths were covered with stones, effectively hiding them from all who did not know the secret. Many people think this site must be the stronghold Sela (or Rock) after which Petra was named. Biblical references are many – for example: 'They sent lambs from Sela, by way of the desert, to the Mount of the Daughter of Zion' (Is. 16:1); 'You who live in the clefts of Sela, though you make your nest as high as the eagle's, I will bring you down!' (Jer. 49:16); 'Your pride has deceived you, you who live in the clefts of Sela' (Obad. v.3).

The Nabataean ruins are at the eastern edge in the middle of which a broad flight of steps takes you to the very brink of a dizzy drop to the city below. A god-statue found nearby suggests this place was a temple, and the reason for the perilous siting of the steps seems obvious enough! It was an excellent place from which to hurl ritual offerings (or unwanted personnel) – the infamous place of sacrifice.

However, it is bad press for the Hebrews. There are many biblical accounts of various populations being 'devoted' to God (i.e. slaughtered), but there are no records of mass executions by Petrans or their Edomite predecessors. As we saw in Chapter 2, the triumphant Jewish King Amaziah once hurled to their deaths no less than 10,000 of the unfortunate Edomites he had captured. Browning commented that 'it would have been a ludicrous exercise to bring 10,000 captives, all most unwilling travellers, up those tortuous and perilous climbs, just to have the satisfaction of tossing them off the top'. But the Hebrew word for 'thousands' (*alaf*) can also mean 'tents' or 'families', which makes the number more realistic.

The highest point of the massif is the north-west corner, overlooking the city. To the south-west the view is of Jabal Harun (Aaron's tomb). Looking west, one can make out the blue-grey humps of the Sinai range baking in the distance.

In 1963 the ruins were excavated for seven weeks by another stalwart female archaeologist, Mrs Crystal Bennett, who did not come down once during that time, despite the local superstition that the place was haunted. She found the courage to stay up there with only one worker, happily enjoying the beauty, the silence and cut off feeling. Her main difficulty was not disturbance by the *afrit* (the troubled spirits of the 'hurled'), but in finding people willing to lumber her requirements up the long, hard slog to the top. (Mrs Bennett believed the biblical Sela to be the village still known as Sela (or Sil) near the village of Tafila.)

The sunset is sheer magic. Descent in the dark, however, is out of the question, so although it is tempting to stay and watch the stars prick out in an ethereal blue sky, you should depart in good time (by 2.30 pm). If caught out by darkness, it is safer to camp, and enjoy the spectacle of the endless stretch of those desolate Sinai mountains at their most inspiring as the first rays of the sun light them up at dawn next day. You need to leave the top very early (before 7 am in summer) to avoid the heat.

Half a mile to the south of the Umm al-Biyara massif is the mountain range called Jabal al-Barra. Continuing south down the Wadi Thughra are the many Southern Graves and a kilometre or so further on the metalworking suburb of Wadi Sabrah (Tour 9). The hillsides here are riddled with disused copper mines. To explore this far out needs a full day, guides, and an enormous appetite for ruins.

The Royal Tombs

This is easy walking, taking about two hours to see the major monuments. Add another hour if you wander back via the Conway Tower, plus two more hours if you climb the Jabal al-Khubtha.

On the eastern side of the city are some of Petra's most spectacular monuments – the so-called Royal Tombs. These include the Urn Tomb, Silk Tomb, Corinthian Tomb, Palace Tomb, and Tomb of Sextus Florentinus, of which only the last is definitely a burial-place. They are cut into the side of Jabal al-Khubtha, the mountain opposite Umm al-Biyara. Argument still rages as to whether the others were tombs, temples or dwellings.

This tour begins some 225m beyond the Nymphaeum. From the Siq, go past the Theatre and follow the mountain road to your right for 200m to the Urn Tomb, also known as Al-Mahkamah or the Royal Court of Justice. Calling it the 'Urn Tomb' seems somewhat unimaginative, since although it does indeed have a grand urn in the centre of the façade,

The Royal Tombs

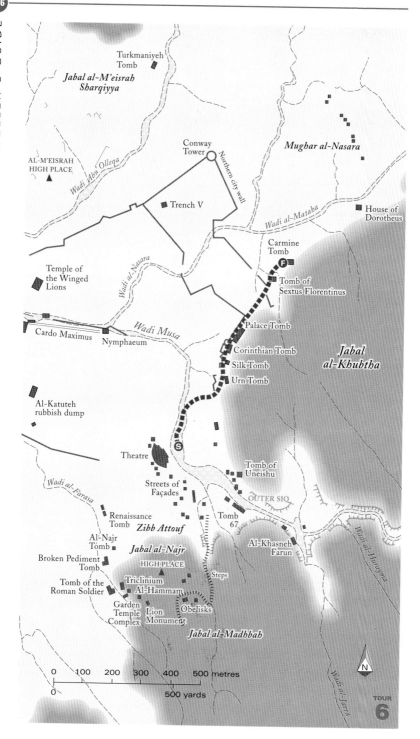

Turkmaniyeh
Tomb

*Jabal al-M'eisrah
Sharqiyya*

Mughar al-Nasara

AL-M'EISRAH
HIGH PLACE

Conway
Tower

Northern city wall

Trench V

House of
Dorotheus

Wadi al-Mataba

Carmine
Tomb

F

Temple of
the Winged
Lions

Wadi al-Nasara

Tomb of
Sextus Florentinus

Wadi Musa

Palace Tomb

Cardo Maximus

Nymphaeum

Corinthian Tomb

Silk Tomb

Urn Tomb

*Jabal
al-Khubtha*

Al-Katuteh
rubbish dump

Theatre

S

Tomb of
Uneishu

Streets of
Façades

OUTER SIQ

Wadi al-Farasa

Renaissance
Tomb

Zibb Attouf

Tomb
67

Al-Najr
Tomb

Jabal al-Najr

HIGH PLACE

Steps

Al-Khasneh
Farun

Wadi al-Huwyma

Broken Pediment
Tomb

Triclinium

Al-Hammam

Tomb of the
Roman Soldier

Garden
Temple
Complex

Lion
Monument

Obelisks

Jabal al-Madhbah

Wadi al-Jarra

0 100 200 300 400 500 metres

0   500 yards

N

TOUR
6

many other monuments also sport an identical feature. Neither is there evidence that it ever had anything to do with the law – although if it was a royal palace it is presumably where supplicants would have had access to the king. Nabataean royalty (like modern sheikhs and Arab royalty) were accessible to all comers, no matter how humble – so long as they were prepared to sit and wait. They dispensed instant justice.

The monument is now believed to have been the tomb of King Malik II (40–70 CE), although the scope of the ruins does not rule out its use as either temple or palace. It involves a bit of a climb up, as it has been excavated quite high up in the hillside, and is an excellent example of an unadorned, classically simple Nabataean façade. Its clean lines and excellent finish are as sharp today as when they were first made.

The Urn Tomb

The Urn Tomb

The Royal Tombs

It is approached across an imposing 21m open courtyard, even more impressive when you realize that the entire hillside above it was removed in order to create it. The colonnaded area on the left was formed by leaving some of the rock in place and chiselling round behind. These columns are now badly eroded – you can see how the sandstorms of centuries have eaten into the bases. Apparently the architect was not satisfied with the size of the courtyard, and a huge extension protruded out from the hillside, resting on an elaborate system of ten vaults (cleared by Professor W. F. Albright in 1936). You will be told that the vaults are dungeons where hapless prisoners languished.

There are three apertures high up the façade which were *loculi*, placed well out of the way of scavenging animals and all but the most determined grave-robbers. The central one is blocked by a large stone depicting the faceless head and torso of a man in a toga – presumably King Malik. The tomb niches can be seen from the interior. The inner chamber (17m x 18m) contains an inscription on the back wall revealing that it was converted for use as a Christian church by Bishop Jason of Petra in 447 CE.

Follow the path round Jabal al-Khubtha to the north for 50m and you come to the next monument, the Silk Tomb (or Rainbow Tomb), a 'must' for the photographer! A tomb made of silk? The rock exposed by this carved façade has some of the best colour variations in Petra, and incredible though it seems, it really does look like rippling shot-silk. The style is deliberately simple, in order that the viewer may concentrate on the colours.

Right next door, very badly damaged by rockfalls and wind erosion, is the Corinthian Tomb, which is rather an oddity. It is decorated in the same style as Al-Khasneh (see Tour 1), but each doorway is of a different style and each room within is a different size. There is no obvious reason for this. It is a very imposing monument, but no suggestions have been made as to whom it was made for or why.

The last 'royal' tomb, 50m away, is the Palace Tomb – a gigantic façade of three storeys, dwarfing all the others, supposedly an imitation of the Golden House of the Roman emperor Nero (which would make it of very late date if this were true). Parts of the top storey are finished in masonry where the hillside was not high enough. This must surely have been a tomb or palace of Nabataean kings, since it is certainly the most vast and elaborate of all the monuments in Petra, and occupies a prime position. Was it built for Harith III? Disappointingly, the four doors lead to smallish rooms, of no particular interest.

You may have had enough by now, but if you have any energy left, you can continue to the Tomb of Sextus Florentinus and the Carmine Tomb (see Tour 7).

The Urn Tomb

The Silk Tomb

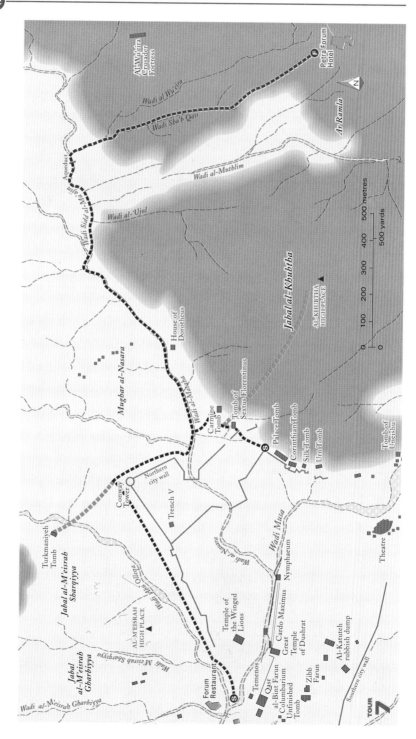

Al-Wu'eira Crusader Fortress

Wadi al-Wu'eira

Wadi Sha'b Qais

Petra Forum Hotel

Aqueduct

Wadi Siyal al-Ma'

Wadi al-Muthlim

Wadi al-'Ujul

Ar Ramla

House of Dorotheus

Mughar al-Nasara

JABAL AL-KHUBTHA HIGH PLACE

Jabal al-Khubtha

Wadi al-Mataha

Carmine Tomb

Tomb of Sextus Florentinus

Palace Tomb

Corinthian Tomb

Silk Tomb

Urn Tomb

Tomb of Uneishu

Northern city wall

Conway Tower

Trench V

Turkmaniyeh Tomb

Jabal al-M'eisrah Sharqiyya

Wadi al-Nmeir

Wadi Musa

Wadi al-M'eisrab Gharbiyya

Jabal al-M'eisrab Gharbiyya

Wadi M'eisrab Sharqiyya

AL-MEISRAH HIGH PLACE

Wadi Kharrubab

Forum Restaurant

Temple of the Winged Lions

Nymphaeum

Cardo Maximus

Great Temple of Dushrat

Al-Katuteh rubbish dump

Temenos

Qasr al-Bint Farun

Columbarium

Unfinished Tomb

Zibb Farun

Theatre

Southern city wall

TOUR 7

0   100   200   300   400   500 metres
0   500 yards

N

North and north-east Petra

This is a continuation of Tour 6, but can be done separately if necessary. It's all walking, unless you also include the ascent of Jabal al-Khubtha. From the Palace Tomb to the Carmine Tomb and back to Nazzal's Camp via the Conway Tower takes a good two hours at an easy pace.

Beyond the Palace Tomb (see Tour 6) the cliff drops drastically to become a low promontory, and a trek of some 200m brings you to the Tomb of Sextus Florentinus (Qabr al-Hakim or the Grave of the Ruler). Sextus Florentinus was a professional soldier and politician, who ended his career as Governor of Arabia, retiring in 127 CE. The Latin inscription at the entrance lists all his official positions – he had been Triumvir for coining gold and silver, Military Tribune of the First Legion (the Minerva), Quaestor of the province Achaia, Tribune of the Plebs, Legate of the Eighth Legion (the Hispania), Proconsul of Narbonensis in Gaul, Legate of Augustus, and ended up Propraetor of Arabia. Apparently, Florentinus had enjoyed his tour of duty in Petra so much that he requested his remains to be taken and interred there when his time came. The tomb, which was cleared by Albright in 1936, could date back a hundred years before Florentinus. It is badly battered and, as it faces north, rarely has the sun on it – and so appears rather more gloomy than the other tombs.

Beyond it is a track going up to the High Place at the summit of Jabal al-Khubtha – a tricky route up from the wadi and the ceremonial staircase from the tombs area. To do it would add about two hours to your itinerary. If you have a guide, he could take you either along the route that comes down at the Urn Tomb near Abu Saksouka's refreshments, or along another in the wadi north of Al-Khasneh.

A 20-minute walk from the Tomb of Sextus Florentinus up the Wadi al-Nasara brings you to

Mughar al-Nasara (Caves of the Christians) a kilometre away. These caves are so called because of the number of crosses carved on walls and doorways. The road eventually reaches the mini-Petra of Al-Barid (the Cold), the northernmost suburb, a trek of 5 miles there and back, which is entered through its own mini-Siq. If you head back to the city ruins, go via the Wadi al-Mataha which takes you to the Nymphaeum; this route will take you about two hours from the Tomb of Sextus Florentinus.

Back in the valley, the final important monument, another 60m beyond Sextus Florentinus, is the Carmine Tomb – a photographer's dream in dramatic deep purplish red with bands of blue and white. By this time many visitors have really had a surfeit of tombs and are flagging, but don't give in and miss it. It is rarely visited, but it is worth making the extra effort just to see the colours.

At this point you decide whether to simply retrace your steps back to the Nymphaeum, or whether to veer westwards, across the valley to your left and return via the Conway Tower, Turkmaniyeh Tomb (described below) and city walls, ending up at the Camp, which would add another hour to your tour. Behind the Turkmaniyeh Tomb the peaks of the Meisrat mountains all have High Places similar to that in Tour 2. They are accessible, although you need a guide and plenty of time.

CONWAY TOWER TO THE CAMP

Traces of a city wall can be seen running across the Wadi al-Nasara to the northernmost point, now called the Conway Tower after Agnes Conway, yet another female archaeologist who worked there in 1929 with her future husband, Mr Horsfield (inevitably known to the Bedouin as Mr Horse). The tower (Al-Mudawwara or the rounded one) is a bastion built at the northernmost point of the Nabataean city walls, surrounding a rocky outcrop. This may have been a sacred rock approached by a processional way, but opinion is divided. The line of the wall is clearly discernible from the tower.

Following the wall down, you come to Trench V, possibly the site of a private gazebo, specially sited to catch any breeze there might be. A gruesome find nearby was the grave of a young person whose sex could not be determined since the entire pelvis had been completely removed. The hands and feet had also been amputated. Some horrific punishment? A murder? We do not know. The body had a posh grave lined and roofed with stone slabs, and there was iron jewellery buried with the corpse.

You can also veer to your right through thickets of oleander to see the Turkmaniyeh Tomb, a 15-minute walk away. Rarely visited, it is a splendid tomb with a Nabataean inscription of considerable length carved above the façade. It is a wonderful piece of lawyer's jargon. It reads:

> This tomb and the large and small chambers inside, and the graves made as *loculi*, and the courtyard in front of the tomb, and the porticoes and dwelling-places within it, and the gardens and the *triclinium*, the water cisterns, the terraces and the walls, and the remainder of the whole property which is in these places, is the consecrated and inviolable property of Dushrat, the God of our lord, and his sacred throne, and all the gods as specified in deeds relating to consecrated things according to their contents. It is also the order of Dushrat and his throne and all the gods that, according to what is in the said writings relating to this property, it shall be carried out and not altered in any way. Nothing shall be withdrawn, nor shall any man be buried in the tomb except him who has a written contract to be buried according to the said writings relating to consecrated things, for ever.

That is all that remains; sadly, the bones intended to rest inviolate 'for ever' are no more. No forlorn spirit may return to take temporary abode, or cast a baleful eye over anyone attempting to smuggle a corpse inside without the appropriate written contract! The base of this tomb has been completely worn away by flash-flooding. The top half looks as though it might come down at any moment.

HEADING NORTH

If you continue along the Wadi al-Mataha and round the Jabal al-Khubtha (you need a guide for this) a walk of about three kilometres brings you to the Petra Forum Hotel.

The most interesting site on this tour is a complex known as the House of Dorotheus, a group of some twenty door and window openings. Dorotheus's name is incised twice in Greek. The complex was probably the private dwelling of this wealthy citizen and his extended family. Directly facing his house is the Mughar al-Nasara with its Christian dwellings and tombs.

Continue walking east until you pass the junction with Wadi Sidd al-Ma'ajin on your right. This was revered as a holy area, but is not practicable for most visitors as the route is blocked with pools of water even in summer. Instead, keep going until you reach a Roman aqueduct, still standing to eight courses of stone. Keep to the right of it and enter Wadi Sha'b Qais, now heading south-east. At one point you have to squeeze through a place in a rock corridor where a large boulder has fallen. When you get to the end of the wadi you will see the Petra Forum Hotel in the distance. The whole walk takes about three hours at an easy pace from the Tomb of Sextus Florentinus.

Al-Barid, a mini-Petra

From Nazzal's Camp to Al-Barid and back is a very long walk or ride. Best to go by car from outside the Siq. Allow half a day. A guide is necessary, and vital if you decide to go on foot. No climbing is involved unless you want to go to a High Place.

If you feel 'claustrophobic' in Petra, and would like a mini ghost-city all to yourself, head for Al-Barid. A whole day could easily be spent in this region. Al-Barid was the main caravanserai north of Petra, a kind of goods depot on the old main road to Arabia. The road heads north from the Visitors' Centre past Al-Wu'eira.

A ten-minute drive from the Petra Forum Hotel brings you to a T-junction where you turn left onto the road to a mini-Siq. At the entrance is an enormous Nabataean cistern still used by the Bedouin and a tomb-temple. The entrance was once controlled by a gate which kept out intuders. The whole area is riddled with tombs, houses and monuments, and there are few tourists. Best is the Painted House, a *triclinium* with a plaster finish still decorated with grapevines and flowers, with cupids playing amongst the branches. The climb to an easily accessible High Place starts about 200m beyond the *triclinium*.

This region is also, by report, riddled with voracious fleas from the Bedouin livestock since the tribespeople are in residence at certain times of the year when there is grazing. The Bedouin are usually very hospitable, and will fetch mattresses and tea for you to enjoy a comfortable break. The village school is not far away, and the noise of children can be heard at playtime.

If you want to visit modern cave-dwellers, head out for another half kilometre or so to Al-Baidha (Baida). The region abounds in monuments and tombs, but you need time, enthusiasm, a horse and a guide, preferably a villager from Al-Baidha, as the local Bedouin, who have given in and 'allowed' tourism to take place around the major sites, do not expect to

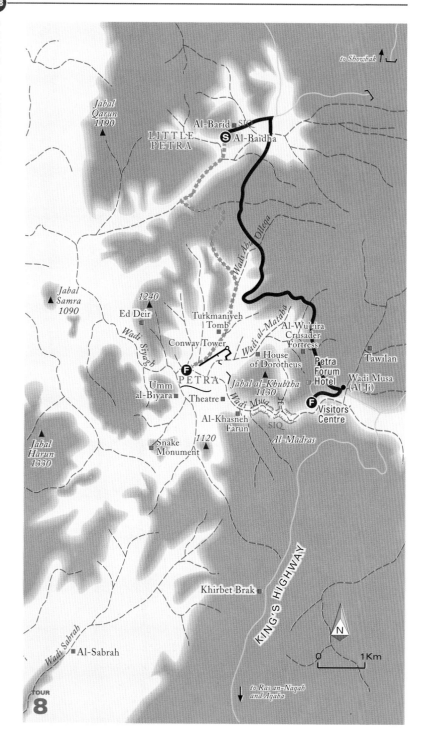

have their privacy disturbed this far out, and can be touchy. It is also possible to reach Al-Baidha via the Wadi Turkmaniyeh (Tour 7) on the road from Mughar al-Nasara, a long trek requiring the best part of a day; it is essential to start early to avoid crossing desert flats in the full heat.

Bear in mind that these basic facilities are people's homes. Think how you would feel if a bunch of noisy strangers suddenly walked through your back garden, or peered into your living room uninvited, especially if they appeared to be rudely laughing at you, and then proceeded to photograph your relatives, and couldn't understand a word you said to them to make them go away. Waving a stick with as menacing expression as possible, or getting their kids to flip small warning stones often makes a quick point.

Such antiquities as there are to see are once more by courtesy of Miss Kirkbride, who spent six months there on her own in charge of excavations in 1956, and continued work from 1958 to 1983. Having discovered an Upper Palaeolithic rock shelter (*c.*10,000 BCE) in one valley, and several Neolithic villages, she excavated this one – which proved to be one of those places where humankind made the transition, some 10,000 years ago, from nomadic hunter-gatherer to settled villager and animal domesticator. The settlement rivals Jericho for antiquity and, as in Jericho, it was found that adults were subjected to the same rather macabre decapitation before burial, their severed heads then covered in clay and decorated. Infants found buried beneath living room floors may have been sacrificed.

Miss Kirkbride uncovered six main levels (the excavation has now reached level seven, the Mesolithic), the earliest (*c.*7000 BCE) featuring stone tools and utensils, before the use of pottery. Al-Baidha contains the remains of the earliest Neolithic houses yet found anywhere. They were unique – circular with strong central posts, rather like wigwams. Stone walls were erected round beam buttresses, and thatches were laid

Little Petra

across the roof beams to support a thick layer of clay. Each level of occupation lasted about 75 years. The latest level was difficult to study because of Nabataean terracing. By 6500 BCE the buildings were rectangular – good houses with very thick walls, which may have supported upper storeys. One notable ruin, a room 8 x 6m, with a central hearth, may have been a 'factory canteen', for it is surrounded by buildings resembling workshops; bone and stone tools have been found, along with grinders, polishers, axes and a box containing 114 choice flints. The most visible things from the visitors' point of view are the Stone Age grinding querns, remains of stone walls and paved floors.

THE VALLEY OF MOSES (AL-WU'EIRA)

The main Crusader fortress in the Petra area is known as 'the Valley of Moses' or 'La Vaux Moise', because of Petra's connections with the Old Testament prophet Moses; it lies about 1.5km to the north-east of Petra. It can only be approached only with difficulty, being perched over 1000m high on the summit of Jabal Wu'eira, surrounded by terrifying crevasses. 'Moses' changed hands several times during the course of its long history. In 1144 the Muslims gained possession, and massacred the Frankish garrison. The 13-year-old leper-king of Jerusalem, Baldwin III, took his army there and burnt all the trees in the nearby valleys to reduce it. This particularly outraged the Muslims, since destruction of trees is forbidden under the rules of *jihad* or Holy War. The fortress was strengthened in 1192 by a knight with the wonderful name of Pagan the Butler, and is now known as Al-Wu'eira.

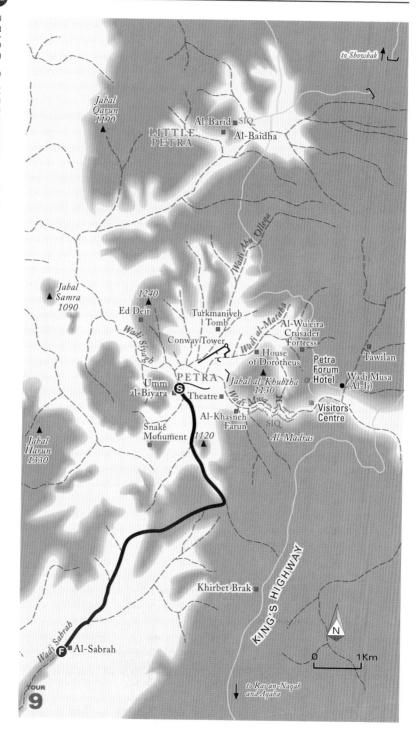

to Showbak

Jabal
Qarun
1190

LITTLE
PETRA

Al-Barid   SIQ
Al-Baidha

Wadi Abu Ollequa

Jabal
Samra
1090

1240

Ed Deir

Turkmaniyeh
Tomb

Wadi Siyagh

Wadi al-Mataha

Al-Wu'eira
Crusader
Fortress

Tawilan

Conway Tower

House
of Dorotheus

Petra
Forum
Hotel

Wadi Musa
(Al-Ji)

PETRA

Umm
al-Biyara

S

Theatre

Jabal al-Khubtha
1130

Wadi Musa

Al-Khasneh
Farun

SIQ

Visitors
Centre

Snake
Monument   1120

Al-Madras

Jabal
Harun
1330

Khirbet Brak

KING'S HIGHWAY

N

Ø   1Km

Wadi Sabrah   F   Al-Sabrah

to Ras an-Naqab
and Aqaba

Wadi Sabrah

TOUR
9

For this full-day excursion you need a guide. The Nabataean suburb of Al-Sabrah is a two-hour journey each way, on foot, and you should take food and water. No climbing unless you want to.

There are several temples, a wall, a bridge, and a mountain-top fortification at Al-Sabrah. The two most notable things are its columns coated with plaster and lime and painted deep red (which suggests that the bright scarlet interiors fashionable in Rome and Pompeii were not unknown here), and a compact theatre which could apparently be flooded for *naumachia*, or naval games. The spring flood-waters were collected in a reservoir located some 25m above the theatre, then conducted by pipe into the theatre.

Sabrah also has the remains of a barracks, perhaps for a garrison defending the southern approaches to the city. It is not known whether these barracks were Nabataean or Roman – they were possibly used by both. Another possibility is that since the hillsides in this region are riddled with copper mines, these remains may have been the housing for expatriate mineworkers and smelters.

You can return to Petra by a more difficult route through Ragbat al-Btahi, west through Ras Sleiman and Ragbat al-Barra, past the Snake Monument and into Petra through Wadi Thughra.

**The Theatre at
Sabrah (Laborde)**

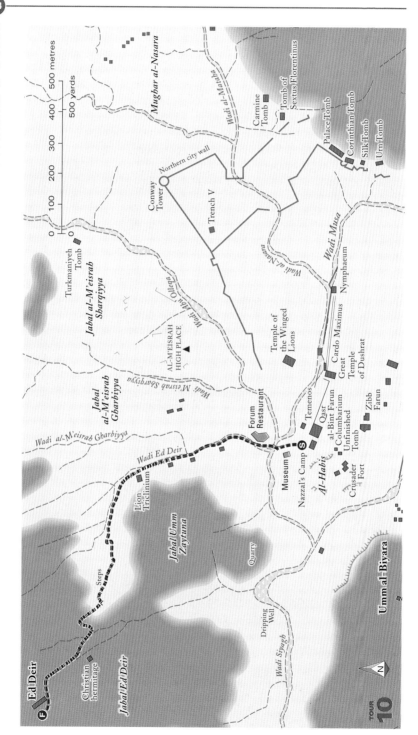

Ed Deir

If you can only face one mountain top, and can cope with 808 rock steps but are nervous about climbing, this pilgrimage to Ed Deir (known as the Convent) is the one for you. It is quite safe and the route is obvious, but a long haul up. You should be prepared for a strenuous trip of at least three to four hours there and back (and also be prepared to stumble back to base after dark). Take a torch and a guide. It is best to attempt this excursion after noon so that you will not be climbing in direct sunlight; you will arrive in time to see the temple set on fire by the late afternoon sun and then switch off. At other times of the day you would miss this spectacle.

Setting out from Nazzal's Camp, cross the Wadi Siyagh to a rock-cut road, in many places running along the edge of a precipice, going up the Wadi Ed Deir. The way is sometimes paved, and chipped into steps where it mounts a cliff; in places great slices of rock have been quarried away to dignify the path for the processions that wound up to the temple.

On the way, take a small detour at the Department of Antiquities sign to see the so-called Lion Tomb (in fact a *triclinium*), with its two very weathered lion reliefs guarding the entrance and giving the clue that we are once more on the track of the Goddess. The odd keyhole effect over the doorway was caused by wind erosion. To the left is a large carved block dedicated to Dushrat, set in a niche, and two graves which still contained bones as late as 1924. At this point the path becomes a staircase. A worthwhile detour (20 minutes) on the way up will take you to Qattar ad-Deir, a large rock ledge sheltered by an overhang. Nearby is the one cistern in Petra that remains perennially full, the water seeping through the rocks and dripping through ferns and moss into a grotto of overhanging sandstone. Thousands of grateful pilgrims must have stopped here to drink as they progressed up the sacred way. When it seems as if you have been plodding up forever, a sudden gap opens out and gives a view over a precipice, with Jabal Harun across the chasm. To the north is a pinnacle with some caves where there was once a Christian hermitage.

Eventually, after much winding and clambering, the path squeezes through a narrow space between two boulders, drops down a pebbly slope, and you arrive at a wide plain, to the north side of which stands Ed Deir, Petra's largest façade between two gigantic walls of cliff. It is the best-preserved monument in Petra, besides Al-Khasneh.

Although it has been suggested that it was originally the tomb of Rabbel II and the last important Nabataean monument to be built in Petra, it was in fact a temple and not a tomb. The open plain in front of it was hewn by hand, a vast artificial platform, this time large enough to accommodate a congregation of thousands.

HOW THE HERMITS SURVIVED

Christian hermits and desert monks are often mistakenly believed to have survived in solitude, presumably miraculously, at various inaccessible places. In fact, one cannot survive in these conditions for more than a few days without help. These monks certainly wished to be cut off from worldly life, but it is a mistake to think they were not highly organized in matters of food supply and defence. Most holy places could only tolerate the luxury of supporting an occasional saint in his desire for solitude, for some poor soul would always have the chore of trailing out or up with his or her rations, however meagre (as Mrs Bennett discovered up Umm al-Biyara). So very few can have had the privilege of being fed by ravens like the prophet Elijah (I Kings 17:6). Incidentally, with different vowels, the Hebrew word for 'raven' becomes 'Arab' or 'trader'.

Ed Deir

After you climb the most welcome sight is possibly the drinks vendor who has lumped his warm load all the way up in anticipation of your arrival! Opposite the Deir is his stall in a cave complete with TV aerial, where there is a row of seats so that you can rest and contemplate the façade in comfort while Bedouin preside over the teapot. Some ten minutes further on is the *triclinium* now used by the Petra Forum Hotel to serve lunches.

The Deir stands 50m wide and 45m high at the top of its striking 9m urn (remember that an average two-storey house rarely tops 8m). The entrance alone is 6m high, and one really only gets the full idea of the size of this monument when attempting to photograph someone standing at its doorway. The solitary plain chamber within features a niche at the back that originally held the sacred god-block and in the centre a little dais with steps leading up to it on either side. There are a few crosses carved on the wall, which may indicate that it has done time as a Christian church.

Summon all remaining reserves of energy and climb the staircase to the left of an open-air altar; it leads up to a rocky platform where there is a circle of hewn stones, and beyond that a solitary cell. Traverse a narrow isthmus of rock, and you are actually on the roof of the temple. Do not attempt to scale the urn unless you are very well insured. From this dizzy vantage point you gain a panorama of the whole site of Petra and the Wadi Arabah to the south some 1,200m below. The Wadi Arabah is part of the Great Rift Valley that extends to the Red Sea and beyond, down the east coast of Africa. (The word *arabah* implies 'rapid river' in Arabic, but the corresponding word in Hebrew means 'desert'.) To the west you can see the Sinai range. As dusk sets in, the brief magical phenomenon occurs – the sun bathes the façade with brilliant golden light, making the rock glow, then the shadow travels dramatically up its face until the secret glory has once again departed.

A MYSTICAL MOMENT

Three thousand worshippers, their faces bathed in golden rays of light that seem to shine from the rock, draw their hours of meditation to an end as the sun slowly withdraws its touch and is gone. A sigh, as if a spell has been broken, escapes those trembling lips. The Pure Goddess, deep in the cave (*ma'ra*, which also means womb), has been lit up by its burning shaft, warmed, and left full of life. The Virgin is with child. The shadows of approaching night return, and it is time to go home. And these are all but phantoms.

Ed Deir (Laborde)

According to Numbers 20 and Josephus (*Antiquities*, 4.4.5–7) it was in this region that Moses' sister Miriam died and was buried. Her mountain-top tomb – at a place simply known as 'Kadesh' (meaning 'the Holy') – was shown to pilgrims at the time of St Jerome (fourth century CE), but has not been identified since. It is quite possible that Ed Deir is the site of her grave. The labour that went into the structure certainly indicates that it was a pre-eminently sacred place, but very likely its sanctity predated any connection with Miriam.

The reason for the vast platform? Obviously, a major ritual event. The second-century Christian saint Epiphanius recorded that a ceremony took place on 6 January to celebrate Dushrat's birth from the Virgin Mother-Goddess – perhaps the result of what the Bible calls 'sacred prostitution' (I Kgs 14:24; 15; 12) back in the Qasr. In the Eastern Orthodox tradition, 6 January is the date of Christmas. And the name of the Mother is Mary, simply a variant of Miriam, and also of Ma'ra or Myrrha or Maira, or Maha-Maya – all the many 'womb' names by which the various virgin mothers have been called.

Many people think that Dushrat's birth ceremony would have taken place at the Qasr al-Bint complex, and it may indeed have been so. However, if the 'vibes' are anything to go by, this hill-top holy place with its light-associations and carved platform for the hushed and expectant worshippers keeping their vigil is far more likely. Maybe, inside the dark and secret room, there was a holy stone or statue waiting to be touched by the sun's ray, like the sanctum of the Egyptian temple at Abu Simbel. Maybe the Christians here followed the scriptures of the Copts, which suggested that Mary did not give physical birth as do other mortal women, but that she withdrew to a cave; a brilliant glow of light was then seen to surround the entrance and a ray pierced the gloom. The observers watched in amazement as the holy infant was materialized, in mortal perfection, at the bosom of the virgin mother.

And what did it mean? What did it all mean? That God can be made flesh, and dwell among us, full of grace and truth, so that we can behold His glory? (John 1:1–18). Whatever your beliefs, here on this naked mountain under the vast bowl of the sky, you draw close to something – and whatever the circumstances of your own journey through life, with all its toils and upheavals and heartbreak, you feel throbbing strongly within you the eternal truth that light shines in the darkness, and darkness is not able to overcome it.

To get back, you must retrace your steps: there is no other way down. Since it will be dark by the time you reach the valley, you may decide to camp at the top and watch the sunrise next day, a good swap for a sprained ankle.

BIRTH OF DUSHRAT

Epiphanius also described the ceremonies and ritual for the birth of the holy baby, Dushrat, at Elusa and Alexandria. There, they took place on 25 December:

'All night long they keep vigil, chanting to their idol [Al-Uzza] with songs and flutes. The nocturnal service over, at cockcrow torchbearers go down into an underground chamber and bring up an image of the infant in gold, lying naked on a litter, with the imprint of a golden cross on its forehead, two similar imprints on its hands, and another two on its knees; all told, five golden marks impressed upon it. They carry the image itself seven times round the central part of the temple with flutes, timbrels and hymns. And after the procession they bring it down again to its underground quarters. If asked what they mean by this mystery, they make answer, "This day and hour Kore [the Virgin] has given birth to her child."'

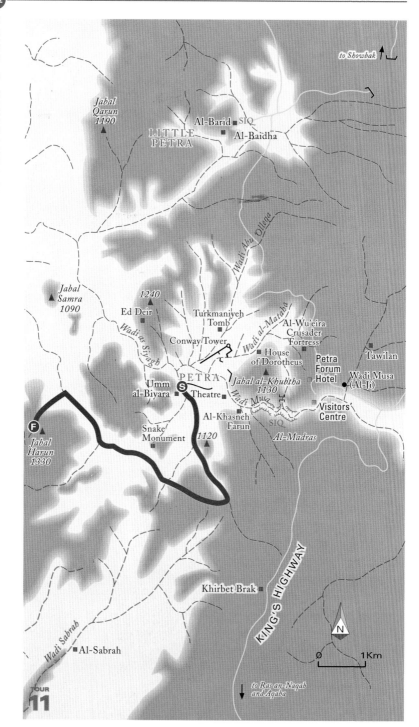

to Showbak

Jabal
Qarun
1190

Al-Barid   SIQ
LITTLE
PETRA   Al-Baidha

Wadi Abu Ollega

Jabal
Samra
1090

1240

Ed Deir   Turkmaniyeh
Tomb

Al-Wu'eira
Crusader
Fortress

Wadi ar Siyagh

Wadi al-Mataha

Conway Tower

House
of Dorotheus

Tawilan

Petra
Forum
Hotel

Wadi Musa
(Al-Ji)

PETRA

Umm
al-Biyara

S

Theatre

Jabal al-Khubtha
1130

Wadi Musa

Visitors'
Centre

F

Al-Khasneh
Farun

SIQ

Snake
Monument

1120

Al-Madras

Jabal
Harun
1330

KING'S HIGHWAY

Khirbet Brak

N

Wadi Sabrah

Al-Sabrah

Ø   1Km

to Ras an-Naqab
and Aqaba

TOUR
11

Jabal Harun

TOUR
11

A full day's excursion (perhaps overnighting). Jabal Harun (Mount Hor) can be reached on horseback (between two and three hours on horseback from Qasr al-Bint), followed by a stiff six-hour climb to the summit and back. Collect the keys from the Bedouin in the tent at the bottom. Take food and drink. The summit is 1,395m, the highest mountain in the Petra region consisting of twin peaks with the grave of Aaron perched on the truncated cone of the higher peak. If you think all this effort would not be worthwhile in order to see a rather delapidated shrine festooned with old rags, then let this opportunity pass. It is much too arduous for people without a genuine pilgrim mentality, and most tourists do not bother to get beyond a glimpse of the white-domed *weli* from one of the High Places. In any case, there is still local resentment here against casual visitors – Bedouin do not appreciate people with no religious feeling bumbling about their sanctuaries – so put on the right attitude if you must go.

Believers in the 'numinous universe' accept that certain localities can be impregnated with the life-giving force of some saint or hero – transforming the sites into powerhouses of spiritual blessing. Traces of their essential virtue would cling to their mortal leavings, even though their spirits had passed to another and better world. Holiness was seen as a kind of invisible substance, which clung to whatever it touched. So the virtues (the Latin word *virtu* means 'power') of saints would remain and be continually renewed and built up by the constant stream of prayer and devotion emanating from the pilgrims who found their way there. These places are visited to gain healing, or fertility, or protection against dangers psychic and physical, or to gain whatever is the desire of the heart. Jabal Harun is such a place.

The difficulties of reaching the shrine were graphically described by two travellers in the 1860s, Captains Irby and Mangles:

We engaged an Arab shepherd as our guide, and leaving … with our servants and horses, where the steepness of the ascent commences, we began to mount the track, which is extremely steep and toilsome, and affords but indifferent footing. In most parts the pilgrim must pick his way as he can and frequently on his hands and knees. Where by nature it would have been impassable, there are flights of rude steps, or inclined planes, constructed of stones laid together, and here and there are niches to receive the footsteps cut in the living rock.

Much juniper grows on the mountain almost to the very summit, and many flowering plants which we had not observed elsewhere; some of these are very beautiful; most of them are thorny.

Travels in Egypt and Nubia, Syria and Asia Minor

Until the thirteenth century the shrine was in the care of Greek Christian monks. In the seventh century the guardian of this tomb was a certain Bahira. The Prophet Muhammad – then aged about ten – was travelling to Damascus with the caravan of his uncle Abu Talib. The uncle climbed up to pay his respects, and was met by the very excited monk who had seen a vision of the lad. Muhammad was duly fetched, and it was there that the Christian Bahira prophesied that he would become a messenger of God who would change the entire course of world history.

The shrine became Muslim, and was restored by the Mameluke Sultan Qalawun in the thirteenth century. The present domed building was constructed in 1459 – the date is given in the Arabic inscription above the entrance. It is still a Muslim holy place. A goat is sacrificed there every year at Eid-al-Adha, the feast at the end of the *hajj* pilgrimage which commemorates Abraham's sacrifice of his son. (Muslims believe it was the eldest son, Ishmael (Ismail), who was sacrificed, and not Isaac as in the Old Testament.)

THE DEATH OF AARON

Aaron was the brother of Moses and Miriam, whose eloquence made up for Moses' embarrassing stammer when he was obliged to face Pharaoh (Ex. 4:10–14). His death and burial are recorded in Numbers 20:23–29. What many Bible scholars miss is the fact that his death may actually have been a human sacrifice on the High Place – it certainly took place at the command of the Lord:

'The Lord said to Moses and Aaron at Mount Hor on the border of Edom, "Aaron shall be gathered to his fathers; for he shall not enter the land which I have given to the people of Israel, because you rebelled against My command at the waters of Meribah. Take Aaron and Eleazar his son, and bring them up Mount Hor; and strip Aaron of his garments and put them upon Eleazar his son; and Aaron ... shall die there."

And Moses did as the Lord commanded; they went up Mount Hor in the sight of all the congregation. And Moses stripped Aaron of his garments and put them on Eleazar his son; and Aaron died there, on the top of the mountain.' (Num. 20:28 and Deut. 10:6)

Numbers 33:37–38 also recorded the death of Aaron, and Numbers 20:29 that when they had all witnessed that he was dead, they mourned him there for 30 days. The fact that he may have been sacrificed is never commented upon, but it seems to be the implication of these passages.

Although visitors are not encouraged, if you do get to the *weli*, you will either be totally perplexed by the enormous amount of fuss and effort over nothing, or will pick up the atmosphere of centuries of prayer. There is nothing there, really, and no one to watch you – so why should you remove your shoes, or leave an offering? Only you can answer this.

Inside, the ancient cenotaph is covered with a much-faded pall of silk striped in red, green and white. Against the pillar which supports the roof hang rows of coloured rags, threads of yarn, snail shells, seashells and ostrich eggs – a common practice throughout the Middle East at holy places which are connected with healing. The little rags last much longer than the candles left alight in Roman Catholic holy places. Incidentally, if the shrine guardian gives you one such little rag, you are expected to make him an offering, and to leave this trophy amongst the others at the top. Bear in mind that the devout might make a very generous gift in return for that little scrap of cotton. You, an affluent visitor from the West, can afford to be generous. Think of the blessing your gift would bring to that poor community.

A wooden bowl is also provided in the *weli* for offerings that reimburse the guardian, who is traditionally a healer, for his prayers on your behalf. Pilgrims are trusted to give, and not to take. A *mihrab* (niche in the wall) points the direction of Mecca, for those Muslims who wish to perform *salah* (prayer) here.

In the corner is a flight of stone steps down to Harun's cave-crypt, much blackened by the smoke of lamps, where the corner of a stone sarcophagus can be seen at a place where the plaster has fallen away. A Muslim traveller in 925 reported that a 'dreadful noise' was often heard inside the cave, but there is no later comment on this strange phenomenon. Could the grave be genuine? It certainly has an atmosphere. There seems to be no real reason why this, like other tombs of prophets and saints dotted around the

Middle East, should not be the genuine resting-place of the claimed incumbent.

BURCKHARDT'S SACRIFICE

The explorer Burckhardt got as far as the hewn rock ledge called Settuh Harun (Aaron's Terrace) at the base of the climb – a place in sight of the Blessed Harun for the convenience of those not climbing up. There Burckhardt cut a goat's throat and covered its spilt blood with a heap of stones. His Arab companion was not at all impressed by his offering, and implored the prophet to 'be content with his good intentions, for it is but a lean goat!' It was cooked and eaten as quickly as possible, the guide explaining that light from the fire would attract other tribesmen with possible fatal consequences for them both. Equally likely was the fear that other tribesmen might turn up and join them for the feast since the size of the poor goat was so derisory, and they would be left hungry!

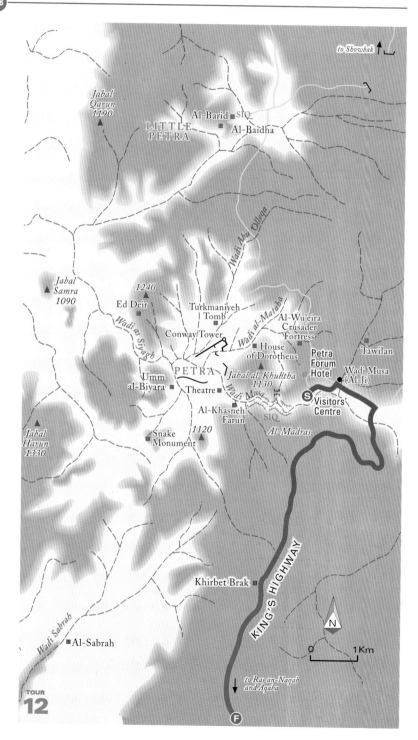

to Showbak

Jabal
Qarun
1190

Al-Barid   SIQ
LITTLE
PETRA   Al-Baidha

Jabal
Samra
1090

1240
Ed Deir   Turkmaniyeh
Tomb
Conway Tower   Al-Wu'cira
Crusader
Wadi al-Mataha   Fortress

Wadi as Siyagh   House
of Dorotheus   Petra
Forum   Tawilan
Hotel
Umm   PETRA   Wadi Musa
al-Biyara   Theatre   Jabal al-Khubtha   (Al-Ji)
1130

Wadi Musa

Al-Khasneh   S   Visitors'
Farun   SIQ   Centre
Snake   1120
Monument   Al-Madras

Jabal
Harun
1330

Khirbet Brak

KING'S HIGHWAY

N

Wadi Sabrah   0   1 Km

Al-Sabrah

to Ras an-Naqab
and Aqaba

F

Petra environs

These excursions are for visitors who have plenty of time to spend in the area. Tawilan is a half-day trip. The others are usually visited on the way down to Aqaba. No climbs unless you want to.

In 1967–68, just north of Ain Musa, Mrs Bennett excavated Tawilan and found a large Edomite settlement – possibly the site of the biblical Teman, the home of Job's friend Eliphaz (Job 2:11). There were traces of occupation going back to 4000 BCE. Tawilan lies exposed on a stony, windswept hillside, the winds having caused severe erosion. Mrs Bennett put down five trenches and found an enormous pit filled with Iron Age pottery and buildings dating from the ninth century to the sixth century BCE. Some of these were of grand dimensions. In one of these large buildings, with three central pillars and a plaster floor, she found a scarab with a crescent moon and star, the symbol of the Edomite god Qaush, and later Al-Uzza. The storage pits revealed all manner of agricultural tools and equipment, and masses of fine pottery, some pieces still intact after 2500 years. A 'watchtower' on the southern trench was thought to date from the Arabic period (636–1099 CE), since all the skeletons found in the nearby graveyard had their faces turned towards Mecca; but other scholars think they are Nabataean.

At Khirbet Brak, another suburb of Petra, a head of Atargatis and relief of a winged figure were found.

Near Ghassul (Tuleitat Ghusul) is a large and heavily fortified site called Jawa, with a cleverly devised water system. It has proved to be another very old settlement. When the bold red, white, yellow and black wall frescoes were carbon-dated by an Australian team in 1978, it was found they were some 6,000 years old. One fresco shows a group of figures before a religious shrine. Jawa is now being restored by a team of UNESCO conservationists from Rome.

At Gharandal, on the new road through Wadi

Arabah, is a small village that may once have been an important Edomite city. It is now notable only for a Chinese pagoda, erected in honour of the labourers who built the road.

THE ROAD TO AQABA

Travelling by car from Petra to Aqaba, you can either return to the Desert Highway at Ma'an, or cut along a rougher road to Ras an-Naqab.

Ma'an is the biggest town in southern Jordan, and the administrative centre of the region, but there's nothing much to see there. There are a few hotels including the Khoury Rest House which stands on the fringe of the desert and you can look east across a vast, empty stretch of country. The old town is made almost entirely of sun-dried mud-brick. The ruined buildings crowning several nearby hills were put up when Sherif Hussein prepared for his last stand against the Saudis, after the First World War. Some Palaeolithic bric-à-brac has been found in the wadi bed.

The scenery is pretty dull until you reach Ras an-Naqab, when a turn in the road suddenly reveals what could be the most startling and beautiful view in Jordan, a great cliff dropping to a plain of pink sand some 600m below. Jutting out of the plain are the jagged outlines of the sandstone mountains of Jabal Rum. It is an unforgettable sight in early morning, when there is a hint of mist. The Nabataean fort that used to be here was used as a stone-quarry for roadbuilding during the Second World War.

You begin now to descend tortuously down the most dangerous section of Jordanian mountain road. Tankers and trucks racing for the bends will age you ten years. Follow the scenic route down to the Red Sea, or turn off for Wadi Rum just beyond Quweira, where there is a small fortress occupied by the Desert Patrol, still making use of a huge Nabataean cistern. The uniforms have changed since Nabataean times, but little else.

Wadi Rum

The fortress at Aqaba (Laborde)

At Khirbet al-Khaldi is another Nabataean fort (they were sensibly placed a day's march apart) with more rock-cut cisterns still in use. The final fort in the series is Khirbet al-Kithara. From this junction the wadi narrows considerably and is littered with huge granite boulders, and confined by sheer mountain walls on either side. When the road emerges again, you can see the Red Sea and Aqaba in the distance.

PRACTICAL
MATTERS

Jordan: basic information

JORDAN TODAY

Jordan is a constitutional monarchy and the king has wide powers. The National Assembly consists of the Upper House (Senate), whose members are appointed by the king, and the lower House of Representatives, elected by the populace. Women have been allowed to vote since 1989.

Jordan's standard of education is one of the highest in the Middle East with 87 per cent literacy and 97 per cent of children attending school. The population stands at about four million, over half of whom are Palestinian. Jordan has a rich mix of ethnic and religious groupings, including the Bedouin who number about 40,000. The vast majority of Jordanians are of Arab descent but there are also Circassians (25,000), Armenians and Chechens. About 92 per cent of Jordanians are Sunni Muslims but 6 per cent are Christian and a tiny minority are Druze or Bahais.

ECONOMY

Agriculture, using modern mass production methods, which produces goods mostly for export, accounts for about 8 per cent of the GDP. Copper, phosphate and potash are also major exports.

Tourism is an important foreign currency earner and continues to grow. After the Six Day War in 1967 Jordan lost 40 per cent of its GNP and 90 per cent of its revenue from tourism. The industry is now reviving, and Jordan has begun to realize the value of the historical treasures on the east of the River Jordan – the wonderful ruins of Jerash, the wild, windswept ghost city of Umm al-Jamal, the grim castles in their high places built to ward off the Crusaders, the vast empty stretches of sand desert or black flint desert, the sunsets, the Grand Canyon of the Wadi Majib, and of course the mystery of the lost city of Petra. In fact the decision to open the borders with Israel has boosted tourist numbers considerably, almost to the point of 'too many', but many of these numbers are day-trippers and ways to encourage people to spend more hotel nights in Jordan are being sought.

The economy suffered another major setback during the Gulf War when it lost its main trading partner, Iraq, becoming one of the biggest financial casualties of that conflict. A lengthy blockade of the port at Aqaba caused further hardship. Despite dire predictions Jordan has rallied round since the war ended and continued to grow economically, the continuing peace process helping the situation enormously.

Perhaps the most valuable resource of Jordan is its people – their friendliness, honesty, pride and sheer hospitality, the Bedouin impish sense of fun and excitement, the generosity of its hosts, the dignity of its sheikhs, and the refreshing lack of dishonesty, begging and misery so often encountered in travels in the East.

GEOGRAPHY

Jordan is a very small country with a curious layout. The total area is about 240,000km^2. It is only about 690km from the northern border to Aqaba in the south. There are three main geographical regions: the Jordan Valley which runs north/south emptying into the Dead Sea, the East Bank plateau traversed by gorges of the extensive wadi system and the desert which stretches east, north and south to Iraq, Saudi Arabia and Syria.

Everyday life in Petra today

PETRA DAYS

Devout Muslims in Petra, as everywhere, go to bed early because they get up before first light, at the moment when 'a black goat's hair thread can be distinguished from a white one'. It is usually quite chilly before dawn in the caves, tombs and tents, so this is no great hardship; attuned to this regime, most will have already become restless waiting for the day to begin. (They usually catch further needed sleep during the heat of the day.)

PREPARING FOR THE NEW DAY

Although it is still pitch black, animals and humans are very sensitive to the slight change in the sky. The seemingly empty landscape suddenly reveals its inhabitants as the sleepers stand and shake out their blankets, roused by the call to prayer. At the same time, animals and wild birds also sense the moment, and there is almost a race for the human worshippers to break the night before the animal kingdom does so. Sounds travel a great distance, and it is a moment of brotherhood to hear the first cry of the *adhan*, joined by many others, as Muslims make ready for the prayer before dawn.

After the ritual wash of hands, arms, face, head and feet, the men usually join together and form lines behind a leader, kneeling in the sand. The women pray in their tents, and then get on with the business of stirring the fire into life and making the day's bread and the first cup of sweet tea. All around the birds are giving out the dawn chorus, the cocks crowing and the sheep and goats bleating and shuffling into life.

The tents

Tents are surprisingly large, made of woven goat-hair. Sometimes these days sacks and modern tarpaulins are disappointingly incorporated into the designs, or erected alongside the traditional ones. The design is not like a Western tent, but very long and low, with barely enough room to stand up in. It is supported by a sturdy central pole or a line of them, depending on the wealth of the incumbents. They are used to hang things on, including the camel-leather, hammock-type cradles for babies. It takes about two hours to pack up the tent and its entire contents, ready to move on.

Inside the tent is a cosy refuge from the outside world of emptiness and desolation. These Bedouin homes are tidy and well ordered, divided into separate living quarters by woven wall-sections called *gata*. Folded quilts, rugs and blankets are piled against these, and called into use when necessary. One section of the tent is always kept for the men and their guests, and it is not considered polite for visiting men to show interest in the females living there. Even if there is no dividing veil, women sit in their section and do not expect to be stared at or even noticed by any visitor, which is rather disconcerting for the Westerner, who feels it is rude to ignore them. In Bedouin culture, the opposite is the case. Women will soon join in if they want to, but they are usually shy.

The women's section is where the family provisions are stored – grain, coffee, beans, yoghurt, water-bags, and other fruit and vegetables, especially dates. The intriguing bright blue 'spice' sometimes glimpsed in sacks is washing-up powder! Sometimes they have acquired a few basic commodities of Western civilization – paraffin lamps, stoves and heaters, a sewing machine, a crackling radio, maybe even a cold box for the cans of soft drinks. In more settled areas electricity is laid on, and they have rotating fans and TV. This part of the tent is where everyone sleeps, and where the cooking is done. Tents are usually owned by the senior women of the family who have actually made them. A hedge of brushwood often guards the front of the tent, giving greater privacy and shelter, and providing firewood.

In a typical camp, there are usually around twenty to thirty tents. The entire group moves on when the grazing is exhausted in that area. The trail followed is not haphazard, because if other people help themselves to their grass and shrubs it would cause great hard-ship and inconvenience, and be a serious matter. Despite what seems to be their poverty, the Bedouin do not regard themselves as the poor relations of settled folk. In fact, they are totally convinced of their superiority. They are not burdened, for a start, by the need to own things. Everything they possess has to be carried around on the backs of camels and donkeys, and since this drastically limits what one can take, it marvellously clarifies the mind as to what is valuable and what is not.

Westerners are sometimes surprised to see the respect paid to some tatty old fellow dressed in what seems to be a few rags; they may be witnessing the honour paid to a man who might have been wealthy, but who has given it all away. I once gave a shirt to an Arabic friend and he reacted with surprise. He already had two – why did I think he needed another? I believe he gave it to a less fortunate friend. It strikes a chord of respect in all who have read the account of the meeting of Jesus with a rich young ruler, who was not able to put into practice what Jesus demanded of him:

> You lack only one thing; go, sell what you have and give to the poor, and you will have treasure in heaven; and come, be my disciple.
>
> Mark 10:21

The most valuable thing any Bedouin possesses is honour. Their lives are governed by rules consisting of their own desert code and the precepts of Islam, and anything which breaks these rules is considered to be shameful.

Hospitality

Hospitality is the most important aspect of honour; if any stranger cannot expect to be fed and watered and granted rest, lodging and protection, then the host (and perhaps the whole group) is shamed. It used to be impossible to find a shop selling food in a Bedouin village because it was considered an insult to their hospitality to expect a traveller to pay for this. The massive influx of tourists has put paid to this.

Yet, in the camps even now, when it is obvious to Western eyes that repayment would not come amiss, it is not done to hand over money to one's host; if anything like this is given, it must be as a present to a child. A woman who accepted money without her husband's permission would be in serious trouble, because she would have shamed him.

If a guest expressed a liking or admiration for any particular thing belonging to the host, the host will offer it immediately. This has embarrassed many unwitting travellers, who have sought only to compliment their hosts, and did not wish to deprive them of their treasures. If offered something, there arises the further embarrassment of how to refuse to take it without giving offence – the implication of a refusal being that the guest has rejected it as being unworthy of their status. This is not a trivial matter, as Bedouin are very sensitive to insult. The problem is generally solved by the Bedouin either having the sense not to display in their public reception area anything that is not easily replaceable, or else accepting the philosophy that material things simply do not matter, but hospitality and a good name do.

Accepting Bedouin hospitality is a very personal decision. In practical terms, you would encounter the most wonderful friendly ambiance if you were lucky enough to be invited as a guest; hospitality is legendary. Be quite sure that if your safety or property were jeopardized in any way, your host would answer for it 'on his life'. But you would have to be prepared to lay aside the normal Western comforts, and cope with the fact that your host will be unlikely to speak more than a few words of English, French or German. (See also 'Going Bedouin' on p. 212.)

A male guest would probably find it less wearing than a female, who can expect to be submerged beneath more wide-eyed children than she might be used to, and would possibly be quartered

amongst them for the night – although it is more likely that the entire family would move out and vacate the tent-space for the guests. Having said that, don't expect Bedouin to rush up to offer you their homes. Whereas some may be delighted to give hospitality to strangers just for the fun of it, if they did it too often without reward they would be bankrupted.

Few tourists are brave enough to part from their groups, so the novelty of gracing a tent with your presence is still a rare enough adventure to be appreciated by the Bedouin; but the flush of novelty has long since departed, and to many you are just regarded as 'business'. Those Bedouin who ignore you have had enough intruders, want to get away from tourists and relax amongst their relatives in the evening, and do not enjoy being pestered or photographed.

Daily tasks

These are taken in leisurely manner, for 'hurry is the devil's work'. Extreme heat and undernourishment do not make for a wildly active existence. Most things are done slowly, and with care. The women are responsible for cooking and cleaning, looking after the small children, making yoghurt, weaving cloth, and dismantling and setting up camps. Many prefer living in the caves in Petra because erecting the tents is a heavy task, and the men do not help much. However, they find the caves dirty by comparison. Fetching water is probably the most laborious task, as it still has to be drawn from a well and carted to the camp on the back of an animal. You can frequently see a donkey struggling along with half a dozen battered cans strapped to its sides. Today's Bedouin now prefer to use pick-up trucks if they have them, and store the water in old oil-drums.

During the day, someone has to sit and watch the flocks and herds grazing, and keep them out of trouble. Men usually take the camels out in the morning, women and children generally look after the sheep and goats. Girls and small boys spend a lot of time collecting brushwood for the fires, and carrying it back in large bundles. This job is much easier for families who own a pick-up truck. The truck has made a great difference to sheep-breeding, since the shepherds can now not only bring water to their flocks, which need watering daily, but can take the animals by truck across barren regions which they could not traverse on foot, to find good grazing on the other side. New areas of grazing have thus become open to them by this increased mobility. Sheep-rearers move less frequently than camel-herders, and

many only move a few times in a region of around a hundred miles during the cool season. For the rest of the year they stay in village houses and the caves, their tents folded up for the duration. They sometimes cultivate alfalfa and grain.

Social customs

Bedouin men and women enjoy largely separate social lives, the men ganging up to enjoy their evening's coffee, and the women clustering together with the children. However, Bedouin women are not cut off from male company like many town and village women in the Middle East. Segregation is not possible, and the women's work is necessary for the survival of the community. Many women spend long hours alone in the desert, their safety protected by the strict code of honour, since the men go away for long periods to earn money in the town.

As women are not prevented from meeting and talking to men, their marriages are mainly love matches rather than family arrangements, but a woman's cousin has first right to her, so his permission must be sought if she has fallen for someone else. In practice, Bedouin marriages are rarely forced against the woman's wishes, and many last a lifetime.

Weddings are an occasion for feasting, with goats and sheep

slaughtered and very large numbers of guests gathering. Most young couples then live near the husband's parents. Muslim men are allowed to marry up to four wives, but in practice few have more than one because of all the problems and expense involved. Divorce is easy, and quite common. Most men have too much pride to live with a woman who has ceased to love them. Women are not allowed to divorce their husbands, but they can and do return to their father's tent and ask for a divorce, which is usually granted since the man has been 'shamed' so publicly.

Western women who succumb to the attractions of Bedouin men should be aware of the general Bedouin opinion of their moral state and a sudden switch from seduction to callousness. If any Western man tried to seduce one of the Bedouin women it would be regarded as a very serious matter, possibly even resulting in the death of the woman concerned, so Bedouin women do not encourage gossip by lingering round tourist men.

PETRA NIGHTS

The nights of Petra are magical, palpitating with a host of unseen lives, as a sharp sliver of moon slides onto a sheet of indigo velvet. The brilliant luminance of Venus is as hard as a diamond, closer and brighter than it ever is when seen

from the dusky atmosphere of living cities.

I once had the glorious but unnerving experience of picking my way through the pitch-black gorge at midnight with only a bicycle lamp, after fulfilling the urge to declaim classical soliloquies at the Theatre in the floodlight of an enormous full moon. This adventure was not accomplished without hazards underfoot, and other hazards from an amorous guide who had totally misunderstood the purpose of the excursion! Our exit – rather more precipitate than I had desired, owing to the carryings-on of the said guide – was accompanied by mysterious, intermittent and very eerie howling.

The Urn Tomb

NIGHT FALLS ON THE CITY OF THE DEAD

At night a different Petra begins to emerge: first the bold dark outlines of tombs cut from the living rock, as high as a four-storeyed house, their gaping black entrances sinister, holding unknown menace. Then, as ray after ray of moonlight begins to light up the details and flood the plain with silver, the holes become mouths, with silent stone lips pledged to everlasting silence. All around you stretch the vast wastes of the so-called 'City of the Dead', tomb after tomb carved out to take the sarcophagi of royal flesh, mummified aristocrats and priestly dignitaries, heads of families and the families they dominated. Who can wonder that the Bedouin who live in the nearby village of Wadi Musa (Al-Ji) and amongst the ruins themselves have plentiful tales to tell of *afrit* and ghosts flitting at night across the moon-struck plain and howling mournfully from the rocky heights?

Perhaps the night is the most appropriate time in which to gaze upon the desolation that is Petra, for in those bewitching hours the spirit world seems closer, and our minds become more sensitive to previously unfelt sensations, and our hearts begin to beat in tune with an ancient rhythm, a heartbeat of the Earth itself, unutterably old.

Despite the distant intermittent barking of dogs, or the eerie howl of jackals on high places, or the ticking, scratching shuffle of the large insects and beetles making their nocturnal rounds, a silence as thick as velvet settles over the ruins. It does not matter that the daytime sees a motley assortment of tourists from all the world's countries, every night the babble ceases and the silence returns to reassert its prehistoric eminence.

Soon comes the vague feeling that one is not alone, an eerie life pulsating through the darkness. You almost expect a ghostly presence to drift out from the necropolis; the darkness presses on your head like an iron weight. The primeval dread of the supernatural, the inexplicable fascination for the horrific and unknown grips the imagination. Shadows begin to flit to and fro, dark apparitions with menace in their hooded eyes, age-old spirits gliding from the rocks intended to house them and channel their power, until the watcher stands up with dry throat and beating heart and aims the torch into the howling void, hopefully sending the malevolent invaders scuttling back into the obscurity whence they came.

The extremely nervous Bedouin explained the origin of the howling in several ways: as watchers from the crags, who were annoyed because their sleep had been disturbed; as vengeful *afrit* or ghosts, who were also annoyed because their sleep had been disturbed; and as a pack of marauding jackals.

I tried to compose my mind, assuring my friend that I was not afraid of ghosts, and that I would very much like to see them anyway. For a few moments we stood our ground, and I boldly addressed the unseen howlers, inviting them to come forth. But I was lying when I said I was not afraid. Rocks clinked down on us from the heights. As the sounds seemed to be approaching, the last kilometre or so of exit from the Siq was made at full pelt!

And so it was that I, a visitor from the twentieth century, felt for myself the sinister magic of Petra. Holy city? Cursed city? All figments of the imagination? Maybe there are no elemental spirits, no earth forces, no psychical 'superpowers' lurking to entice and trap the minds of the unwary. All my life I was a Christian and then I became a Muslim. Yet here, in the glinting blue moonlight of Petra, I experienced the seductive whispers of the ancient gods, and felt the powerful grip of fascination and fear. Strange how instinctive it was to clutch my prayer beads and utter the protective mental cry: 'I seek refuge in Allah from Satan, the rejected one. In the name of God, the Compassionate, the Merciful! There is no God but One!'

Poor shades of Petra, they had been cursed again. In the gloom enclosing the Siq behind me – could I hear a laugh, or a cry?

The cemetery

Planning your trip

WHEN TO GO

The two high seasons for visiting Petra are:

Autumn (September–November) when the temperatures are warm, but not too hot for comfort. It can be fairly crowded on the site at this time of year.

Spring (mid-March–mid-May) which is probably the best time to visit. The weather is good and you get the benefit of spring flowers and the greenery of shrubs. This is the most crowded time of year though.

The low seasons are:

Winter (December–mid-March) when the cooler temperatures make it more comfortable for climbing or more strenuous trekking, but the nights can be very cold and few hotels have adequate heating. Rainy and cloudy days are not unusual which makes good photography less certain. Also it is the season for wadi floods (although this hazard is now largely tamed due to the new barriers).

Summer (June–August) has soaring daytime temperatures which can reach furnace level. Few people visit Petra in high summer. If hot weather bothers you then definitely avoid it. If heat doesn't bother you then the advantage is having the site practically to yourself.

OTHER CONSIDERATIONS
Ramadan

Visitors should be aware of the dates of the holy month of Ramadan, which varies each year, belonging as it does to the lunar calendar. At the moment it is occurring in early winter; it gets about ten or eleven days earlier each year.

As a general rule travelling in the Middle East during Ramadan can be a bad idea for non-Muslim visitors. The fast for Ramadan lasts from dawn to sunset and involves a total ban on eating and drinking.

Tourists do not partake in fasting and tourist restaurants are still open, but it is considered very impolite to eat, drink or smoke in front of fasting Muslims. Do not do any of these things outside of the tourist restaurants if there is anyone about (a Muslim Arab caught breaking the fast in Jordan can actually be sent to jail until the end of the thirty-day fast – and few would feel sorry for him).

The rigours of the fast mean that energies are depleted, tempers are shorter and everything works at just a basic level. Tourists should consider carefully visiting during this time.

HOW TO GET THERE
Visas

These are required for all visitors. Charges vary greatly from nationality to nationality. For UK passport holders the charge is JD 23 for a single-entry visa, available on arrival for tourists.

Flights

The national carrier, Royal Jordanian, has direct flights from London to Amman every day except Monday. An APEX return ticket costs £535, so it will pay to shop around for a cheaper alternative.

Olympic Airways offers London to Amman via Athens for around half the price. Also Turkish Airlines offers a good low season fare via Istanbul.

Other airlines offering deals to Amman are: Cyprus Airways, Alitalia and Air France. The British Airways subsidiary British Mediterranean mainly serves Beirut but flies on to Amman twice a week.

An increasing number of travellers are flying direct to Eilat in Israel on holiday charter flights and crossing over by land to Aqaba. This is mostly for reasons of cost (charter flights can cost as little as £160 return) but also for convenience as Petra is far nearer Aqaba than Amman. Beware though, the airport at Ovda which serves Eilat is 60km (one hour by bus) north of Eilat. There is also an exit tax from Israel leaving by the land border.

Overland

Jordan has land borders currently open with Israel, Saudi Arabia, Syria and Iraq (although it is very unlikely that a Western traveller will be using the latter route for the foreseeable future).

The establishment of the Palestine National Authority and the peace accord has changed the picture for travellers enormously. There are now two new border crossing points in addition to the old Allenby Bridge crossing point to the West Bank (Jisr al-Malek al-Hussein in Arabic). One is in the north at Jisr Sheikh Hussein near Beit She'an on the Israeli side. There is a minibus to/from Irbid on the Jordanian side and a bus connction to Beit She'an on the Israeli side.

The most useful new crossing point for travellers is between Eilat and Aqaba. Called Wadi Araba (Arava in Hebrew) it is convenient for those flying in to Eilat or coming overland from Taba in Egypt. The border is open from 6.30 am to 10 pm Sunday to Thursday and 8 am to 8 pm Friday to Saturday. There are no buses yet running between Eilat and Aqaba, although there are plans afoot. At the time of writing you need to take a taxi to and from the border crossing (about a ten-minute ride from both town centres).

The only border post between Jordan and Syria is at Ramtha and it can take a few hours to cross if the traffic is heavy. There are regular air-conditioned buses (at least twice a day) between Amman and Damascus. There are also service taxis (shared taxis) and minibuses. These arrive and leave from the Abdali bus station in Amman and next door to the Karnak bus station in Damascus and leave more or less when full.

There is a border post with Saudi Arabia just south of Aqaba which is often used by expat families working in Saudi wishing to explore the region and visit Petra. Most bring their own cars but there are bus services to/from Jeddah, Riyadh and Dammam.

Taking your own car

It is quite easy to take your own car in to Jordan – just be prepared for a lot of paperwork. Firstly you need a *carnet de passage en douane*. This can be arranged through the Automobile Association or RAC in the UK. They will require a financial guarantee in the form of a bank indemnity which could be up to three times the value of the vehicle. What the carnet basically does is act as an import waiver for your vehicle and guarantees payment should you fail to export it again.

Once your vehicle is registered as having re-entered its country of origin your bank indemnity will be cancelled. It is *very important* that you check that the *carnet* is

correctly filled in at the border post, otherwise you could be in serious trouble when you come to leave the country or later on your return home and find yourself liable for a large sum of money. If you are driving an Israeli vehicle you will be fitted with temporary Jordanian number plates at the border.

If you turn up at the border post without a *carnet* it is just about possible to buy a temporary customs waiver on the spot but it is reported to be a lot of trouble and by no means a sure thing.

The second thing you need is insurance valid in the region. Normally this has to be purchased at each border immigration. Your Green Card (normally only valid in Europe) can be extended to include Israel if you request it at the time of issue from your insurance company. Your UK driving licence is perfectly all right for driving in the Middle East (with the exception of Egypt).

Once in Jordan the main roads are good and well signposted in both Arabic and Latin script. Driving is on the right. It is a good idea to carry with you all the spares you are likely to need.

By ferry

There are a couple of daily ferries to/from Nuweiba in Egypt leaving from Aqaba at the terminal south of the main port (about 6km from the town centre). Two types of boat run: a fast catamaran for foot passengers and a car ferry. The catamaran takes only an hour while the car ferry takes three. Tickets can be bought on the day of departure; just turn up an hour or two before the sailing. This approach is best avoided during peak seasons (such as *hajj*) when all sailings can be very full and advance booking is a good idea.

Organized tours

There are two kinds of organized tour: the one you book from the UK which is all-inclusive, or the one you book locally from either Amman or Aqaba. With the latter you will probably be able to set your own itinerary to some extent. The small travel agents often offer tours by taxi. A good source of information about local travel agents can be found at Royal Jordanian offices.

Several UK tour operators offer itineraries to Jordan (sometimes combined with Syria). Most tend to be rather upmarket companies selling cultural tours with an emphasis on Petra. They are also quite expensive but what you get for your money is (hopefully) a trouble-free trip with good catering and accommodation. Nearly all the tour operators fly into Amman on scheduled flights.

A new trend is to combine a diving holiday with a cultural sightseeing tour. There are also tour operators that emphasize the adventure travel aspect. The following is a list of selected British tour operators:

Aquatours
Shelletts House, Angel Road, Thames Ditton, Surrey KT7 0AU
Tel: 020 8398 0505
Fax: 020 8398 0570
E-mail: info@aquatours.com
Website: www.aquatours.com
Jordan specialists who combine diving and cultural excursions.

Bales Tours
Bales House, Junction Road, Dorking, Surrey RH4 3HL
Tel: 0870 241 3208
E-mail: enquiries@balesworldwide.com
Website: www.balesworldwide.com
Bales have a selection of tours from 8 to 19 days, with 2 or 3 nights in Petra.

Caravanserai Tours
1-3 Love Lane, Woolwich, London SE18 6QT
Tel: 020 8855 6373
Fax: 020 8855 6370
E-mail: info@caravanserai-tours.com
Website: www.caravanserai-tours.com
Middle East specialists who offer 8 to 18 day tours of Jordan.

Crusader Travel
57 Church Street,
Twickenham TW1 3NR
Tel: 020 8744 0474
Fax: 020 8744 0574
E-mail: info@crusadertravel.com
Website: www.crusadertravel.com
*Red Sea diving specialists. A good source
for cheap charter air tickets to Eilat.*

Explore Worldwide
1 Frederick Street, Aldershot,
Hampshire GU11 1LQ
Tel: 01252 760000
Fax: 01252 760001
E-mail: info@exploreworldwide.com
Website: www.exploreworldwide.com
*Adventure-style holidays in small groups.
They have tours that stay in Petra for 2 or
3 nights.*

The Imaginative Traveller
1 Betts Avenue, Martlesham
Heath, Suffolk IP5 3RH
Tel: 020 8742 8612
Fax: 020 8742 3045
E-mail: info@imaginative-traveller.com
Website: www.imaginative-traveller.com
*Main tours are 8 days in Jordan or 19
with Syria and Lebanon too. Other
variations are available.*

Jasmin Tours
53–55 Balham Hill,
London SW12 9DR
Tel: 020 8675 8886
Fax: 020 8673 1204
E-mail: info@jasmin-tours.co.uk
Website: www.jasmintours.com

*An established specialist to the Middle
East, they have many programmes which
include Petra.*

Kuoni Travel
Kuoni House, Dorking,
Surrey RH5 4AZ
Tel: 01306 740888
Fax: 01306 744222
24-hour brochure line: 0870 07458664
E-mail: help@kuoni.co.uk
Website: www.kuoni.co.uk

Martin Randall Travel
10 Barley Mow Passage,
Chiswick, London W4 4PH
Tel: 020 8742 3355
Fax: 020 8742 7766
E-mail: info@martinrandall.co.uk
Website: www.martinrandall.com

Prospect Art Tours
36 Manchester Street,
London W1U 5PE
Tel: 020 7486 5705
Fax: 020 7456 5868
Escorted cultural tours.

Ride World Wide
Staddon Farm, North Taunton,
Devon EX20 2BX
Tel: 01837 82544
Fax: 01837 82179
E-mail: info@rideworldwide.co.uk
*Specialist horseriding tours. 10-day tours
starting and ending in Aqaba. Also
custom made itineraries available.*

Saga Holidays Ltd
Freepost, Folkstone,
Kent CT20 1BR
Tel: 0800 300500

Travelsphere Ltd
Compass House, Rockingham Road,
Market Harborough LE16 7QD
Tel: 01858 410456
Fax: 01858 466477
E-mail: telesales@travelsphere.co.uk
Website: www.travelsphere.co.uk
10-day tours of Jordan with 1 full day in Petra.

Voyages Jules Verne
21 Dorset Square,
London NW1 6QG
Tel: 020 7616 1000
Fax: 020 7723 8629
Website: www.vjv.co.uk
8-day tour to St Catherine's Monastery and Petra plus tailor-made itineraries.

HEALTH MATTERS
Vaccinations
Check current health regulations in plenty of time before your departure date. Inoculations are not usually required unless you are travelling from an infected region. Recommended vaccinations are: cholera, hepatitis, tetanus and typhoid. Ask your GP for advice about these. Some vaccines have to be ordered on private prescription. Typhoid vaccine is given in two shots one month apart. If it's your first time the typhoid vaccine can make you feel quite ill for 24 hours or so. (A good tip is for partners to be done on different days.)

More detailed information on health matters can be obtained from:

The Hospital for Tropical Diseases
Mortimer Market,
London WC1E 6AU
Tel: 020 7387 9300
E-mail: administrator@thehtd.org.uk

Liverpool School of Tropical Medicine
Pembroke Place,
Liverpool L3 5QA
Tel: 0151 708 9393
Fax: 0151 708 8733
Website: www.liv.ac.uk/lstm

MASTA (Medical Advisory Service for Travellers Abroad)
Healthline 0906 8224100 (24 hours)
Website: www.masta.org
MASTA will send you a free printout of the current health advice for your journey. Be prepared with your name, address and journey details.

Thomas Cook Vaccination Centre
45 Berkeley Street, London W1
Tel: 020 7499 4000

Health insurance
Take out a traveller's health insurance policy for your trip and read the small print before you go. Some

policies exclude 'dangerous activities' which may include even trekking and scuba diving, so check first if you are planning these activities.

If you fall ill during your journey and need professional medical attention you will probably need to pay and then reclaim the cost when you return home (except in the case of a major medical emergency). It is vital to get a proper receipt and the doctor must sign your original policy form.

If you need to visit a doctor or dentist in Jordan you can get a list of recommended practices from the British Embassy (see useful addresses). Or ask your hotel to arrange an appointment locally.

Stomach upsets

However careful you are in what you eat and drink sometimes you simply can't avoid an upset stomach. These range from mild to serious and it is useful to know what to look out for. Most upset stomachs are a result of unfamiliar bacteria and sometimes just the change of climate. Symptoms are stomach cramps and diarrhoea. In this case avoid food altogether for a day and sip plenty of mineral or soda water (not too cold and no ice added) and drink tea without milk. This kind of tummy upset should pass in 1–2 days at most.

If your problem is more severe you may have picked up a parasite such as those causing dysentery or giardiasis. This can leave you feeling very ill for a week or more unless treated with a course of tablets available from the doctor. Do not ignore any diarrhoea which persists – the dangers from dehydration are serious.

Prevention is better than cure, and if you are prone to stomach disorders take the following precautions:

- Drink only bottled water or water that has been boiled (e.g. tea) or purified chemically (take some fruit squash to disguise the flavour). If you purify water using Puritabs or similar beware that it takes 30 minutes to work and will not protect you against giardiasis or amoebic dysentery.
- Salads and fruit should be washed in purified water. Fruit should be peeled.
- Avoid milk and ice cream, although yoghurt is fine.
- No ice in drinks – ever. It is usually made with tap water.
- In restaurants order meals that have to be freshly cooked, not ready-made dishes that could have been sitting around for hours.

Sunburn and heatstroke

Both of these are hazards to the unwary in the fierce heat of the Middle East from spring to autumn and great care should be taken to avoid problems. When exploring a site such as Petra you are exposed to strong UV rays for most of the time. During the hottest part of the day shade can be hard to find.

- Use a good high-factor sunscreen all the time on any exposed part of your body, not forgetting the back of your neck.
- Wear a brimmed hat to shade your face from the sun and more importantly your eyes from the strong glare. Also a good pair of sunglasses will protect your eyes from damaging UV.
- If you are visiting Petra during a particularly hot time of year consider taking a collapsible umbrella for instant shade. This may sound extreme but it will be very welcome when you really need to get out of the sun and rest.
- Carry a light cotton bandana or scarf that you can wet and wrap around your neck.
- If you do nothing else be sure to take plenty of water when walking around the site and take frequent small swigs rather than long drinks. One litre per person is recommended for a half-day trek, more if you can carry it.
- Take salt tablets or rehydration solution (these come in sachets and you mix them with water). It is vital to maintain your body salts. If too low you may suffer

dizziness, muscle cramps and extreme fatigue.

A traveller's health kit

A small first aid kit will not take up much room in your luggage but is worth its weight in gold if you need it. The following may prove useful:

Salt tablets or sachets; water purification tablets; antiseptic wipes; plasters; a blister kit (available from chemists); aspirin or paracetamol; a crêpe bandage in case of sprains; Immodium or similar to stop diarrhoea (to be used only as an emergency measure when travelling); tweezers; Blisteeze or similar for chapped lips; eye drops; and medicated talcum powder for prickly heat.

Small quantities of all the above will fit into a small toilet bag. Of course, don't forget any prescription medicines you require for the duration of your trip.

Accommodation and restaurants

Jordan in general, and Petra in particular, has now expanded its range of hotels considerably. It is now possible to choose from super-deluxe to small and modest accomodation within walking distance of the site at Petra. The luxury hotels are extremely good and offer a degree of pampering previously only dreamed of on a visit to Petra. The smaller cheapies are very good value if you are on a budget but it pays to look around before making your choice.

With the addition of these new hotels the pressure for rooms in high season has eased considerably. It is now possible to turn up and find a hotel room in most places, although pre-booking is still recommended if you definitely want to stay at a particular hotel.

WHERE TO STAY IN PETRA

Hotels of all classes have sprung up along the road which runs from the entrance to Petra to the village of Wadi Musa up the hill. The distance between Wadi Musa and Petra is easily walkable (about 20 minutes down and 30 minutes up – or 5 minutes by taxi!). As a general rule the hotels which are very close to the entrance tend to be expensive. Wadi Musa has the advantage of more choice at the budget end and places to eat other than in hotels. It also boasts great views.

Those arriving in Wadi Musa by public bus are likely to be met by one or several hotel touts who will try very hard to persuade you of the merits of their establishments. Remember if you agree to go and look at a room you are in no way obligated. If you don't like it a polite 'no' will suffice. The touts

often quote very low prices for rooms or tell you that the hotel is down the hill. Once you go with them you may find the cheap rooms have miraculously gone and the hotel is way up a steep hillside. This doesn't always happen of course but it is as well to be aware.

The following is a list of recommended places which is by no means exhaustive.

LUXURY HOTELS

Grand View Hotel
PO Box 11
Tel: (3) 2156871 • Fax: (3) 2156984
E-mail: nazzalco@nets.com.jo
This hotel, also on the road to Tayyibeh, has a swimming pool, snooker room and two bars. Singles/doubles cost JD 75/100.

King's Way Inn
PO Box 71
Tel: (3) 2156799 • Fax: (3) 2156796
E-mail: resrv@kingsway-petra.com
Way up above Wadi Musa , near the spring, is this luxury hotel with far-reaching views, a swimming pool and good restaurant. Singles/doubles cost JD 70/85

Mövenpick Hotel
PO Box 214
Tel: (3) 2157111 • Fax: (3) 2157112
E-mail: hotel.petra@movenpick.ch
A 5-star Swiss-owned hotel close to the entrance to the site, this is the latest and most luxurious hotel in Petra. It has been

built with no expense spared using traditional Islamic design and decorated with inlaid furniture, marble floors and crystal chandeliers. There is a swimming pool, a health club and a splendid roof garden. Singles/doubles cost US$160/195 including breakfast + tax.

Petra Forum Hotel
PO Box 30
Tel: (3) 2156266 • Fax: (3) 2156977
E-mail: petra@intercont.com
The original luxury hotel in Petra is in a good position overlooking the canyon. These days it is fighting back against the new wave of luxury hotels in the area by offering more in the way of entertainment and facilities. It has a pleasant terrace with pool where nightly classical music concerts take place as well as regular barbecues. Non-residents can use the pool for JD 6. The Forum also runs the excellent Basin Restaurant in the heart of the ruins. Singles/doubles cost JD 90/100 + 20 per cent tax per night.

Petra Plaza Hotel
PO Box 150
Tel: (3) 2156407 • Fax: (3) 2156407
E-mail: exec@btc.com.jo
On the road to Tayyibeh from Wadi Musa this hotel has lovely views across the Petra mountains although it is quite a way from the site entrance (courtesy minibus provided). Singles/doubles cost JD 100/120 plus tax.

Petra Rest House
PO Box 30
Tel: (3) 2156014 • Fax: (3) 2156977
E-mail: petra@intercont.com
The original Government resthouse is now under the management of the Forum and undergoing dramatic refurbishment. Very close to the site entrance this hotel even has a bar in a Nabataean tomb. Guests may use all the facilities of the nearby Petra Forum Hotel. New rooms cost around JD 50/70 and the older rooms JD 40/60 for singles/doubles.

Taybet Zaman
PO Box 2
Tel: (3) 2150111 • Fax: (3) 2150101
E-mail: taybetzaman@jtic.com
Not exactly close to Petra at about 9km away, the Taybet Zaman is nonetheless one of the most interesting hotels in the area. It is a collection of 96 traditional stone-built chalets recreated from old Ottoman houses into a hotel village. It is all very tasteful with an emphasis on arts and crafts and has a pleasant restaurant with good views. There is a courtesy bus to the site entrance at 8.00 and 9.30 am returning at 2 pm. Singles/doubles cost JD 85/110 plus tax.

MID-RANGE HOTELS

Candles
PO Box 181
Tel & Fax: (3) 2156954
A simple but friendly hotel with no air conditioning but fans in the rooms. Close to the site entrance. Singles/doubles cost

JD 25/30 plus tax but including breakfast.

Edom
PO Box 18
Tel: (3) 2156995 • Fax: (3) 2156994
E-mail: edom@go.com.jo
Reasonable but dull, the Edom is part of a new cluster of hotels to spring up near the site entrance. Singles/doubles cost JD 35/45.

Elgee Hotel
PO Box 121
Tel & Fax: (3) 2156701
Rather a dull place in the centre of Wadi Musa this hotel has one distinction: it is the only place selling alcohol in Wadi Musa. Singles/doubles cost JD 25/35 including breakfast.

Petra Moon
PO Box 216
Tel & Fax: (3) 2156220
Close to the site entrance, it is good value at JD 25/35 for singles/doubles.

Petra Palace Hotel
PO Box 70
Tel: (3) 2156723 • Fax: (3) 2156724
E-mail: ppwnwm@go.com.jo
The best of the mid-range hotels this is a very pleasant and friendly, family-owned hotel close to the site entrance and represents good value. The rooms on the fourth floor open onto a large terrace and those on the first floor open onto the courtyard pool area. The hotel boasts its own pub with draught Guinness, no less.

Singles/doubles cost JD 33/47 including tax and breakfast.

Al-Rashid Hotel
PO Box 96
Tel: (3) 2156800 • Fax: (3) 2156801
Right on the small roundabout which marks the centre of Wadi Musa, this hotel is very convenient for buses and taxis. It is also very close to the restaurants in Wadi Musa. Singles/doubles cost JD 15/25 including breakfast.

BUDGET HOTELS

Al-Anbat Hotel
PO Box 43
Tel: (3) 2157200
Higher up the road towards Ain Musa, this hotel is clean and good value with buffet lunches at JD 4. Singles/doubles/ triples cost JD 6/12/18 or there are mattresses on the covered roof for JD 2.5.

Cleopatra Hotel
PO Box 125
Tel & Fax: (3) 2157090
On the upper side of Wadi Musa the Cleopatra is a homely and welcoming place with small, clean rooms. Doubles cost JD 12 or dorms for three or four people cost JD 2 per person.

Mussa Spring Hotel
PO Box 62
Tel: (3) 2156310 • Fax: (3) 2156910
This is the original backpacker's hotel situated high above Wadi Musa offering good budget accomodation and buffet

lunch/dinner for JD 3. Slightly cramped rooms cost JD 10/12 for singles/doubles with bath, somewhat cheaper without, or the covered roof costs JD 2. The hotel has a minibus which runs down to Petra in the morning, returning at about 5 pm.

Qasr Al-Bint Hotel
PO Box 210
Tel & Fax: (3) 2157115
Right in the centre of Wadi Musa this friendly budget hotel has cheap, clean rooms, some with very good views. Singles/ doubles cost 10/13JD. The hotel has heating for the winter.

Sunset Hotel
PO Box 59
Tel: (3) 2156579 • Fax: (3) 2156950
The best by far of the cheaper hotels near to the site entrance. It is understandably popular with young travellers on a budget. Singles/doubles cost JD 15/20. There is a rooftop restaurant and terrace.

The village of Wadi Musa is an hour's hike from the Siq. Among the ten hotels there is the new Petra Student House, a basic facility with beds at JD 1.5–2 per night. The owner of the house, Khalid, will provide a lift down to those who take his fancy. The rest have to hoof it. The Al-Khalil tea house beside the spring has one room with four beds (JD 1 each), but has not bothered to lay on running water.

CAMPING
Camping is permitted in a designated part of the grounds of the Petra Forum Hotel. It costs JD 6 per person to use this facility and tents can be hired for a small charge. There is a shower block for the use of campers but no other facilities.

Apart from the Forum there are no other official camp sites and if you choose to camp 'in the wild' be aware that Petra is already inhabited, not only by Bedouin tribesmen who resent being woken after hours but also by a rich and varied fauna which includes jackals, 10cm-long black centipedes, the omnipresent large dung beetles, cockroaches, spiders and scorpions – most of which are highly active at night.

Do not make a habit of wandering about after dark – it wakes up every dog for miles and sets them all off barking which is very irritating for people trying to sleep. It also causes nervousness in other campers who hear you blundering about. Even a quiet voice carries a long way amongst these rocks. If you must do so, you would be advised to carry a stick – the guard dogs are not bluffing when they bare their teeth.

SLEEPING IN ROCK TOMBS
This is an experience for the hardy. It is very uncomfortable, but can be done if you have your own sleeping-bag and are prepared to

spend most of the night either cursing your stupidity, in a state of high anxiety, or enraptured by the uniqueness of the moment. Take one of those little blow-up neck pillows.

You are not supposed to stay within the city overnight without a permit, which can be obtained from the Ministry of Antiquities in Amman. However, it is quite possible to acquire these locally, and in any case no one would bother to stop you from staying out if you were suddenly seized by a spur-of-the-moment enthusiasm at some remote spot, or were simply caught out by darkness. (Likewise, remember that they would not bother to come searching for you if you got into difficulties either – unless someone was awaiting you. Be warned.) Remember that every time you go in through the Siq, you pay an extra JD 1 entrance fee.

If you have undressed, always shake out clothes and check shoes before putting them back on – most scorpion bites are not much worse than a couple of bee-stings, but do need treatment, and a few varieties are fatal. These chummy little creatures enjoy company, and like to huddle up in warm material towards dawn. So, incidentally, do some snakes.

WHERE TO EAT IN PETRA
Apart from the hotels' own restaurants, eating out in Petra is a limited experience – but one that is improving all the time. Inside the site you have a choice – either bring your own picnic or buy lunch (or a takeaway picnic bag) at one of the many cafés and small snack tents there. Bringing your own picnic is now officially not allowed (you are expected to buy your food inside Petra), but it is a rule which is universally ignored. Even if you do not bring a picnic you should at least bring a bottle or two of water with you.

Along the main street of Petra there are several tented cafés and down near the Qasr al-Bint is a small café/restaurant selling drinks and snacks/light meals. Far and away the best place for lunch if you feel like a splurge is the Basin Restaurant, run by the Petra Forum Hotel down near the museum known as Nazzal's Camp. It offers a vast and delicious self-service hot and cold buffet for JD 7 per person, excluding drinks, outside under shady awnings. It also has the best WCs in Petra.

Outside the site there is a variety of places to eat, mostly on the road up to Wadi Musa and in the town itself. Near the site entrance is Al-Mehbash which serves Arabic dishes in the mid-price range. Just up the hill from the Movenpick Hotel there are a couple of fast food places: Papazzi which serves Italian-style pizzas and snacks and further up Petra Burger. The Sunrise Restaurant underneath the Sunset Hotel sells kebabs and other local dishes at inflated tourist prices.

In Wadi Musa one of the most popular places is Al Wadi, right on the roundabout, which has a vast array of local dishes at reasonable prices. Just off the roundabout is the Kleopetra Restaurant which serves an all-you-can-eat buffet for JD 5. This includes soups, salads, mezze and three or four main dishes. Opposite the Kleopetra is the Petra Pearl Restaurant which specializes in rotisserie and shawarma dishes. Also popular is the Al-Mankal Chicken Tikka, part of the well-known chain, and the Syrian Al-Shamia Flower which sells good *foul* and *felafels*.

Daily provisions

Most people can make do with *khubz* and *jibneh* (flat bread and white cheese) scrounged from the breakfast table. Add an egg and a tomato and you have a feast! There are a few grocery stores in Wadi Musa which sell salad, fruit and vegetables as well as tinned and dairy food. The Bedouin supermarket also sells picnic bags. If you fancy something more elaborate the larger hotels often make up lunch boxes on request – anything from a simple sandwich to a three-course lunch – at a price. Be aware that whatever you take for your picnic will no doubt be eaten very warm, i.e. melted, so forget about chocolate altogether.

WHERE TO STAY IN AMMAN

The capital of Jordan has a vast range of hotels at all levels of comfort. As a general rule the more downmarket hotels tend to cluster around the downtown area, particularly along Sharia Al-Malik Faisal, while the more upmarket hotels are dotted around Jabal Amman. Here is a brief selection of recommended places:

LUXURY HOTELS

Jordan InterContinental Hotel
Queen Zein Street
Jabal Amman
Tel: (6) 4641361 • Fax: (6) 4645217
E-mail: annha@nets.com.jo
The premier luxury hotel in Amman. Double rooms cost JD 130/140 for singles/doubles plus 20 per cent tax.

Amman Marriott Hotel
PO Box 926333
Shmeisani
Tel: (6) 5607607 • Fax: (6) 5670100
E-mail: jomariot@marriott.com.jo
The most expensive hotel in Amman, the Marriott is the favoured choice for well-heeled tourists. Double rooms are JD 145 plus 20 per cent tax.

MID-RANGE HOTELS

Carlton Hotel

Opposite the InterContinental
Tel: (6) 4654200 • Fax: (6) 4655833
E-mail: jcarlton@joinnet.com.jo
*This comfortable and quite luxurious hotel
looks like a bargain compared with the
Marriott and InterContinental.
Singles/doubles cost JD 45/55 plus 20 per
cent tax.*

Hisham Hotel

Zahran Street, Jabal Amman
Tel: (6) 4642720 • Fax: (6) 4647540
E-mail: hishamhotel@nets.com.jo
*This popular and friendly hotel offers
satellite TV, private bathrooms and air
conditioning. Singles/doubles cost JD
40/55 plus 10 per cent tax.*

BUDGET HOTELS

Cliff Hotel

Off Al-Malek Faisal Street
Tel: (6) 4624273
*This is one of the most popular budget
hotels in Amman; its reputation with
backpackers spreads far and wide. Modest
rooms with two beds cost about JD 8.
Showers are extra. Alternatively sleep on
the roof on mattresses for JD 2.*

Lords Hotel

Al-Malek Al-Hussein Street
Tel & Fax: (6) 4622167
*Large rooms with fans (or heating in
winter) are an advantage in this hotel
where singles/doubles cost JD 7/12.*

Select Hotel

Baoniya Street, Jabal Al-Weibdeh
Tel & Fax: (6) 4637101
*Comfortable rooms, many with a balcony,
make this a good choice at the upper end
of the budget range. Singles/doubles cost
JD 11/16.*

WHERE TO EAT IN AMMAN

The city has a wide range of
cuisines and prices so the following
list contains just a few suggestions:

Bukhara Restaurant

InterContinental Hotel
Queen Zein Street
Jabal Amman
Tel: (6) 4641361
*Authentic Indian food in luxurious
surroundings.*

Al Bustan

Jordan University Road
Tel: (6) 5661555
*Live music and a lively atmosphere
accompany the authentic Arabic dishes.
Popular with locals and tourists alike.*

Kan Zaman Restaurant

Airport Road
Tel: (6) 4126449
*A renovated Ottoman village with a
restaurant, shops and handicraft centre.*

Al-Saha Al-Hashemieh

Opposite the Roman Theatre,
downtown
*Well-prepared traditional food served
under a Bedouin tent.*

Seven Hills
Airport Road
Tel: 079 524998
Authentic food in very pleasant
surroundings.

WHERE TO STAY IN AQABA

There is quite a wide range of
hotel accommodation in Aqaba.
The prime locations are those on
or close to the small stretch of
coast in the town. The beachside
hotels are often considerably more
expensive than those in the town
centre. For those planning to visit
the dive sites, having a beachfront
hotel is perhaps not so important
as you will be visiting the Red Sea
beaches anyway. Most hotels run a
shuttle bus to the dive centre and
back again.

The following is a selection of
recommended hotels:

LUXURY HOTELS

Aquamarina I Beach Club Hotel
PO Box 96, Corniche
Tel: (3) 2016250 • Fax: (3) 2032639
E-mail: aquama@go.com.jo
Excellent watersports' facilities, pleasant
pool area and private beach. Singles/doubles
cost JD 48/66 including tax.

Coral Beach Hotel
PO Box 71, Corniche
Tel: (3) 2013521 • Fax: (3) 2013614
One of the original beachfront hotels, it
has a private beach and watersports but

the rooms need some upgrading to really
justify the cost. Singles/doubles cost about
JD 50/60.

Radisson SAS
PO Box 215, Corniche
Tel: (3) 2012426 • Fax: (3) 2013426
E-mail: aqjzh_fo@go.com.jo
This international chain has taken over
the old Holiday Hotel and upgraded it
considerably. Facilities include pool, beach,
tennis courts and watersports. Room rates
start at JD 120.

MID-RANGE HOTELS

Crystal Hotel
PO Box 905
Tel: (3) 2022001 • Fax: (3) 2022006
A new and very comfortable hotel in the
centre of town, near the Corniche. It has
several bars, a good restaurant and a
nightclub. Singles/doubles cost about JD
24/36 which for a hotel of this standard is
a good price.

Nairoukh 2
PO Box 1138, Corniche
Tel: (3) 2012980 • Fax: (3) 2012980
A clean, well-appointed hotel five minutes
walk from the centre of town, which is
justifiably popular with tour groups. It
has a superb position overlooking the Gulf
of Aqaba and has constructed all the
rooms to take advantage of this.
Singles/doubles cost JD 18/30 plus 10 per
cent tax but including breakfast.

BUDGET HOTELS

Dweik Hotel (formerly called
Nairoukh as well)
Next to the Nairoukh 1
E-mail: info@dweikhotel.com
Website: www.dweikhotel.com
*This is one of the better quality budget
hotels. The rooms are clean and have TV
and private bathrooms. Singles/doubles
cost JD 15/20.*

Jerusalem Hotel
Tel: (3) 2014815
and
Jordan Flower Hotel
Tel: (3) 2014377
*These two are both next door to the Petra
Hotel and all offer very similar rooms and
prices.*

Al-Nahr Khaled Hotel
Al-Razi Street
Tel: (3) 2012456
*Friendly place right in the centre of town.
Can be a bit noisy in the evening but
convenient for shopping. Rooms cost JD
12/16 for singles/doubles with bath and
a balcony.*

Nairoukh 1
Round the corner from the Ali
Baba Restaurant
Tel: (3) 2019284
*A friendly, clean hotel which is not
bad value at JD 16/32 for singles/
doubles.*

Petra Hotel
PO Box 587, Main Street (near
bus station)
Tel: (3) 2013746
*A classic backpacker's hotel with various
grades of room or a covered roof terrace to
choose from. Doubles cost about JD 9 or
the roof costs JD 2 for a mattress.*

CAMPING
The National Touristic camp is
situated 11km south of town on
the Red Sea coast. They charge
JD 1 per night to pitch a tent. There
are showers and a Bedouin-style
restaurant. A very good location on
the beach for snorkelling.

WHERE TO EAT IN AQABA
There is no shortage of small
fast food places serving felafels
or snacks around town. Also there
are quite a few snack stalls selling
their wares along the Corniche.
Delicious bags of hot *foul* (broad
beans) can be bought for JD 1.
For a proper meal there are two
restaurants worth trying. The most
popular is the Ali Baba which has
an attractive outside eating area. It
has a long menu including local
and international dishes. It is open
all day and is the best place to stop
for a quiet drink. Next door is the
Hani Ali which has a very good
menu and also specializes in sweet
dishes. It is very popular with local
people especially on Fridays. The
Syrian Palace Restaurant is right

next door to the Shuala Hotel, near the Grand Mosque. Try to get a table outside on the upstairs balcony if you can. The food is OK, if not exceptional.

For a real splurge try the Mina House Restaurant which is on a boat moored near the old harbour. It specializes in fish dishes (expensive) but has other Arabic and inter-national items on the menu. Also by the water, on the stretch below the Corniche, are a series of simple cafés covered with palm awnings where you can sip tea and watch the sun set.

Transport

Once you arrive in Jordan Petra is only accessible by road from either Amman or Aqaba. There is no passenger rail service. The trip from Amman used to mean days on horseback or a full day along a rough track if travelling in a vehicle. Nowadays there are two main road routes to Petra from Amman: the Desert Highway through Ma'an (250km) which takes about three hours in a car, and the more scenic King's Highway via Madaba and Kerak, which takes about eight hours if sightseeing en route. If you are coming the other way from Aqaba the drive takes about two hours by car direct, or if you stop and make a short visit at Wadi Rum you can complete

the journey in time for dinner at Petra.

BUSES

Public minibuses run a semi-regular service to Petra (Wadi Musa) from both Aqaba and Amman. From the Wahadat bus station in Amman minibuses leave several times a day (in the morning), departing when full. The fare to Petra is JD 2 each way. Also the air-conditioned Jett bus leaves from the Abdali bus station in Amman at 6 am. The fare is JD 5.5. It returns to Amman at 3 pm daily.

If your time is very short Jett buses also run an inclusive day trip to Petra leaving from Wahadat bus station at 6 am. The price of JD 32 (children under 12 half price) includes the fare, entrance to the site and a guided tour (packed lunch thrown in). The same bus returns to Amman at about 3 pm, getting back to the capital at about 6 pm.

Leaving Petra, the minibuses for Amman and Aqaba tend to depart early in the morning, although in high season there is also a lunchtime departure for Aqaba. If you find yourself stuck, take a minibus to Ma'an from Wadi Musa roundabout. These run at about one an hour. From Ma'an you can connect with another minibus to Amman or Aqaba, or take a service taxi. From Wadi Musa there is also one minibus a day going to Wadi Rum leaving at about 6.30 am.

TAXIS

If you want a private taxi and driver ask a travel agent in Amman or Aqaba to arrange one for you and fix a price for everything including sightseeing stops en route. This is obviously not a cheap option but if there are three or four of you it can work out to be a reasonable and comfortable way to travel to and from Petra.

Otherwise you can easily get a service taxi in the mornings from either Aqaba or Amman to Wadi Musa. Nothing seems to run in the afternoons. The yellow taxis are a good idea for shorter excursions and you have the flexibility of leaving whenever you want. A taxi to/from Aqaba costs JD 25, to/from Amman non-stop JD 50.

CAR HIRE

Avis, Hertz, Budget and Eurodollar all operate car hire services in Jordan as well as numerous smaller local firms that are usually quite a bit cheaper. To hire a car you must have a valid driver's licence at least one year old and be at least 25 years old yourself. You should be prepared to pay at least JD 25 per day for a small car with unlimited mileage. You will be asked for a deposit of about JD 200 to JD 300. It is worth noting that the driver is usually liable for an excess of up to JD 200 on any insurance claim.

HITCHING

This is possible on the main roads where there is plenty of traffic and Jordanians are often willing to stop for a hitchhiker. Sometimes a small payment is expected and to avoid any embarassment offer a small amount of money when you get out. It is definitely not advised for women travelling without a man to try and hitchhike.

If you are coming from Amman it is a good idea to take a bus to Madaba and start from there as the traffic hurtling out of Amman will rarely be able or willing to stop. Likewise start hitching in Aqaba a the outskirts of town, on the road north and you stand a far better chance of getting a lift.

GETTING AROUND IN PETRA

Once past the ticket office there is a choice: you can either walk through the Siq (3km – around 45 minutes on foot) or you can hire a horse to take you as far as the beginning of the Siq for JD 7 (not exactly a bargain for such a short ride, 300m). In the old days you could ride right through as far as the Treasury or beyond, but the increase in numbers has rendered this impractical nowadays – the horse-droppings alone were causing a major cleaning problem. Exceptions are made for disabled or elderly people who can still use the horse-drawn carriages to get through the Siq. These cost JD 8 per passenger (maximum two).

Once inside, on the main road through the site there is no shortage of Bedouin tribesmen offering camel or horse rides. The Ministry of Tourism is looking into a way in which visitors do not have to walk all the way back out through the Siq, but can be taken out on horseback by another route.

Other practical matters

MONEY

The currency of Jordan is the dinar (JD), commonly called the jaydee, which is divided into 1,000 fils. You may also hear people refer to it as the lira. There are also colloquial names for various amounts of fils.

> JD 1 = 1,000 fils
> 1 dirham (bariza) = 100 fils
> 1 shilling = 50 fils
> 1 piastre (ghirsh) = 10 fils

In round figures the current exchange rate is £1 = JD 1.

You can buy Jordanian money from a bank or *bureau de change* before you go but the exchange rate is the same as in Jordan. There is no limit to the amount of currency you can take into or out of the country, either JDs or foreign currency. Changing money is easy in Jordan (the exception is the New Zealand dollar which they don't accept at any price).

Traveller's cheques: Banks, hotels and some of the larger shops will change travellers cheques.

Eurocheques: Not generally acccepted but the British Bank of the Middle East in Amman will cash them.

Personal cheques with banker's card. These are not accepted.

Visa and Mastercard: Increasingly accepted in shops and restaurants. Cash is available from the many ATM machines now in Jordan. There is one near the entrance to Petra and one in Wadi Musa.

Other credit cards: These are quite widely accepted in shops and restaurants but cannot be used in ATMs at the moment. The Amercian Express office in Amman is at International Traders, Abdul-Hamid Sharaf Street (opposite the Ambassador Hotel), Shmeisani. Tel: 607014. Open from 8 am to 12 pm and from 3 to 6 pm except Fridays. In Aqaba the AMEX office is near the municipality. Tel: 313757.

Cash withdrawal cards: The ATMs in Jordan are compatable with the Cirrus network, which is used now by most British banks and building societies.

BANKS

Hours: 8 am to 12.30 pm. In summer also from 4 pm to 6 pm and in winter 3.30 pm to 5.30 pm. Banks are closed on Fridays and holidays.

If you get caught without cash outside banking hours, the large hotels will change cash or traveller's cheques, but they charge a lot of commission for doing so.

If you are arriving by air into Amman's Queen Alia airport there are several banks which stay open seven days a week. There are also *bureaux de change* on both sides of the border post between Aqaba and Eilat, which stay open as long as the border crossing.

BUSINESS HOURS

Government offices: 8 am to 2 pm daily except Fridays.
Small businesses: 9 am to about 1 pm and 3 or 4 pm until late.
Markets: Open every day including Fridays and most holidays.
Museums: Individual opening times apply, but most are closed Tuesdays. These times are subject to variation and you should expect reduced opening hours during the month of Ramadan.

RELIGIOUS FESTIVALS AND NATIONAL HOLIDAYS

The dates of Islamic festivals are different every year because Islam uses the lunar calendar.

Islamic festivals

Ras al-Sana (New Year's Day): 1 Moharram
Mulid al-Nabi (The Prophet Muhammad's Birthday): 12 Rabi al-Awal
Ramadan (the month of fasting): ninth month of the Islamic calendar
Eid al-Fitr: 3-day feast at the end of Ramadan
Eid al-Adha (also known as **Eid al-Kabeer**) – the big feast (pilgrimage to Mecca): 10–13 Zuul Hijja

National holidays

New Year's Day: 1 January
King Abdullah II's birthday: 30 January
Arab League Day: 22 March
Labour Day: 1 May
Independence Day: 25 May
Arab Revolt and Army Day: 10 June.
The late King Hussein's birthday: 14 November
Christmas Day: 25 December

TELEPHONE, POST, E-MAIL & FAX

Post is generally quite efficient and post offices will hold mail for you (poste restante). Letters and cards from Jordan usually take about four days to Europe and two weeks to the US or Australia. It is now possible to send letters between Jordan and Israel. In telephone offices the system is to queue up and fill out a slip with the number you wish to ring and pre-pay an estimated cost for the call. If your bill is larger you pay the difference and if smaller they give you the change.

Jordan is increasingly using e-mail and it is possible to find hotels and small businesses willing to send and receive e-mails for you for a small fee. In Amman there are one or two Internet cafés where you can rent a terminal by the half-hour.

Amman

The main telephone office is in Sharia Khayyam behind the main post office which is in Sharia Al-Amir Mohammed. Opening hours are from 7.30 am to 11 pm seven days a week. The call rates are cheaper after 10 pm. There are English-speaking operators available to help you and you can also send faxes or telegrams from here.

Petra

There is a small post office near the site entrance open from 8 am to 7 pm daily although it sometimes closes unexpectedly. There is also a post office in Wadi Musa open from 8 am to 7 pm daily except Friday. There is no public telephone office in Petra or Wadi Musa; all international calls or faxes have to be made from the hotels. Local calls can often be made from shops' own phones which are metered.

Aqaba

The post office and telephone office are next door to one another in the town centre. The post office opens from 7.30 am to 7 pm daily except Fridays when it closes at 1.30 pm. The telephone office is open daily from 8 am to 10 pm.

MEDIA

Imported English-language news-papers can sometimes be found in the business-class hotels and a few shops in Amman, occasionally in Aqaba, but they are very expensive and at least a couple of days out of date. Apart from that there is very little chance of buying foreign press in Jordan. Jordan publishes its own English-language daily, the *Jordan Times* which is easily found in most places. There is also a news weekly, the *Star*, which is useful for 'what's on' listings. Journalism is relatively uncensored by the standards of the region and the quality of the press is quite high.

You can pick up English-language broadcasts on Radio Jordan on 96.3 FM in Amman or 98.7 FM in Aqaba. The BBC World Service broadcasts from 4 am to midnight and Voice of America from 4 am to 10 pm on a variety of short-wave frequencies. Jordan TV on Channel Two broadcasts in a variety of languages: English, French and Arabic. The news in English is at 10 pm. Also you can receive Israeli and Egyptian TV in the south of the country and Syrian TV in the north.

EMERGENCIES – THEFT OR LOSS

Of all the Middle Eastern countries, Jordan is one of the safest for travellers and there is very little cause for concern regarding crime. The streets are safe to walk around in, both day and night, and baggage can be safely left in the care of a hotel or office. Given the Jordanian sense of honesty and hospitality the greatest risk of theft comes from other foreigners. It is always sensible to take a few precautions with your belongings – so don't leave valuables in a hotel room; ask the hotel manager to take care of them for you. It is also sensible not to carry all your cash, credit cards and ATM cards in the same wallet together; keep them in separate places or hide some emergency money in your luggage.

DUTY FREE

You can take into Jordan, without paying duty, the following: two hundred cigarettes and one litre of wine or spirits.

ELECTRICITY

Jordan uses 220V, fifty AC electricity with mostly round two-pin plugs (although in Aqaba you sometimes see British-style three-pin sockets).

Take any necessary adaptors with you.

TIME

Jordan is two hours ahead of GMT and three hours ahead of British Summer Time.

WEIGHTS AND MEASURES

Jordan uses the metric system.

WHAT TO TAKE

- Plenty of film. You will no doubt shoot more than you thought you would. Although film is sold almost everywhere in Jordan there is no guarantee that it has been stored properly, so it is best to buy your film from a reliable retailer before you travel.
- A torch – useful for looking around the dark interiors of tombs and for walking around after dark.
- A blow-up neck pillow. These are valuable items when camping, sunbathing or for those long bus or plane journeys.
- An insulated water bottle. These are available now on a waistband and not only keep water cool but keep your hands free.
- Sunglasses and a hat. Buy the best quality sunglasses you can afford in order to cut down on UV damage to your eyes. The best hats for travelling are canvas hats with a medium stitched

brim all round. These can be folded up when not in use. Baseball caps shade your eyes but offer no protection to the back of your neck, so are not a good idea.

- Clothing. As a general rule when packing for a trip in the hot season, stick to cotton, silk and linen. Natural fibres absorb perspiration and keep you cooler far better than man-made fibres. For women loose trousers are far more comfortable than skirts – it is also the custom in Jordan to keep the legs covered. A loose cotton shirt over the top is ideal. One problem that affects quite a few people in the hot weather is a heat rash on the inner thigh which can become very sore. If you are prone to this condition take a pair of fine knitted silk long-johns (available in above-the-knee or full length). You can buy these from outdoor activity shops.

- If you only take one luxury you could do worse than carry a large woven raffia fan or perhaps a folding fan. The less romantically minded acquire little mechanical fans.

- If you could carry one more book besides your guide book consider taking the Bible. Whether you have never read it before or whatever your religious stance, nothing opens the eyes quite so much as actually going to the places mentioned there and seeing them for yourself. If you don't take it with you at least read the Book of Genesis when you get home. You could surprise yourself and turn into a lifelong Bible addict.

- Foods. If you get tired of unfamiliar foods and crave something from home take some boiled sweets and packets of instant soup or noodles for variety. If you really must have milk in tea and coffee take some powdered milk. In fact Arab tea is not harsh and you may not miss the milk. When ants found their way into mine, my Arab friend was undaunted. 'Don't worry,' he said. 'They all float to the top.'

OUT AND ABOUT IN PETRA
Photography

Petra is a photographer's dream, presenting new and enticing views at every turn. With a little forethought even the most novice photographer can come home with some striking images which provide a lasting souvenir of your visit. If you don't already own one, investing in a good quality point-and-shoot camera will pay dividends. For those of you who are a little more advanced with your photography the possibilities are very great indeed. It all depends on how much equipment you want to lug around with you – an important consideration when you will be walking over quite rough terrain in the heat for several hours. For this reason alone it is worth considering taking a zoom lens rather than several fixed focal length lenses.

One of the most important considerations is to protect your camera, lenses and film cassettes from heat and dust. Simple plastic carrier bags (one for each piece of equipment) inside a larger day pack or camera bag is fine. A padded fabric bag is by far the most comfortable option; if you don't want to pay a lot for a fancy camera bag line a small rucksack with foam padding (or even bubble wrap) and use that. Remember to return shot film to the plastic pot it came in as grit can work its way into the cassette and scratch an entire film. A holster-style camera bag on a waistband will hold one body plus a couple of lenses plus several films and leave your hands free.

Despite its obvious photogenic properties, to get the best out of Petra you have to shoot your pictures at the right time of day. In most cases this means either early morning or latish afternoon, when the sun is warmer and slanting against the rock face. In most cases if the rock face is in shadow in the morning it will be lit in the afternoon and vice versa. An exception is the narrow Siq itself when shooting at midday means that the dark recesses are lit somewhat more than usual. The best view to the east is Ed Deir at sunset, to the west from the High Place of Sacrifice in the early morning. Al-Khasneh is in full sunlight at mid-morning and the deepest pink is around 4 pm.

Generally, shooting around midday will produce heavy, blue-tinged shadows so is best avoided. For the odd time when you are stuck somewhere in the middle of the day and want to take a picture a simple warm-up filter over the lens will often do the trick; also a lens hood will help to cut out glare. A flash is useful for filling in shadows and photographing dim cave interiors.

When it comes to choosing what film to shoot the best advice is to buy a well-known brand. Fuji and Kodak are both of the highest quality and make films, both negative and slide, in a wide variety of film speeds. The rule of thumb is to shoot the slowest film you can manage. A good all-round choice where there is plenty of light is 100 ASA. Whatever your choice bring plenty of film with you. Although film is widely sold in Jordan it has frequently been sitting around in a hot shop for longer than is good for it.

Do not be tempted to get your films processed in Jordan (especially slide films) as the quality is very poor, apart from being expensive.

Etiquette

Apart from the ruins you will inevitably come across scenes that you want to photograph with local people in them. It is good manners to always ask permission first – no one likes to have a camera thrust in their face and in the case of local women it may in fact cause them considerable embarrassment. Even worse, they may be accused of having encouraged you and become the subject of nasty gossip and backbiting. Sneaking pictures of the old, the ugly, the deformed or the dilapidated is very insensitive. Try to empathize with your subjects. Jordanians have a strong sense of pride and taking pictures of any kind of squalor is likely to provoke a sharp reaction. Children on the other hand appear from nowhere and mug into the camera in every shot if you're not careful.

Sometimes local people ask for money in return for taking their picture, especially the Bdul who are peddling souvenirs in the site. It is up to you if you agree to this. Personally I prefer to buy something and then ask if I can take a picture – charging outright for a snapshot seems a bit too close to an outright hustle in my opinion and shouldn't be encouraged.

Flora and fauna

Although the flora in and around Petra is dominated by the oleander with its tough silvery leaves and pink flowers, other parts of Jordan have somewhat more in the way of greenery. In the far north of the country there are hills covered with Aleppo pine which give way further south to groves of cedar, olive and eucalyptus trees.

In the arid semi-desert and desert areas wildlife is sometimes hard to spot. If you are lucky you may see a gazelle or an ibex. Desert foxes are quite common as are mongoose, jerboa and mole-rat but as they all hunt at night they are rarely seen. Jordan has a few nature reserves such as Shaumari or Dana where a wider variety of animals can be seen, such as the Arabian oryx which was hunted to extinction in the wild and is now being introduced back into the area through zoo breeding programmes.

A more spectacular display of wildlife can be seen in the bird and fish kingdoms. Both in Azraq Oasis in the north-east of the country and around Aqaba in the south huge numbers of migratory birds are attracted by the shallow salt marshes in the area. The Red Sea is well known the world over for the rich diversity of its tropical fish and its coral reef.

For further information about nature reserves contact the Royal Society for the Conservation of Nature (RSCN) in Amman, Tel: 6837931/2, Fax: 847411.

Life-savers

At major sites a man can often be found with water (very warm) in petrol cans strapped to the sides of his donkey – quite safe if you pop in a water purification tablet. In the high season, vendors will appear from the rocks at most major sites.

Carry some boiled sweets or a packet of raisins.

The sun

Choose the sensible times to attempt, for example, the ascent to Ed Deir – it is much more comfortable when the sun has moved round and the steps up are in the shade. If caught out by sunstroke, or heat-exhaustion, the best 'rescue-remedy' back at base is to stick your head under a cold water tap for 15 minutes or so (just trickle it – remember water is precious), to bring the temperature down rapidly; drink plenty of fluids, and rest.

Women with plump legs might suffer the embarrassment of unexpected floods of perspiration in those parts, resulting in rashes and blisters. Wear cotton underwear, preferably knee-length (I'm serious) and take medicated talcum powder. The best defence I know against 'dhobi itch' is to wear long cotton trousers (pyjama bottoms are quite adequate) under a cotton skirt – again, I'm quite serious, and no one will snigger except your tourist friends, who may soon envy you. It prevents chafing, and sweat evaporates quickly from cotton cloth leaving you dry. Wear tights and corsets only if you are quite mad.

Flash floods

It rarely rains in Petra, but occasionally rain up to 50km away can send a wall of water hurtling through the Siq gorge. In April 1963, 28 travellers were caught in the Siq and all were drowned. Two Landrovers were deposited many feet up the sides of the canyon on a ledge, where they remained as gruesome warnings for several years. Recently a barrage dam has been built across the mouth of the Siq to ensure year-round safety (Insha'Allah) by diverting the water through a tunnel through the sides of the mountain – especially cut by the Nabataeans in the first century BCE! Presumably they had the same problems – plus, they wished to utilize every available drop of water for their citizens.

Harriet Martineau described the Wadi Musa in spate in 1847:

> We walked along a water-course and got out of it not far from our platform. Within three minutes, before I had half put off my wet clothes, I heard a shout: the torrent had come down. Down it came, almost breast-high … giving a river in a moment, where we had never dreamed of hoping to see

one! ... Just before sunset I went to look again. The white waterfalls were still tumbling from the steeps ... dashing along, making eddies among the stones.

The water hurtles off through the Wadi Siyagh.

Guides

Guides can be hired from the Al-Ji Police Post, the Petra Forum or the Forum Rest House. They are negotiable, so be prepared to bargain. Horses are JD 7 from the site entrance to the beginning of the Siq. Prices for guides for day trips – try to get the 'inside story' by asking around (i.e. get several estimates before committing yourself).

How much are you willing to pay a man for engaging him for a day? JD 25 per day is what they hope for.

Once away from official eyes, the guides will press for tips urgently and with pitiful expressions, and if this doesn't work and you have made an unlucky choice, can suddenly turn nasty. Ignore both tactics – they are acting. Tourists who weakly give in – mainly out of gratitude for safe return after a gruelling day – simply raise their expectations and make it less pleasant for those who follow on. Best practice is to negotiate your tip beforehand, and stick to it. If you have agreed on your tip, it is

up to them what they choose to do for it. But be reasonable – if you get into difficulties and are helped, or if you receive help over and above the call of duty, it is only fair to reward it.

I was once staggering on the point of collapse and very grateful indeed to discover my horse-man had come up the valley over a mile, on the off-chance, to wait for me and offer to carry my bag. His expression did not change when he found I had filled it with souvenir chunks of 'rose red' rocks. My wallet and camera were loose on the top. He made a point of doing up my purse and carrying it on the shoulder nearest to me, after noticing my unguarded and uncalled for flash of Western anxiety. He absolutely refused my offered tip, but was grateful for the drink I fetched back to him from the camp – he was not allowed to approach the final couple of hundred metres since that would have encroached upon the territory of the Arab camp.

Repayment for services rendered
For those lucky enough to experience genuine hospitality, the most embarrassing problem is working out how to repay it. To offer money used to be an insult, although they are rapidly getting the hang of tourists. Be aware, anyway, that a polite Bedouin will automatically

refuse, many times, even when some kind of payment really is expected. The polite tourist will insist on giving the payment to the children, and not insult the host.

Carrying an endless supply of rather useless small gifts is wearisome, but suitable items could include packets of Disprin or other simple medicines; pencils (biros are useless in the heat and sand, as you will swiftly discover); pen-knives; postcard views of anywhere; headscarves (you can get a cheap supply in advance from shops like Oxfam); cigarettes; photos of yourself. Decent watches seem to be favourite gifts.

If the family likes being photo-graphed, 'instant' family portraits are very acceptable if you have a Polaroid camera. Be warned that although it may be just another snap to you, the mothers and children may take an hour to get smartened up for the event. They will want to be 'done' in their best clothes. Some don't like photography – the superstitious used to be afraid of their souls being trapped and taken away on the paper; and some very strict Muslims regard creating the representation of a living being on paper as blasphemous and get very angry about attempts to involve them in this corrupt practice!

Promising to send things or photos from home is a bit of a non-starter; taking the address is a noble thought, but items probably wouldn't get there.

Climbing

Be very careful – rescue services are very rough and ready, if not non-existent. Always tell someone where you are going, and when to expect you back. Take guides when recommended. Don't attempt anything you know you can't do. Wear tough shoes – you can't climb in strappy sandals. If you're really serious about climbing, there are specialized tours and guidebooks available (see list of tour operators and Further Reading). Carry as little as possible, but take drinks. Boiled sweets or a few raisins can be life-savers.

Shopping

You can buy souvenirs at the Tourist Information Centre near the Forum Rest House; they also claim to sell postage stamps, but seem to run out very frequently. Bedouin bring bits and pieces to Al-Khasneh, the High Place of Sacrifice, Nazzal's Camp and the Royal Tombs in the City Ruins, and Ed Deir.

There is a small post office at Wadi Musa, but it is not always reliable. Beware of leaving post-cards and money with volunteer helpers – although usually honest, things can get left lying around, and be subsequently 'binned'. If you have said something offensive or hurtful about the Bedouin on your open postcard, it may be 'tactfully removed'. Post moves in a mysterious way in Jordan; it is quite possible to post twenty cards, and only see five reach their destination, many weeks later!

'Going Bedouin'

Do not attempt such an adventure if you cannot work out for yourself a satisfactory answer to the problems of how to go to the toilet during the night (and don't forget those tummy troubles!) and how to sleep fairly rough amongst a group of people. You would also be expected to share food and drink probably without cutlery, possibly served on to your plate by hand, and you might have to drink unpurified water if no bottled drinks were available (but they usually are; take water purification tablets anyway, or better, stick to tea made with boiled water).

Bedouin tents do not generally supply running water (they will have a tank somewhere and a jar or tin), and any people who keep livestock (a goat or two may well wander in there with you!) can be plagued by fleas which seem to have the uncanny ability to sense the arrival of a new and juicy 'host'. (Take flea powder.)

Romantic encounters

Female tourists who wander off alone can expect to be invited into caves for an experience not necessarily of a cultural nature. Promises to reveal the 'treasures of Jordan' may include treasures the innocent had not expected. Since many of these tribesmen are good-looking, one can only assume their importunity pays off frequently enough for them to persist. (At least one Western woman has married a Bedouin and now lives in his cave home.)

It is rather unnerving to be pursued by an ardent swain clasping his stomach and repeating sombrely 'I am dying, I am dying', only to discover that the cause of his malady is his overwhelming desire for you. (Whoever sold them this dreadful line?) However, Arabs respect honourable women, and a friendly but firm refusal is quite enough. If the offending suitor is the horse-man with whom you are stuck for the next few hours, the offer of a cigarette heals the 'fatal wound' thus inflicted. Bear in mind that the sweetest moments can turn ugly, and that these days payment can even be demanded for services rendered!

Remember AIDS, and that contraceptives are not available.

Do not wander off alone

This is the best way to avoid the

problems described above. Groups of two or three are sensible. And on a more practical note, it would be no fun to collapse or faint in that heat without anyone to fetch help or locate you in due course. If you are wandering about alone, a luminous sticker on your pack makes you easily spottable.

Insects

If you don't like them, take insect powder. (This has its disadvantages. As I went to sleep one night I was vaguely aware of what I thought were mice scurrying around the bed. I took no notice, and never saw a single insect, despite rather obvious splat-marks on the wall. My friend in the next room dutifully spread her insect powder, and in the morning discovered she was hemmed in by around fifty large cockroaches in various stages of dying. Her screams spoiled the morning's meditations!)

If you have undressed, always shake out clothes and check shoes before putting them back on – the safest way to avoid being bitten by a scorpion (or any other unpleasant temporary occupant of your discarded raiment); in any case, the messy business of excavating crushed dung-beetles and cockroaches from your hiking boots is not a pleasant chore.

The best attitude is to 'go with nature' and try to enjoy it.

Incidentally, if you are offered a large spider for your room, it is because they like you – spiders are supposed to keep the cockroaches at bay!

Toilets

Remember that if water-pressure is low toilet-paper may not flush away and will soon block the system, in which case someone will have to go in after you and remove it. Notice two things – the plastic bag often found in the corner of the toilet is for the tourist's paper, embarrassing and dirty though this may seem to you; and somewhere, usually directly beneath you, there will be a little tap. This is for use instead of paper, and is much more hygienic anyway. Do not plump down unwarily on a toilet-seat in case the tap is dangerously positioned!

Where facilities are very basic, a considerate person will find the can or jug, fill it from a tap that will surely be found nearby, and flush the loo in readiness for the next person. The very squeamish sometimes take comfort in carrying a bottle of disinfectant.

There are no conveniences out in the wilds of the lost city apart from one on the Cardo and one at the Basni Restaurant. Despite your prudery, it is very bad form to nip into the cave-tombs if caught short. When tombs get fouled by visitors, they are either left like this to the detriment of later explorers, or some poor soul has to go and clean it up. The Bedouin who live in the caves would never foul them in this way, and can be disgusted by the ignorance of Western visitors. Paper droppings (from those who think they are so clever bringing their own toilet rolls rather than washing, like the Arabs) are not appreciated either. They don't biodegrade easily, and goats sometimes eat them, to their general detriment.

A note for women: It is difficult indeed to find a suitable cover in desert conditions; one cannot nip behind a bush. Amongst the rocks of Petra, you can never be completely sure that you are unobserved. Wearing a skirt over trousers eases the trauma and provides instant privacy if caught out. No full moons. And, be sociable – bury it!

A warning: You may spot a nice little clump of bushes or trees and head there for your emergency; bear in mind that this is probably the favourite picnic spot for local family outings. The behaviour of tourists in this respect causes much ill-feeling. They have the whole wilderness to choose from, but they have to go and squat just where Gran always sits for her pitta and eggs, and spoil the only bit of view worth looking at (to the Arabs).

Manners and modes

PUBLIC BEHAVIOUR AND DRESS

The respect felt by Jordanians for people of other nations is much reduced by the lack of dignity of some of these visitors. It is considered to be bad manners to shout, laugh loudly, or play the fool in public. The first culture shock that hits the traveller returning from the Middle East is no longer the greenness of the grass but the noisy, aggressive behaviour of many people. It is a very rare Jordanian who behaves like this.

Jordanians always dress with dignity, and are extremely clean and smartly turned out – whatever rank, from king to poor villager. The visiting Western woman may slip into a long dress and feel quite correct on the streets. The author has accomplished many a shopping trip wearing a long-sleeved cotton night-dress plus headscarf. Most Jordanian women cover their hair when out on the streets, but many are abandoning this custom. However, a woman's hair is still a matter for comment – a Western woman with a very vivid colour might consider covering it purely to avoid too much attention.

Women's arms are also covered. Unfortunately many Western

blouses have see-through sleeves, and this counts as naked – wearing them will provoke a reaction from some Jordanian women, who might express their disapproval of you tempting their men by hissing at you, or pinching your arm as you pass by. Be warned, though, that even the simple cotton tops ubiquitous in the West can be considered too low-cut or clinging. You can get away with them only so long as you stick to tourist areas. Tight jeans are also disapproved of, although many Jordanian girls wear trousers or denims under a skirt. Incidentally, when a Jordanian says 'mini-skirt' he means a garment that clears the ankle!

One of the funniest things I saw was a 'punk', a woman with spiky hair dyed pink, very exaggerated make-up, and an outfit that featured various deliberate holes and zips. No doubt she had dressed like that to create an impression. She must have been very surprised, for no matter what she did no one took the slightest notice of her – until she had gone by. Then the Jordanians could stand it no longer, and were doubled up with mirth. I trailed her for about twenty minutes, so fascinated was I by the entire phenomenon. About fifty Jordanians were also trailing her – all of us 'freezing' and politely gazing into shop windows every time she stopped.

Incidentally, it is important for Western men to be aware that in Muslim society many of these rules apply to them! It is considered very impolite, if not offensive, for a man to bare the chest or legs. After spending some time in Jordanian company, it comes as a real culture shock to find yourself sitting next to a large, pinky-brown man with sweat pouring from bared hairy chest, and naked legs – often totally unaware of the embarrassment he is causing.

VISITING

Jordanian manners vary from the completely Westernized to the traditional, unchanged over thousands of years. In many places Jordan is completely Westernized, for example in much of Amman, where there are plenty of hotels, night clubs, shopping precincts. Elsewhere life goes on much the same as it has done for centuries, except that tents have been exchanged for small houses or apartments.

The reception rooms are 'public' and normally used by men; the domestic section will be separate, and women may be shown straight into it, although Western women will probably sit down at first in the men's room and take coffee. If they are to enter the 'haram' or 'forbidden' – i.e. private – section, a considerate husband will go in first to warn his family to expect guests, so that they can quickly tidy up. It is considered unthinkably rude to enter anyone's private rooms unannounced.

When visiting, a man should knock at the outer door and wait. If only female voices reply, he should go away again – it would be most impolite if he insisted on entering a house occupied only by women. If a man is at home, the visitor should still wait outside to give time for the women and children to retire should they so wish.

Western men are often fascinated by the thought of the seclusion of Arab women, and try to catch glimpses of them. Sometimes women will cross the room or courtyard, or fetch refreshments. He should pretend not to notice them. This is the polite reaction, not rude, as it may seem to us. If a woman wishes to be 'seen' she will soon make it obvious. Most men these days will introduce their wives and children. If they are all happy about it, that's fine. But a tactful visitor should not inquire after their wives, only 'the family'. It might be thought, mistakenly, that the women are being kept prisoner, or subservient. Most women are quite able to get their husbands to bring them in and introduce them, if they want to.

There is usually little furniture in the room, but the floor may be spread with rugs (take your shoes off) and mattresses to sit on and bolsters will be spread round the walls to lean against. Remember, therefore, to have clean feet (or there will be embarrassing malodours), and women to have their legs covered. If you have inadvertently walked into this situation with a short skirt on, you can ask for something with which to cover your legs, and it will be instantly provided – thus you will be in no danger of revealing your underwear!

Precedence is important, but politeness is everything. When entering any room, one should hang back and give way to the other person – who will naturally refuse. In formal arrangements, it will usually be obvious that a couple of places are for the most important guests. You should not make straight for them assuming that you are the most important (since you may only have been invited to be shown off to a revered grandparent!). If you are shown to the best seats, refuse once, then accept when pressed. If someone else comes in (who might be more important – or older than you), it is polite to go through the motions of vacating your place for them, even if they refuse.

Correct behaviour when dining

Any meal will have been prepared with considerable time and trouble, often tender chunks of meat on top of a mountain of rice, boiled wheat (couscous) or bread soaked in gravy. The dish is placed in the centre (it could be on the floor, or on newspaper – that makes clearing up a great deal easier), the guests sit round it, and usually eat with their hands.

You may be offered a spoon, but don't expect a knife and fork unless the host is fully Westernized. Don't expect not to make a mess, or get greasy. Never eat with unwashed hands, or your hosts will be disgusted; and remember that the left hand is considered unclean. Accept anything passed to you, and eat, with the right hand.

Do not be alarmed if your host fishes around by hand in the dish to pick out what he considers to be the best bits for you. He will press on you far more than you can eat, and look as if he is never going to stop. If you are in family company, you will probably notice that the children are not getting much; anything you can't manage should be accepted on to your plate graciously, and then passed along again, to them.

Your host and his family may not eat with you at all – it is good manners to let the guests eat first. The host, and possibly his entire family, will watch attentively to observe your slightest need. This can be unnerving if you don't enjoy people watching you eat, and are not used to having people wait upon you. The sight of you enjoying your meal will, however, give them the greatest pleasure, even if it makes conversation a little difficult.

It is ill-mannered to show haste, or eagerness to be served. Others should always come before you. When you have had enough, you should continue to pretend to be eating, or slow down and eat tiny mouthfuls, so as not to embarrass those with larger appetites or slower mechanics who have not finished.

If a glass of water is placed in front of you and there are no others in sight, don't assume it is just for you; it will probably be shared by all at the meal. It depends on how many glasses they own. Don't be alarmed or offended if it is picked up and drunk from by someone else after you have put it down.

Tea and coffee come in little cups. It is polite to have three, then refuse any more by shaking the cup. Again, you may find yourself being watched; this is sometimes because the same cup will be used for the next guest after you have finished.

Muslims will say a blessing at the beginning and end of a meal. Diners leave the table together.

Smoking and drinking alcohol
Cigarettes will be offered, but it is not common for a woman to smoke in public, nor for a grown

man to smoke in front of his father as a matter of respect. Take your cues from what is going on around you. It is extremely discourteous to smoke in front of abstaining Muslims in Ramadan.

A devout Muslim will not drink alcohol, but this is not a universal prohibition in Jordan. A very popular local tipple is the fiery Arak, which can be diluted with water like the other aniseed drinks (pernod, ouzo, raki).

OFFENSIVE BEHAVIOUR (YOURS!)

A word of caution – the natives are not always friendly. The behaviour of some tourists can be very irritating, if not downright offensive. Loud transistors, drunks, strident women, men who insist on trying to look at, speak to or photograph Muslim women, and those who urinate in public, never go down well. The attitude of the Bedouin around you often depends on who has just been before you – although they are used to culture shocks. Musicians who are good and know when to stop can draw crowds – so can good dancers. Give full value of yourself. Entertain by your appreciation, conversation, and any little talent you possess, but try to be sensitive to the moment when your efforts become wearing. A friend of mine worked wonders by playing his mouth organ; another

could do simple conjuring and tricks with a pack of cards. Do not offer alcohol, or show photos of your female relatives in bikinis.

RACIAL STEREOTYPING (THEIRS!)

Amongst the Bedouin this stereotyping is as widespread as anywhere else. The English are honest, well-meaning, gullible and very poor – you can tell them anything and they will believe you, but they have nothing much to give you. Americans are loud and insensitive, patronizing, amazingly dressed, ladies with blue hair – but often kind and very generous; ask what you like. Germans are over-sexed and arrogant, also loud, treat hotel staff like dirt. Scandinavians are either hippies with guitars and large socks, or very gentle and scholarly.

BEGGARS

Unlike many places in the Middle East, you will virtually never come across hands stretched out or demands for *baksheesh*. Jordanians are taught from infancy to be too proud to ask. The only exceptions are at holy shrines, where you may spot cripples sitting around – but there is good medical care in Jordan, and professional beggars who cherish or even aggravate their ailments in order to arouse sympathy are not approved of.

Appendices

The teachings of Islam

Islam is not considered by Muslims to be a new faith, but a continuation of the stream of revelation that began with the first couple, Adam and Eve, continued through the prophets of the Jewish Old Testament (especially Noah, Abraham, Moses and Solomon) and their campaign against polytheism, and reached a wonderful climax in the life and ministry of Jesus, but was then corrupted by the 'error' of Trinitarian theology so that a fresh messenger became necessary. Muslims are 'those who submit' to the will of God (Allah); that will is made known in the pages of the Holy Book, the Qur'an.

The Bible is revered as a holy text, but Muslims believe that it was created by human editors with very human motives, and that occasionally texts are so unreliable that no credence can any longer be placed in the Testaments as a whole. What Muslims call the Gospel (*Injil*) was the pure revelation taught by Jesus, and not the Christian gospels that now exist.

Muslims, like Jews, do not believe that the Supreme and Absolute God has a 'human' son; they believe that Jesus, like all the prophets, was a messenger of God to humanity. He was a wonder-worker, the Messiah, a martyr, the greatest of the prophets up to his time – but Muslims believe that Christians have made a mistake in allowing their devotion to him to elevate him to the status of Godhead. They do not accept the idea of a Trinity. As Jesus himself taught: 'The Lord our God the Lord is One, and He Alone should be worshipped with all one's heart, soul, mind and strength.'

Muslims do not accept the need for an atoning saviour, for they believe that God forgave Adam and Eve, and teach that God is supreme Compassion. It only takes our genuine repentance to be forgiven – there is no need of an atoning sacrifice or a divine incarnation. The justice of God is perfectly fair, and His compassion far greater than that of any created human being. They believe that when any prodigal son repents and returns home, the father is already coming out on the road to receive him, with open arms.

The Prophet Muhammad is regarded as the last of the messengers, the Seal of all the prophets who went before. A man of great understanding and compassion and justice, his exemplary life earned him a special place in every Muslim heart. The Qur'an was not written by Muhammad, but was a series of revelations given to him and written down verbatim over period of 23 years. The Qur'an is divided into chapters (*surahs*) and verses (*ayats*), but these are not in chronological order. Before Muhammad's death he was instructed by God to put these revelations into a particular revealed order; and Muslims believe that to this day not one word has been changed or altered. True Muslims always try to study the Qur'an in its original language (Arabic), because any translation is always subject to personal interpretation. (The extracts given in this book are the author's own translation, and illustrate the point exactly.)

Muslim life is based on two things: the instruction in the Qur'an and the *sunnah* (or practice) of the Prophet Muhammad.

Muslims practise five 'pillars' – *shahadah* (bearing personal testimony), *salah* (prayer), *sawm* (fasting), *zakah* (taxing one's surplus income) and *hajj* (pilgrimage to Mecca).

If one can say the *shahadah* with commitment, one has become a Muslim in the heart. It states that a person believes that there is no god but Allah, and that Muhammad is his genuine messenger. *Salah* involves certain ritual movements, including kneeling with the head touching the earth. It does not include personal prayers and supplications, which are a separate devotion known as *du'a*, and are extra. *Salah* has to be performed five times per day, commencing just before sunrise.

Sawm means physical discipline, a going without food or drink or sexual gratification during all the hours of daylight for the whole of the month of Ramadan. One's success in this is only valid if the mind and intentions are also kept free from unkindness and impurity. The *zakah* tax is not voluntary giving to charities – anything which might be spurred on by appeals to our compassion. It consists of the giving as a duty of one-fortieth of one's surplus income, after the needs of family and dependants are taken care of.

The *hajj* is the pilgrimage to Mecca and should be undertaken once in a lifetime in the *hajj* month by every Muslim able to do it without causing personal or financial hardship to their dependants. A pilgrimage done at any other time of the year is known as *Umrah*, or Lesser Pilgrimage.

Muslims believe that Allah is the Creator and Sustainer of the entire universe, including all its beings. Every person has the duty to live a good life, without harming others. Two guardian angels are assigned to each individual, and these record all the deeds and thoughts and motives at every moment of human life. This record is what judges a person at the Day of Judgement and it cannot be falsified or avoided. God certainly cannot be bribed or corrupted. Individuals are responsible for their own actions, and no other person can bear someone else's burdens; therefore the idea of a 'saviour' is a nonsense in Islam. Muslims believe in miracles, since everything is possible to God; in the existence of a jealous Satan, ultimately under God's judgement; and that the whole of human life is a test, in accordance with the will of God. On no human soul does God place any burden greater than it can bear; therefore suicide is considered a gross lack of faith in God. God is the source of all things, and unto Him we return.

A SELECTION OF VERSES FROM THE QUR'AN

The Qur'an is divided up into *surahs* or chapters and *ayats* or verses.

> He is my Lord, there is no God but He, who created me and guides me, who gives me food and drink, who heals me when I am sick, who will cause me to die, will raise me up again, and who, I hope, will forgive me my sins on the Day of Reckoning.
>
> **Surah 26:78–82**

It is not righteousness to turn your face towards east or west; but this is righteousness: to believe in God and the Day of Judgement, and the angels, and the Book, and the messengers; to give from your wealth out of love for God to your family, to orphans, to the needy, to the warfarer, to those who ask, and for freeing of slaves; to be steadfast in prayer, and practise regular giving; to fulfil all the promises which you have made; to be firm and patient in pain and suffering or any other adversity, and through all periods of panic. Such are the people of truth, the God-fearing.

from Surah 2

By the glorious light of morning, and by the stillness of night! Your God has never forsaken you and He is not angry with you. Surely your future will be better for you than your past, and in the end God will be kind to you, and you find satisfaction. Did He not find you an orphan, and gave you a home? Were you not lost and wandering, and He showed you the way? Were you not in great need, and He took care of you? As to you, therefore, do not wrong orphans, do not turn away those who ask your help; spread and increase your Lord's blessings.

Surah 93

No vision can grasp Him, but His grasp is over all vision; He is above all comprehension, yet Himself knows all things.

Surah 6:103

God is in the splitting of the seed-grain and the sprouting of the date-stone, who causes the living to come from the dead … who splits the daybreak from the darkness.

Surah 6:95–96

God is the Light of all worlds; His light may be compared to a shrine in which there is a lamp; the lamp is in a crystal; the crystal is, as it were, a glittering star kindled from a blessed olive tree. The oil would burst into flames even though fire had never touched it; Light upon Light.

Surah 24:35

If all the trees on earth were pens, and the oceans were ink with seven oceans more, yet the words of God would not be exhausted, for God is the supreme source of power and wisdom.

Surah 31:27

THE PROPHET MUHAMMAD

Muhammad, peace be upon him, was a Quraish tribesman of the clan Hashim, born in Mecca in about 560 CE. His father died before he was born, and his mother when he was six years old. He was reared by his grandfather Abdul Muttalib, then an uncle, Abu Talib. Abu Talib trained him as a shepherd and taught him how to be a good merchant. When he was 26, Muhammad married his employer,

Khadijah, a devout and wealthy widow. He was already very well known for his piety and life of prayer, and his new security in life gave him further opportunity to devote his time to the service of God. Mecca was an important sanctuary town, with a temple believed to have been built over the foundations of an original one dedicated by Adam and later rebuilt by Ibraham and his son Ismail. At the time of Muhammad it contained around 360 idols. When Muhammad received his revelations from the One True God, he began to teach that veneration of these idols was misplaced, and thus incurred the wrath of his family who profited by the pilgrim trade.

The night of Muhammad's first revelation, when he saw the angel Gabriel, was known as the Night of Power. After this momentous event, he received no further revelation for several years and began to doubt his calling. However, the messages began again, and continued at intervals until his death. In the year that both his beloved wife and his uncle died, and he faced rejection in the city of Taif, he received his second special 'night' – the Night of Ascent, in which he miraculously journeyed to Jerusalem, and was allowed to ascend through the seven heavens to glimpse the Throne of God.

Muhammad may have been vilified in Mecca but he was highly venerated elsewhere, and eventually migrated to Medina where he was welcomed as ruler. His followers had left all their possessions behind in Mecca, and were 'adopted' by families in Medina. The people of Mecca continued to oppose him, and battles broke out, but such was the quality of Muhammad's life that the numbers of converts grew swiftly. The campaigns culminated in the capture of Mecca without bloodshed or reprisal, and the destruction of all the idols in the Kaaba Temple.

In c.632 Muhammad died and his empire passed to a series of Khalifas, or successors, the first four being Abu Bekr, Umar, Uthman and Muhammad's nephew Ali (whom Shi'ite Muslims claim should have been the first successor. Their name comes from Shiat'Ali – or 'faction of Ali').

A SELECTION OF THE SAYINGS (HADITHS) OF THE PROPHET MUHAMMAD

Control your anger, then forgive your brother. Do you not wish to be forgiven?

Do not take part in corrupt practices, or do anything of which you would be ashamed if it became known.

Gladden the heart of the afflicted, feed the hungry, give comfort to the sorrowful, and remove the wrongs of the injured.

You shall not enter Paradise until you have faith, and you cannot have faith until you love one another. Have compassion on those on earth, and God will have compassion on you.

God does not accept beliefs if they are not expressed in deeds; and your deeds are worthless if they do not back up your beliefs.

On the Day of Judgement you shall answer concerning four things: your body and how you used it; your life and how you spent it; your wealth and how you earned it; your knowledge and what you did with it.

He is not a believer whose neighbour cannot feel safe from his harm. He is not a believer who eats his fill while his neighbour goes hungry.

If you think of God, you will find Him there before you.

Useful addresses

UK

Association of British Travel Agents Ltd
68-71 Newman Street,
London W1T 3AH
Tel: 020 7637 2444
Fax: 020 7637 0713
Website: www.abtanet.com

British Airways
Website: www.britishairways.com

Jordanian Embassy
6 Upper Phillimore Gardens,
London W8 7HB
Tel: 020 7937 3685
or (09001) 655 089 68 (recorded visa information; calls cost 60p per minute)
Fax: 020 7937 8795
Website: www.jordanembassyuk.org
Opening hours: Mon – Fri 9 am – 12 pm (consulate enquiries),
Mon – Thurs 2 pm – 3 pm and
Fri 12 pm – 1 pm (visa collection)

Jordan Information Service
(address as Embassy above)
Tel: 020 7937 9499
Fax: 020 7937 6741
E-mail: info@jiblondon.com

Jordan Tourism Board
Brighter Resolutions,
Lee House, Second Floor,
109 Hammersmith Road,
London W14 0QH
Tel: 020 7371 6496
Fax: 020 7603 2424
E-mail: info@jordantourismboard.co.uk
Website: www.see-jordan.com.

Royal Jordanian Airlines
32 Brook Street,
London W1K 5DL
Tel: 020 7878 6333
Fax: 020 7629 4069
E-mail: lontbrj@rja.com.jo
Website: www.rja.com.jo

USA

Embassy of the Hashemite Kingdom of Jordan
3504 International Drive NW,
Washington, DC 20008
Tel: (202) 966 2664
or (202) 966 2861 (consular section)
Fax: (202) 966 3110
or (202) 686 4491 (consular section)
Website: www.jordanembassyus.org

Jordan Tourism Board
2000 North 14th Street,
Courthouse Place, Suite 770,
Arlington, VA 22201
Tel: (703) 243 7404/5
or (877) 733 5673 (toll free)
Fax: (703) 243 7406
E-mail: info@seejordan.org
Website: www.seejordan.org

AMMAN
British Embassy
PO Box 87,
Amman
Tel: (6) 5923100
Fax: (6) 5923759
E-mail: info@britain.org.jo
Website: www.britain.org.jo

The British Council
First Circle,
Jabal Amman,
PO Box 634,
Amman 11118
Tel: (6) 4636147/8
Fax: (6) 4656413
Website: www.britcoun.org/jordan

Embassy of the USA
PO Box 354,
Abdul,
Amman 11118
Tel: (6) 5920101
or (6) 5923293 (consular section)
Fax: (6) 5920121
Website: www.usembassy-amman.org.jo

AIRLINE OFFICES IN JORDAN
American Airlines
Tel: (6) 5669068 • Fax: (6) 5688919

British Airways
Tel: (6) 5828801 *or* (6) 5866151
Fax: (6) 5862277 *or* (6) 5866150

British Midland
Tel: (6) 5694801 • Fax: (6) 5694803

AIRPORTS
Queen Alia International Airport
Tel: (6) 4453200
or tel: (6) 4453013 / (6) 4453014 for
flight information
Fax: (6) 4451136

Amman Airport
Tel: (6) 4891401
Fax: (6) 4891653

Aqaba International Airport
Tel: (3) 2012111
Fax: (3) 2012397

MUSEUMS AND GALLERIES
Jordan Archaeological Museum
Citadel Hill,
Amman
Tel: (6) 4638795
Fax: (6) 4615848
Opening hours: 9 am – 5 pm in
winter, 9 am – 7 pm in summer;
except 10 am – 5 pm Fridays and
Public Holidays (open daily except
Tuesdays)
Entrance charge: JD 2
*Excellent collection of pottery, metalwork
and glass Jordanian antiquities dating from
prehistoric times until the fifteenth century.*

Jordan Folklore and Jewellery Museum
Adjacent to Roman Amphitheatre
Downtown Amman
Tel: (6) 4651742
Fax: (6) 4615848
Opening hours: 9 am – 5 pm

(open daily except Tuesdays)
Entrance charge: JD 1
*On display are antique Jordanian
costumes and jewellery, as well as mosaics
from Jerash and Madaba dating back to
the fifth and sixth century.*

Jordan Museum of Popular Tradition

Adjacent to Roman Amphitheatre,
downtown Amman
Tel: (6) 4651742
Fax: (6) 4615848
Opening hours: 9 am – 5 pm
(open daily except Tuesdays)
Entrance charge: JD 1
*Various artefacts of traditional life:
costumes, home furnishings, musical
instruments and handicrafts dating back
to the nineteenth century. The museum is
divided into four sections: Palestinian,
Jordanian, Syrian and Bedouin.*

Jordan National Gallery of Fine Arts

Jabal Al Weibdeh
Tel: (6) 4630128
Fax: (6) 4651119
Opening hours: 10 am – 1:30 pm
and 3 pm – 6 pm (open daily except
Tuesdays)
Entrance charge: free
*Fine collection of contemporary
Jordanian, Arab and Muslim paintings,
sculptures and ceramics, as well as
European Oriental paintings.*

The Martyr's Memorial (Military Museum)

Sports City,
University Road,
Amman
Tel: (6) 5664240
Fax: (6) 5664240
Opening hours: 9 am – 4 pm
(open daily except Fridays)
Entrance charge: free
*Chronological display of military
memorabilia dating from the Arab Revolt
of 1916 to the present.*

Further reading

Complete Works by Flavius Josephus, translated by William Whiston (Hendrickson Publishers: 1987)

Freya Stark in the Levant edited by Malise Ruthven (Garnet Publishing: 1994)

In Search of Lost Worlds by H.-P. Eydoux (Hamlyn: 1972)

Petra by I. Browning (Chatto & Windus: 1973)

Petra: A Guide to the Capital of the Nabataean Kingdom by Rami G. Khouri (Longman: 1986)

Seven Pillars of Wisdom by T. E. Lawrence (Penguin: 1976)

The Antiquities of Jordan by G. Lankester Harding (Lutterworth: 1959)

The Holy Bible – revised standard edition (Collins: 1952)

The Jewish War by Flavius Josephus (Penguin: 1981)

The Qur'an: A Modern English Translation translated by Majid Fakhry (Garnet Publishing: 1996)

The Pleasure of Ruins by Rose Macaulay (Thames and Hudson; 1964)

Travels in Egypt and Nubia, Syria and Asia Minor by Captain Charles Leonard Irby and James Mangles (John Murray: 1868)

Travels in Syria and the Holy Land by Johann Ludwig Burckhardt (John Murray: 1822)

Treks and Climbs in the Mountains of Wadi Rum and Petra by Tony Howard (Jordan Distribution Agency: 1987)

Voyage de l'Arabie Pétrée by Léon de Laborde (Girard: 1830)

By the same author
Islam (Heinemann Educational: 1989)

Teach Yourself Islam (Hodder: 1994)

The Qur'an (Heinemann Educational: 1991)

The Separated Ones – Jesus, the Pharisees and Islam (SCM Press: 1990)

Useful words and phrases

The following Arabic words and phrases may be helpful. If you want to go into the language more deeply, then there are tapes and books available, or try a local evening class. Take a pocket dictionary or phrase book.

Yes – *aywa, na'am*
No – *la*

Greetings and courtesies
Please – *min fadlak (min fadlik)*
Thank you – *shukran*
Thanks very much – *shukran jazeelan*
Good morning – *sabah el khair*
    (reply) – *sabah el noor*
Good evening – *masa el khair*
Good night – *laileh saeedah*
Hello – *marhaba*
    (reply) – *marhabtain*
Welcome – *ahlan wa sahlan*
Peace be with you – *as salaam alaikum*
    (reply) – *wa alaikum as-salam*
Goodbye – *masalama*
Go with God – *fi aman allah*
Praise God – *alhamdu lillah*
God bless you – *yarhamukallah*
God willing – *inshallah*

Language
I don't know – *ma baraf*
Never mind – *malesh*
Excuse me – *muta'assif, afwan*

Do you speak English? – *hal tatakallam(i) ingleesi?*
I understand – *ana afham*
I don't understand – *ana ma afham*
I do not speak Arabic – *la atakallam arabi*

Time
When? – *mata*
Tonight – *il-leylah*
Tomorrow – *bokra*
Today – *il-yom*
What is the time? – *kam sa'a? kam issa'a?*

Obtaining assistance
Can you help me, please? – *mumkin tsa'edni lao samaht?*
How much is that? – *hada addaysh?*
What? – *shu?*
What do you want? – *shu biddak?*
What is this? – *aish hada?*
Where is the …? – *wayn …?*
Where is the toilet? – *wayn twalet?*
I don't want – *ma biddi*
Please give me – *min fadlak (fadlik) ateeni*
It doesn't matter – *malesh*
Again, more – *kaman*
Bring me – *jeebli*
Go away – *imshi*
That's enough, please stop – *bass*

Adjectives
Big/small – *kabeer/sagheer*
Good/nice – *kwayyis*
Bad – *mush kwayyis*
Open/closed – *maftooh/mughlaq*
Cheap/expensive – *rakhees/ghaaly*

Tourist essentials

Let's go – *yallah*
Slowly – *shway shway*
Take me to the hotel – *khudni ala otel*
Wait here – *istanna hona (istanni honi)*
Car, taxi – *sayyara, taxi*
Shared taxi – *servis*
Post office – *maqtab bareed*
Bus station – *mahattat albas*
Bank – *masraf, bank*
Money – *fuloos*
Suitcase – *shanta*
Market – *souq*
Mosque – *jami'*
Church – *kaneesah*
Museum – *mathaf*
Hospital – *mustashfa*
Shop – *dukkan*
Street – *shari*
Bill – *hisab, fatoora*
Breakfast – *iftar*
Restaurant – *matam*

Directions

Right – *yameen*
Left – *shemal*
Straight ahead – *dughri, sida*
Where is the road to …? – *wayn al-tareeq al …?*
How many kilometres? – *kam kilometer?*

Problems or emergencies

I don't have – *ma fi, ma indi*
I'm hungry – *ana ja'an*
I'm thirsty – *ana atshan*
I'm lost – *ana dayi'*

I'm tired – *ana taban*
I feel ill – *ana marid*
Policeman – *bolis*
Doctor – *hakeem, doctoor*
Pain – *waj'a*
Sunstroke – *darbit shamis*
Diarrhoea – *is-hal*
Fever – *harara*
Sick, vomit – *rah-araj'a*
Stomach pain – *waj'al batn*
Headache – *waja ras*

Numbers

zero – *sifr*
one – *wahad*
two – *ethnain*
three – *thalatha*
four – *arb'a*
five – *khamsah*
six – *sitte*
seven – *sab'a*
eight – *tamanya*
nine – *tis'ah*
ten – *ashra*
twenty – *ishreen*
hundred – *mia*
thousand – *alf*

Archaeological periods in the Holy Land

Some readers may not be familiar with the abbreviations 'BCE' (before the Christian Era) and 'CE' (Christian Era). This style of dating takes into account the fact that not all cultures use the same system of dating. The Christian system is as relative as any other. All dates in the earlier periods are approximate, since even scholarly studies disagree.

Palaeolithic	200,000 – 14,000 BCE
Mesolithic	14,000 – 7,000 BCE
Neolithic	7,000 – 4,000
Chalcolithic	4,000 – 3,000
Bronze Age	3,000 – 1,200
Iron Age	1,200 – 330
Hellenistic	332 – 63
Roman	63 BCE – 330 CE
Byzantine	330 CE – 636
Arab	636 – 1099
Crusader	1099 – 1291
Mameluke	1247 – 1507
Ottoman	1517 – 1917

Index